Microsoft®

PROGRAMMING MICROSOFT® SQL SERVER™ 2000 WITH XML

Principal Technologist, Content Master Ltd.

Graeme Malcolm

Microsoft® .net™ Enterprise Servers

PUBLISHED BY
Microsoft Press
A Division of Microsoft Corporation
One Microsoft Way
Redmond, Washington 98052-6399

Library of Congress Cataloging-in-Publication Data
Malcolm, Graeme, 1971-
Programming Microsoft SQL Server 2000 with XML / Graeme Malcolm.
p. cm.
Includes index.
ISBN 0-7356-1369-9
1. SQL server. 2. Client/server computing. I. Title.

QA76.9.C55 M343 2001
005.75'85--dc21 2001030648

Printed and bound in the United States of America.

1 2 3 4 5 6 7 8 9 QWE 6 5 4 3 2 1

Distributed in Canada by Penguin Books Canada Limited.

A CIP catalogue record for this book is available from the British Library.

Microsoft Press books are available through booksellers and distributors worldwide. For further information about international editions, contact your local Microsoft Corporation office or contact Microsoft Press International directly at fax (425) 936-7329. Visit our Web site at mspress.microsoft.com. Send comments to *mspinput@microsoft.com.*

Acquisitions Editor: David Clark
Project Editor: Kathleen Atkins
Technical Editor: Julie Xiao
Manuscript Editors: Kathleen Atkins, Rebecca McKay

Body Part No. X08-05015

This book is dedicated to Charles and Andy, who bet me that I couldn't get the phrase "Turkish oily man wrestling" into a Microsoft Press publication.

Table of Contents

Acknowledgments

It's traditional in the acknowledgments section to make the point that writing a book is an enormous task and the author couldn't have done it without the help and support of a cast of thousands, which generally turns the whole section into a kind of Oscar acceptance speech. Of course, this kind of acknowledgment means that the author gets all the credit if the book is a success but supplies a convenient list of scapegoats to take the blame if it all goes horribly wrong.

So I'd like to make the point that writing a book is an enormous task and I couldn't have done it without the help and support of a cast of thousands. First of all, I want to thank my partner, Rose, for her willingness to put up with my part-time life while this book was written and for managing to look suitably interested every time she heard me describe what it was that I was actually writing about. I also want to mention the great team of people I work with at Content Master Ltd. for their tremendous breadth of technical expertise and willingness to share it. Finally, I'd like to thank my editor at Microsoft Press, Kathleen Atkins, for making my passive voice active and coping with all manner of bizarre Scottish colloquialisms, and technical editor, Julie Xiao, for her amazing attention to detail in checking my example code. (Although any errors are of course my fault, not Julie's!) We've worked hard to produce this book, and I hope you enjoy reading it.

Graeme Malcolm

Introduction

Over the past few years, XML has emerged as the computer world's favorite three-letter acronym. At first, XML was a curiosity about which a few technological boffins were getting a little over-excited—an interesting technology looking for a place to happen. Gradually, however, developers came to realize the enormous potential of a platform-neutral way to exchange structured data over the Internet, and we started to see people using XML in new and interesting ways. Of course, there's nothing particularly noteworthy about this trend; in an industry where new technologies are often obsolete before they even get to market, it's not unusual to see a mass adoption of the latest and greatest technological fashion. But XML has proved to have more staying power than many of the other techniques and technologies that have risen and fallen in the computing world. One reason for XML's continued support is that unlike many new ideas, it doesn't require us to throw away all our old ones. In fact, XML makes it easier to retain your existing systems and integrate them with new ones. It also makes it possible to integrate your applications with those of your trading partners, even if they're using platforms and systems completely different from yours.

Integrating applications and businesses has long been the holy grail for many developers, and as the Internet has become the environment in which more and more development takes place, we're constantly looking for ways to build integrated applications on the Web. XML is the key to this kind of integration. By adding support for XML to Microsoft SQL Server 2000, Microsoft has made it easier than ever to integrate SQL Server–based solutions with existing systems, Web applications, and trading partners.

Who Is This Book For?

Let's start by understanding who this book is *not* for. It's not designed to teach you XML (in spite of what the title of this book's appendix suggests). Bookstores are already filled with shelves groaning under the weight of XML texts, and there's enough information on the Web to help you become an XML guru, if that's your ambition in life. I've generally assumed in this book that you're familiar with the basic structure of an XML document and that you're aware of XML-related technologies such as XSL style sheets and schemas. If you have no working experience with XML, you should read the appendix, "Introduction to XML," before reading the rest of the book. The appendix will familiarize you with basic XML knowledge that you need to work with XML and SQL Server. Similarly, I didn't write the book with the intention of teaching all there is to know about SQL Server or the Transact-SQL language. In fact, I'm counting on your already being familiar with the basic Transact-SQL statements, such as SELECT, INSERT, UPDATE, and DELETE, and knowing something of the basic architectural and security concepts in SQL Server.

I wrote this book for anyone who needs to understand how to use XML to integrate applications or organizations that store data in a SQL Server database. The book covers XML-related functionality in SQL Server 2000 and describes how this functionality can be used to build a solution that exchanges data in XML format. Because a great deal of the emphasis in this book is on Internet-based applications, you'll need to be familiar with some basic Web-development techniques for the Microsoft Windows platform, such as Microsoft Internet Information Services (IIS), Microsoft Active Server Pages (ASP), Hypertext Markup Language (HTML), and the Hypertext Transfer Protocol (HTTP). This book shows you how to use the XML functionality in SQL Server together with these technologies to build integration solutions that work across the Internet.

What's in the Book?

With only nine chapters, this book is pretty short. I've tried to stick to the main points and avoid lengthy explanations of basic issues or architectural irrelevancies so that you can find the information you need quickly and easily. After all, you're an advanced developer, and if you're anything like me, you'll want to get straight to the code you need to write in order to solve a particular business problem.

The first chapter offers a rationale for using XML in integration solutions and describes ways in which relational data can be mapped to XML. Chapters 2 through 7 examine the various XML-related features in SQL Server 2000 and show how these features can be used to build an XML-based data exchange application. I based code examples on the Northwind sample database, and many of the examples are provided as demonstrations on the companion CD. Chapter 8 describes the additional XML functionality provided in the XML For SQL Server 2000 Web Release 1, which you can download from the MSDN Web site at *http://msdn.microsoft.com/downloads*. These new tools consolidate the existing XML features in SQL Server, and I've included some sample code on the CD to help you get started with them. Finally, I describe in Chapter 9 a sample case study application that uses most of the techniques described in the book and integrates the XML functionality of SQL Server with Microsoft BizTalk Server 2000. The sample application is on the CD, so you can take the time-honored approach favored by most developers and simply dismantle it to see how it works.

Throughout the book, I've tried to emphasize the key challenges in integrating solutions with XML and focus on the code or configuration required to meet them. I hope you find the information and sample code useful in building your own integrated solutions with SQL Server and XML.

Using the Companion CD

The CD included with this book contains all sample programs and demos described in the book, a fully searchable electronic version of the book, and helpful tools. (See the Readme.txt file on the CD for information on using these tools.)

To view the contents of the CD, insert the CD into your CD-ROM drive. If the startup application doesn't begin automatically, run StartCD.exe in the root directory of the CD.

Installing the Demonstration Files

You can view the demonstration files from the companion CD, or you can install them onto your hard disk and use them to create your own applications.

Installing the demonstration files and the sample application requires approximately 3.4 MB of hard disk space. To install the demonstration files, insert the companion CD into your CD-ROM drive and execute Setup.bat in the \Demos folder. To install the sample application for Chapter 9, execute Setup.bat in the \Sample Application folder. Some of the demonstration programs require that the full version of Microsoft Internet Explorer 5.5 be installed to work properly. If your computer doesn't have Internet Explorer 5.5 installed, run ie55setup.exe in the MSIE55 folder to install Internet Explorer 5.5. If you have trouble running any of the demonstration files, refer to the Readme.txt file in the root directory of the companion CD or to the text in the book that describes the demonstration programs.

Tools

Two tools have been provided on this CD: the Microsoft XML Parser 3 and XML For SQL Server 2000 Web Release 1. They are located in the \Tools folder.

To install the tools, run the Setup program in the \Tools folder and follow the Setup instructions. You can also run these tools directly from the CD.

eBook

This CD contains an electronic version of the book. This eBook allows you to view the book text on screen and to search the contents. For information about installing and using the eBook, see the Readme.txt file in the \eBook folder.

System Requirements

To see the demonstrations and sample applications provided on the companion CD, you'll need a computer with the following configuration:

- Microsoft Windows 2000 Server (or Advanced Server)
- Microsoft SQL Server 2000 (Standard or Enterprise Edition)
- Microsoft Internet Explorer 5.5
- The Microsoft XML Parser (MSXML) 3 (installed in Replace mode using Xmlinst.exe)
- The XML For SQL Server 2000 Web Release 1 (required for the Chapter 8 demonstrations)
- Microsoft BizTalk Server 2000 (optional, but required for the full case study application)

You can download evaluation editions of Windows 2000, SQL Server 2000, and BizTalk Server 2000 from *http://www.microsoft.com/servers*.

Microsoft Press Support Information

Every effort has been made to ensure the accuracy of this book and the contents of the practice files CD-ROM. If you do run into a problem, Microsoft Press provides corrections for its books through the World Wide Web at

http://mspress.microsoft.com/support/support.htm

If you have comments, questions, or ideas regarding the presentation or use of this book or the companion CD, you can send them to Microsoft using either of the following methods:

Postal Mail:

Microsoft Press
Attn: Programming Microsoft SQL Server 2000 with XML Editor
One Microsoft Way
Redmond, WA 98052-6399

E-mail:

MSPINPUT@MICROSOFT.COM

Please note that product support isn't offered through the preceding mail addresses.

1

SQL, XML, and the Business Internet

The Internet is changing the way we do business. That's the inescapable conclusion of many organizations seeking to use technology to gain a competitive advantage in an ever more Internet-based business environment. Increasingly, the Web is seen as a compelling way for businesses to communicate with their customers, their employees, and their trading partners.

Of course, technology has always had an impact on the way businesses operate. Few companies don't use software applications to automate and enhance their core business processes, and most organizations with more than a handful of employees use a computer network for file and print services and applications. What makes the Internet such a major business issue is the way it removes boundaries and makes previously unimaginable levels of communication and cooperation possible. When businesses use the Internet, financial transactions can take place in a fraction of a second and customers can shop around for the best deal without leaving their chairs. If companies are to survive, let alone prosper, in the Internet marketplace, they need to examine what they do and how they do it very closely and identify ways to make their business processes adaptable to the Web.

Relational Data and SQL

Most, if not all, business applications function by processing business data. In fact, early business solutions were described as *data processing* applications. The efficient storage, processing, and communication of data is such an important part of running a business that companies make huge investments in developing computerized systems to handle those tasks in the most effective manner possible.

One of the ways data processing can be made more effective is by ensuring that an efficient mechanism for storing and retrieving data is used. By far, the most common approach to data storage is to use a *relational database*, such as those managed by Microsoft SQL Server 2000, and *structured query language* (SQL) to retrieve and manipulate the data contained in the database.

You're probably familiar with relational databases, and because there are many excellent reference books about SQL Server already available, I won't delve too deeply into a discussion of its features here. In any case, the database itself is simply a tool for storing data; the important thing to concern ourselves with is the actual data itself. Data is central to the success of a business or an organization, so we need to understand what it actually represents.

The data that is stored and processed by a business represents the real-world *entities* that the business is concerned with. When designing a database for a business, your first task is usually to identify the entities that need to be represented. For example, a retail organization might use data to represent retail industry entities, such as products or suppliers, while a bank uses data to represent banking entities, such as accounts or customers. The entities can be thought of as *classes,* or *types,* that define the important things the business needs to deal with.

The database designer then identifies the individual properties or characteristics of an entity. These characteristics reflect the properties of real instances of each entity that are important to the business. For example, each customer in a bank might have a name, an address, and a telephone number, while each product in a retail database might have a description and a price. To make the data as granular as possible, most database designs break the characteristics down into *nondecomposable* units. For example, a *name* property could be broken down into *firstname, middle initial, lastname, title,* and so on. Usually, one or more properties are used to define a unique characteristic for each entity. For example, each product could be assigned a unique *Product ID.* This is the *primary key* by which an individual instance of the entity is identified.

Finally the database designer identifies the relationships between instances of the entities. For example, in a retail database, a product has a supplier. At this stage, the model can be refined to include some conceptual entities that enable the relationships. For example, the designer can create an *order* entity to facilitate the relationship between a *customer* and a *product* (because a customer places an order for a product).

This logical model of the business is implemented physically in the database when the designer creates tables to represent the entities. Each characteristic of an entity is represented as a column, and each instance of an entity is represented by a row of data in the table. Relationships between the entities are represented by using common key columns in the tables.

> **Note** The logical and physical design of a database is an extremely complex task, and I've only mentioned the main points briefly. You'll find some excellent documentation on the subject in the "Creating and Maintaining Databases" section of SQL Server Books Online.

The relational approach to storing data has proved to be one of the most important developments in building business software. Most large organizations in the world use relational databases for most of their business data, and the relational database is the foundation for most of the business applications written today.

The Challenge of Integration

As the use of technology to manage a business has become more and more pervasive, business analysts recognize that they need to integrate the different systems in use throughout the various parts of the organization if it is to function efficiently as a whole. After all, there's little point in having a highly effective marketing system if the ordering system can't cope with the volume of sales generated.

Designers face a number of difficulties, however, when they attempt to integrate different applications. For example, the definition of a particular business entity used by one system might be different from the definition used by another and some programmatic logic might have to be written to handle the translation issues.

The problems become even more pronounced when the applications you need to integrate belong to different organizations. It's increasingly desirable for trading partners to be able to integrate their systems and enable cross-organization business processes. For example, a retailer might want to improve the efficiency of the ordering process by sending all orders to the appropriate suppliers electronically. However, this ambition needs to be achieved in such a way that differences in the platforms, operating systems, programming languages, database management systems, and protocols can be tolerated, as well as differences in business entity definitions.

> **Note** Solutions for cross-organization integration have existed for many years in the form of Electronic Data Interchange (EDI) applications. However, EDI solutions are extremely costly and complex to develop and often don't provide the flexibility required by today's Internet-enabled organizations.

XML to the Rescue

Extensible Markup Language, or XML, has in recent times become one of the most talked about technologies since the relational database. Indeed, if you believed everything you heard, you'd assume that XML is the solution to just about every software development problem in the world. Of course it's not, and we need to be wary of using it inappropriately, but it is a tremendously useful technology for building integration solutions.

The key to identifying solutions in which XML is useful is to understand what it does well. And the thing that XML does well is describe data. In the same way that relational databases provide an efficient way to *store* business data, XML provides a great way to *communicate* business data.

XML is well-suited to solving integration problems for a number of reasons. First, it's completely neutral with respect to platform, operating system, programming language, and so on. XML documents are simply streams of text that can be sent and received by any application on any platform, in a similar way to its close relative HTML. Second, XML is an Internet standard, approved by the World Wide Web Consortium (W3C), so parsers for reading and processing XML documents are available on almost any platform you care to mention—including Microsoft Windows, UNIX, LINUX, and Macintosh. Third, developers can make use of a number of related standards for defining, processing, and transforming XML documents, including Document Type Definitions (DTDs), XPath query language, the Document Object Model (DOM), the Simple API for XML (SAX), and Extensible Stylesheet Language (XSL). Additionally, more XML-related standards are in the process of being approved, including XML schemas, which provide a way to define XML business documents.

> **Note** Microsoft supports the XML-Data W3C recommendation for XML schemas, and many Microsoft products use XML-Data Reduced (XDR) schemas, which use a subset of the XML-Data definition. Microsoft has confirmed that when it is approved, Microsoft products will support the final standard for XML schemas as well as the current XDR implementation.

Representing Business Entities with XML

So, XML and relational databases are both concerned with representing business entities. The key thing is to understand the differences in the way that they do it.

Relational databases represent entities using tables; XML does it using *documents*. An instance of an entity in a relational database is represented by a row in a table, while in XML an instance of an entity is represented by an *element* in a document. So far, so good. However, when we start to represent an entity's attributes, the correlation between relational data and XML becomes a little more murky.

Mapping Table Columns to XML

In a relational database, as I've said, an entity's characteristics are represented by columns in a table. In an XML document, the characteristics can be *attributes*, element *values,* or *subelements*. For example, examine the following relational table:

Customers

CustID	Name	Phone
1001	Graeme	555 111222
1002	Rose	555 222111

To represent this table in XML, we could create an XML document named *Customers* containing two *Customer* elements. The columns could be represented in an *attribute-centric* fashion—the columns in a table are mapped to attributes in an XML document, as shown in the following example:

```
<Customers>
    <Customer CustID='1001' Name='Graeme' Phone='555 111222'/>
    <Customer CustID='1002' Name='Rose' Phone='555 222111'/>
</Customers>
```

Alternatively, we could use an *element-centric* mapping. In this mapping, all columns are returned as subelements of the element representing the table they belong to, as shown in the following example:

```
<Customers>
    <Customer>
        <CustID>1001</CustID>
        <Name>Graeme</Name>
        <Phone>555 111222</Phone>
     </Customer>
    <Customer>
        <CustID>1002</CustID>
        <Name>Rose</Name>
        <Phone>555 222111</Phone>
    </Customer>
</Customers>
```

Of course, there's no reason why a mixed approach couldn't be taken, as shown in this example:

```
<Customers>
    <Customer CustID='1001'>
        Graeme
        <Phone>555 111222</Phone>
    </Customer>
    <Customer CustID='1002'>
        Rose
        <Phone>555 222111</Phone>
    </Customer>
</Customers>
```

This example is interesting because it uses all three ways of representing the characteristics of an entity. *CustID* is represented as an attribute, *Name* is represented as the value of the element representing the entity instance, and *Phone* is represented as a subelement.

The particular mapping of database columns to XML is largely a matter of style, although a couple of considerations are worth bearing in mind. Attribute-centric documents result in smaller XML streams, so for large amounts of data, they're more efficient. However, each element (and therefore each entity) can have only one of each attribute. Subelements are useful for potentially multivalued characteristics. For example, in the preceding sample code, a customer can have only one ID or name, but he can have more than one telephone number, as shown here:

```
<Customers>
    <Customer CustID='1001'>
        Graeme
        <Phone>555 111222</Phone>
```

```
        <Phone>555 111333</Phone>
    </Customer>
    <Customer CustID='1002'>
        Rose
        <Phone>555 222111</Phone>
    </Customer>
</Customers>
```

So as you can see, you can choose from many ways to represent the same business data using XML. So far, we've seen how XML can be used to represent a single entity. Let's now turn our attention to representing relationships among multiple entities.

Representing Relationships in XML

Relational databases, as their name suggests, are designed to enable you to represent relationships between entities. For example, an *order* entity can contain one or more *item* entities, as shown in the following tables:

Orders

OrderNo	Date	Customer
1235	01/01/2001	1001
1236	01/01/2001	1002

Items

ItemNo	OrderNo	ProductID	Price	Quantity
1	1235	1432	12.99	2
2	1235	1678	11.49	1
3	1236	1432	12.99	3

The most common approach to representing this data in XML is to use a nested XML document, as shown here:

```
<Orders>
    <Order OrderNo='1235' Date='01/01/2001' Customer='1001'>
        <Item ProductID='1432' Price='12.99' Quantity='2'/>
        <Item ProductID='1678' Price='11.49' Quantity='1'/>
    </Order>
    <Order OrderNo='1236' Date='01/01/2001' Customer='1002'>
        <Item ProductID='1432' Price='12.99' Quantity='3'/>
    </Order>
</Orders>
```

In most circumstances, XML documents such as this will be used to exchange data that involves relationships. However, for large data transfers where the elimination of duplication is important in order to keep the document size down, an alternative approach can be taken. XML-Data schemas support the use of the ID, IDREF, and IDREFS data types when you're defining XML attributes, and you can use this strategy to create relationships between entities in XML documents.

For example, suppose a supplier needed to send a catalog document listing all products by category. You could use the following schema to define the XML catalog document elements:

```
<Schema name='catalogschema'
    xmlns='urn:schemas-microsoft-com:xml-data'
    xmlns:dt='urn:schemas-microsoft-com:datatypes'>
    <ElementType name='Category' model='closed'>
        <AttributeType name='CategoryID' dt:type='id'/>
        <AttributeType name='CategoryName' dt:type='string'/>
        <attribute type='CategoryID'/>
        <attribute type='CategoryName'/>
    </ElementType>
    <ElementType name='Product' model='closed'>
        <AttributeType name='ProductID' dt:type='i4'/>
        <AttributeType name='ProductName' dt:type='string'/>
        <AttributeType name='Category' dt:type='idref'/>
        <attribute type='ProductID'/>
        <attribute type='ProductName'/>
        <attribute type='Category'/>
    </ElementType>
    <ElementType name='Catalog' content='eltOnly' model='closed'>
        <element type='Category' maxOccurs='*'/>
        <element type='Product' maxOccurs='*'/>
    </ElementType>
</Schema>
```

This schema defines a *Category* element and a *Product* element. The *Category* element has two attributes (*CateogryID* and *CategoryName*), and the *Product* element has three attributes (*ProductID*, *ProductName*, and *Category*). Finally, this schema defines a *Catalog* element that can contain multiple *Category* and *Product* elements. Using this schema, the catalog data could then be represented by the following XML document:

```
<Catalog xmlns='x-schema:catalogschema.xml'>
    <Category CategoryID='1' CategoryName='Games'/>
    <Category CategoryID='2' CategoryName='Educational'/>
    <Product ProductID='131' ProductName='TicTacToe' Category='1'/>
    <Product ProductID='1432' ProductName='Chess' Category='1'/>
    <Product ProductID='1678' ProductName='Spelling' Category='2'/>
</Catalog>
```

You can see an example of an XML document based on a schema by viewing Catalog.xml in the Demos\Chapter1 folder on the companion CD. Because the schema defines the *CategoryID* attribute in the *Category* element as an ID field and the *Category* attribute in the *Product* element as an IDREF field, a link can be discerned between products and categories. When processing the document using the Microsoft implementation of the DOM, you can use the *nodeFromID* method of the *XMLDOMDocument* object to retrieve related data for a given element. An IDREFS datatype could have been used to allow products to belong to multiple categories, represented by a comma-delimited list.

> **Note** Explicit references using ID, IDREF, and IDREFS datatypes rely on XML parsers that can use XML-Data schemas. Because the standard for schemas isn't yet officially defined, many parsers don't support the XML-Data grammar and therefore can't use this technique to represent relational data. As an alternative approach, XSL Transformation (XSLT) style sheets containing the *<xsl:key>* instruction are often used to define relationships in XML documents. For more information about XSLT, visit *www.w3c.org/TR/xslt.*

Web-Enabling a Business Using XML

As you've already seen in this chapter, XML can be a very effective way to represent business data for transfer between different systems and organizations. With the increasing importance of the Internet and related technologies, XML can be a key factor in helping organizations move their businesses to the Web.

Using XML in Business to Consumer (B2C) Solutions

When most people think of using the Internet for business, they think of online retailers selling goods and services through a Web site. Retail e-commerce solutions such as these usually rely on HTML pages accessed by means of a Web browser. The pages show product data from a database and allow customers to place orders, the details of which are also stored in a database.

XML can be an extremely effective way to pass data from the database to the Web application. XSL can then be used to easily transform the XML data into HTML for display in the browser. This approach is usually more efficient than retrieving data as a rowset and writing presentation logic in a Web page script or component to render the data. In addition, as more devices are used to connect to the Internet, the same XML data can be transformed using different style sheets to suit different client devices. For example, an XML product catalog could be transformed into HTML for display in a browser or into Wireless Markup Language (WML) for display on a Wireless Application Protocol (WAP)–enabled cell phone. This flexibility makes XML a great choice for developing Web-based applications that will be accessed by multiple client types.

Using XML in Business to Enterprise (B2E) Solutions

Of course, Internet technologies such as HTTP are often used to build internal applications. This is particularly helpful in environments where multiple platforms and development languages are used because an Intranet-based solution allows any application that can communicate over TCP/IP to be integrated.

For applications that allow users to access and manipulate data, XML-aware browsers such as Microsoft Internet Explorer can be used to download and render the data. Users can then manipulate the data in the browser using XML data islands before sending the updated data back to the server for storage in the database.

Existing applications running on platforms such as mainframes or UNIX can use XML as a neutral way to describe data. For example, suppose a mail-order company with a large existing Information Management System (IMS) application running on a mainframe decided to build a Web-based e-commerce program using Windows 2000 and SQL Server. Existing telephone sales orders can continue to be entered into the IMS application as before, and new orders placed through the Web site can be represented as XML and passed to the mainframe to be stored in the IMS application.

Using XML in Business to Business (B2B) Solutions

One of the most important aspects of Web development is the integration of business processes across trading partners. Most interbusiness processes involve an exchange of business documents, such as orders, invoices, delivery notes, and so on. XML provides an ideal way to describe these business documents for exchange across the Internet. XML schemas can be used to define the XML representation of the business documents, allowing trading partners to agree on a format for the data being exchanged. Of course, each organization can represent the data differently internally and use XSL to transform data for exchange.

Because XML is a text-based language, business documents can be exchanged by using any protocol, such as HTTP (or more likely HTTPS), SMTP, or FTP, or by using a message queuing solution. This flexibility makes it possible for any business to integrate with its trading partners over the Internet.

Web-Enabling Northwind Traders with XML

Throughout the rest of this book, I'll be examining various ways in which XML can be used to Web-enable the fictional Northwind Traders organization. I've chosen Northwind Traders as the basis for the examples because it represents the kind of organization that will benefit most from the use of XML to integrate with trading partners and customers, and because the Northwind database comes with a standard installation of SQL Server 2000.

The Northwind Traders company is a fictional wholesaler that supplies food and drink products to various companies throughout the world. A SQL Server database is used to store employee, product, customer, order, and shipment data.

The Northwind Traders organization can benefit in a number of ways from Web-enabling the application. Customers could be allowed to browse the catalog over the Web or even download it as an XML document to display to their own customers. Business documents, such as orders and invoices, could be exchanged with customers and trading partners as XML, and employees could use browser-based applications to access business data over the corporate intranet. In each of these scenarios, two basic tasks need to be accomplished: relational data needs to be extracted from SQL Server as XML, and XML data needs to be inserted into SQL Server tables. In the following chapters, I'll examine how the XML support in SQL Server 2000 can be used to perform these fundamental tasks.

2

Retrieving XML Data Using Transact-SQL

In Chapter 1, I described the use of XML in business integration solutions and the relationship between relational data and XML documents. Now let's turn our attention to extracting data from Microsoft SQL Server in XML format.

Most database application developers are accustomed to retrieving large sets of data from a database server in a rowset format, such as a Microsoft ActiveX Data Objects (ADO) recordset. In a typical application, a SQL SELECT statement is used to select rows from one or more tables in the database and return those rows to the client for processing. SQL Server 2000 extends the SELECT statement to enable the retrieval of data as XML.

The ability to extract SQL Server data as XML is extremely useful in a number of scenarios. Most important, the data is retrieved in a neutral format, which is essential for the creation of business integration solutions in which business documents might need to be exchanged between different systems and different organizations. In this chapter, I'll show you how the developers of the Northwind Traders' e-commerce solution can extract order data to generate XML invoices that can be sent to customers over the Internet.

The SELECT...FOR XML Statement

To help you retrieve XML data from the database, SQL Server 2000 provides an extension to the Transact-SQL SELECT statement in the form of the FOR XML keywords. By appending FOR XML to a SELECT statement, you can indicate to the SQL Server query processor that you want the results to be returned as an XML stream instead of a rowset. In addition to including the FOR XML keywords, you must also specify a *mode* to indicate the format of the XML that should be returned. This mode can be specified as RAW, AUTO, or EXPLICIT. Here's the basic syntax for the SELECT...FOR XML statement:

```
SELECT select_list
FROM table_source
WHERE search_condition
FOR XML AUTO | RAW | EXPLICIT [, XMLDATA] [, ELEMENTS] [, BINARY BASE64]
```

You use the XMLDATA option to return an XML-Data Reduced (XDR) schema defining the document being retrieved. You use the ELEMENTS option with AUTO mode to return columns as subelements rather than as the default attributes, and you use BINARY BASE64 to specify that binary data should be returned in BASE64 encoding. We'll look at each of these options at greater length later in this chapter.

Before we examine the SELECT...FOR XML statement in detail, you need to understand one important issue. The stream that's returned by a SELECT...FOR XML query isn't a complete XML document but an XML fragment containing an element for each row returned by the query. You must include code in the client application to add a root element to the stream to create a full, well-formed XML document. For example, the following XML fragment could be returned by a SELECT...FOR XML query:

```
<OrderItem OrderID="10248" ProductID="11" Quantity="12"/>
<OrderItem OrderID="10249" ProductID="42" Quantity="10"/>
```

Well-Formed XML

The rules for describing data using XML are fairly strict. Although the rules can cause headaches when you're trying to figure out what's wrong with the document you've created, they're necessary so that XML parsers can easily read and expose XML documents.

First, XML elements must be strictly nested: each opening tag must have a closing tag. Second, XML tags are case sensitive. When you're creating an element using an opening and a closing tag, the case used in the opening tag must match that of the closing tag. Third, all elements in the document must be contained within a single root element. You can have only one top-level element per document. Fourth, all subelements must be wholly contained within their parent element.

An XML document that obeys all these rules is described as being *well formed.*

This sample would be considered a valid XML document only if a root element was added to the fragment, as shown in the following example:

```
<Invoice>
    <OrderItem OrderID="10248" ProductID="11" Quantity="12"/>
    <OrderItem OrderID="10249" ProductID="42" Quantity="10"/>
</Invoice>
```

Using RAW Mode

RAW mode is probably the easiest of the FOR XML modes to understand. Queries executed using RAW mode simply return an XML element for each row in the resulting rowset. The element contains an attribute for each column retrieved. The elements returned are simply given the generic name *row*, while each attribute of a row element takes the name of the corresponding column.

To generate an invoice, for example, the developers of the Northwind Traders' e-commerce solution need to extract a list of items in a particular order as XML. The following FOR XML query could be used:

```
SELECT OrderID, ProductID, UnitPrice, Quantity
FROM [Order Details]
WHERE OrderID = 10248
FOR XML RAW
```

This query would produce the following XML fragment:

```
<row OrderID="10248" ProductID="11" UnitPrice="14" Quantity="12"/>
<row OrderID="10248" ProductID="42" UnitPrice="9.8" Quantity="10"/>
<row OrderID="10248" ProductID="72" UnitPrice="34.8" Quantity="5"/>
```

You can execute this query by running RAW.vbs in the Demos\Chapter2 folder on the companion CD.

Using Joins in RAW Mode Queries

Note that since each row in a RAW mode result set is represented by a single element, all elements in the fragment are empty—that is, they contain no values or subelements. All data is contained in attributes. As I mentioned, mapping columns in a table to attributes in an XML document is referred to as *attribute-centric mapping*. RAW mode queries always return attribute-centric XML, including queries containing a join. For example, to generate an invoice containing order data such as the order date as well as the list of items ordered, the query would need to retrieve data from both the Orders and Order Details tables, as shown in the following example:

```
SELECT Orders.OrderID, OrderDate, ProductID, UnitPrice, Quantity
FROM Orders JOIN [Order Details]
```

(continued)

```
ON Orders.OrderID = [Order Details].OrderID
WHERE Orders.OrderID = 10248
FOR XML RAW
```

This query returns the following XML fragment:

```
<row OrderID="10248" OrderDate="1996-07-04T00:00:00" ProductID="11"
    UnitPrice="14" Quantity="12"/>
<row OrderID="10248" OrderDate="1996-07-04T00:00:00" ProductID="42"
    UnitPrice="9.8" Quantity="10"/>
<row OrderID="10248" OrderDate="1996-07-04T00:00:00" ProductID="72"
    UnitPrice="34.8" Quantity="5"/>
```

Using Column Aliases to Specify Attribute Names

Column aliases can be used to change the names of the attributes returned or to provide a name for a calculated column. However, in a RAW mode query, there's no way to change the name of the elements; you must always use the generic *row*. The following example shows how to use an alias to specify the names of the attributes returned:

```
SELECT OrderID InvoiceNo,
       SUM(Quantity) TotalItems
FROM [Order Details]
WHERE OrderID = 10248
GROUP BY OrderID
FOR XML RAW
```

This query returns the following XML fragment:

```
<row InvoiceNo="10248" TotalItems="27"/>
```

You can execute this query by running RAWGroupBy.vbs in the Demos\Chapter2 folder on the companion CD.

Using AUTO Mode

AUTO mode gives you more control over the XML returned. By default, each row in the result set is represented as an XML element named after the table it was selected from. For example, data could be retrieved from the Orders table using an AUTO mode query, as shown in this example:

```
SELECT OrderID, CustomerID
FROM Orders
WHERE OrderID = 10248
FOR XML AUTO
```

This query returns the following XML fragment:

```
<Orders OrderID="10248" CustomerID="VINET"/>
```

In cases in which table names contain spaces, the resulting XML element names contain encoding characters. For example, we could retrieve our invoice data from the Order Details table using the following AUTO mode query:

```
SELECT OrderID, ProductID, UnitPrice, Quantity
FROM [Order Details]
WHERE OrderID = 10248
FOR XML AUTO
```

However, the resulting XML fragment would look like this:

```
<Order_x0020_Details OrderID="10248" ProductID="11" UnitPrice="14"
    Quantity="12"/>
<Order_x0020_Details OrderID="10248" ProductID="42" UnitPrice="9.8"
    Quantity="10"/>
<Order_x0020_Details OrderID="10248" ProductID="72" UnitPrice="34.8"
    Quantity="5"/>
```

You can execute this query by running AUTOSpaces.vbs in the Demos\Chapter2 folder on the companion CD.

Using Aliases in AUTO Mode Queries

To get around the problem of the resulting XML element names containing encoding characters, we can use aliases. As with RAW mode, column aliases can be used to rename attributes. In AUTO mode queries, however, you can also rename the elements using table aliases, as shown in the following example:

```
SELECT OrderID InvoiceNo,
       ProductID,
       UnitPrice Price,
       Quantity
FROM [Order Details] Item
WHERE OrderID = 10248
FOR XML AUTO
```

The XML fragment returned by this query follows. Note that the element name has been returned as *Item*, which is the alias used in the query.

```
<Item InvoiceNo="10248" ProductID="11" Price="14" Quantity="12"/>
<Item InvoiceNo="10248" ProductID="42" Price="9.8" Quantity="10"/>
<Item InvoiceNo="10248" ProductID="72" Price="34.8" Quantity="5"/>
```

You can execute this query by running AUTOAlias.vbs in the Demos\Chapter2 folder on the companion CD.

Joins in AUTO Mode

Queries with joins in AUTO mode behave differently from RAW mode queries containing joins. Each table in the join results in a nested XML element. For example, a query to generate an invoice from the Orders and Order Details tables could be written as an AUTO mode query, as shown here:

```
SELECT Invoice.OrderID InvoiceNo,
       OrderDate,
       ProductID,
       UnitPrice Price,
       Quantity
FROM Orders Invoice JOIN [Order Details] Item
ON Invoice.OrderID = Item.OrderID
WHERE Invoice.OrderID = 10248
FOR XML AUTO
```

When executed in AUTO mode, the XML fragment returned is significantly different from the results of a JOIN query using RAW mode, as shown by this partial result set:

```
<Invoice InvoiceNo="10248" OrderDate="1996-07-04T00:00:00">
    <Item ProductID="11" Price="14" Quantity="12"/>
    <Item ProductID="42" Price="9.8" Quantity="10"/>
    <Item ProductID="72" Price="34.8" Quantity="5"/>
</Invoice>
```

You can execute this query by running AUTOJoin.vbs in the Demos\Chapter2 folder on the companion CD.

Using the ELEMENTS Option

Another difference between the RAW and AUTO modes is that the ELEMENTS option can be used in AUTO mode to produce element-centric XML results. When ELEMENTS is specified in an AUTO mode query, all columns are returned as subelements of the element representing the table they belong to. For example, here's how the query used to retrieve invoice data would look with the ELEMENTS option specified:

```
SELECT Invoice.OrderID InvoiceNo,
       OrderDate,
       ProductID,
       UnitPrice Price,
       Quantity
FROM Orders Invoice JOIN [Order Details] Item
ON Invoice.OrderID = Item.OrderID
WHERE Invoice.OrderID = 10248
FOR XML AUTO, ELEMENTS
```

The resulting XML fragment contains an *Invoice* element with a subelement for each column. The *Invoice* element contains an *Item* element, which also has a subelement for each column, as shown in this partial result set:

```
<Invoice>
    <InvoiceNo>10248</InvoiceNo>
    <OrderDate>1996-07-04T00:00:00</OrderDate>
    <Item>
        <ProductID>11</ProductID>
        <Price>14</Price>
        <Quantity>12</Quantity>
    </Item>
    <Item>
        <ProductID>42</ProductID>
        <Price>9.8</Price>
        <Quantity>10</Quantity>
    </Item>
    <Item>
        <ProductID>72</ProductID>
        <Price>34.8</Price>
        <Quantity>5</Quantity>
    </Item>
</Invoice>
```

You can execute this query by running AUTOJoinElements.vbs in the Demos\Chapter2 folder on the companion CD.

> **Note** The ELEMENTS option is an all-or-nothing choice; either all columns are returned as elements or all columns are returned as attributes. You can't use AUTO mode to retrieve XML containing a mixture of element-centric and attribute-centric mappings.

AUTO mode's greater control over the format of the XML returned means that it allows you to retrieve more flexible document structures than RAW mode does. However, GROUP BY queries and aggregate functions aren't supported in AUTO mode, so if you need aggregate data in an XML document, you might want to stick with RAW mode.

Using EXPLICIT Mode

EXPLICIT mode requires a more complex query syntax but gives you the greatest control over the resulting XML. EXPLICIT mode queries define XML fragments in terms of a universal table, which consists of a column for each piece of data you require and two additional columns that are used to define the metadata for the XML fragment. The Tag column uniquely identifies the XML tag that will be used to represent each row in the results, and the Parent column is used to control the nesting of elements. Each row of data in the universal table represents an element in the resulting XML document.

Identifying the Required Universal Table

The easiest way to understand the EXPLICIT syntax is to begin with the XML document fragment that you want to produce and work backward to figure out the universal table needed to create that particular XML structure. Let's take a simple example to begin with—imagine that we need to produce a simple list of UK-based customers in the following XML format:

```
<Item InvoiceNo=OrderID>ProductID</Item>
<Item InvoiceNo=OrderID>ProductID</Item>
⋮
```

The task of figuring out the universal table required to produce this XML structure requires that you identify the columns needed to define the metadata and data in the document. To identify the metadata columns, you need to examine the hierarchy of elements in the document, noting the different tags in the document that map to tables in the database and the parent/child relationships between the elements. In this case, that's fairly simple. The required XML fragment contains only one tag that's mapped to a table: <Item>, so all Tag fields will have a value of 1. Elements at the top level of the fragment have no parent element, so the Parent of each element is NULL.

Having worked out that each row in the universal table will contain 1 in the Tag column and NULL in the Parent column, we must now turn our attention to the columns required for the data. In our document, we have two pieces of required data, both of which belong to the *Item* element. One is an attribute of the *Item* element, while the other is the actual value of the *Item* element.

Universal tables use the name of the data columns to dictate how the data will be defined in an XML document. Column names in a universal table consist of up to four parameters, as shown here:

```
ElementName!TagNumber!AttributeName!Directive
```

The *ElementName* and *TagNumber* parameters are required to specify the name and tag number of the element the data belongs to, so in our example the column names must all begin with *Item!1* to indicate that the data belongs to an element named *Item*, which is represented by tag number 1. Column names with no attribute name or directive result in element values, which is what we want for the ProductID column. So the column name for the ProductID column is simply Item!1.

Adding the *AttributeName* parameter creates an attribute in the specified element, which is what we want for the InvoiceNo column. To create a column with the required attribute, we need to name the column Item!1!InvoiceNo.

> **Note** The use of the *TagNumber* parameter together with the *ElementName* parameter might at first appear to be redundant because each column in a query against a single table must always use the same ElementName and Tag values. However, when we retrieve data from multiple tables to produce a nested XML hierarchy, the *ElementName* and *Tag* parameters are used to map the values in the columns into the appropriate element in the XML hierarchy.

So we now know that we're looking for the following universal table:

Tag	Parent	Item!1	Item!1!InvoiceNo
1	NULL	ProductID	OrderID
1	NULL	ProductID	OrderID
...	...	...	...

The Transact-SQL code required to produce this table from the data in the Customers table is shown here:

```
SELECT   1 AS Tag,
NULL AS Parent,
ProductID AS [Item!1],
OrderID AS [Item!1!InvoiceNo]
FROM [Order Details]
WHERE OrderID = 10248
```

Note that the Tag and Parent values are explicitly assigned in the SELECT statement. This ensures that every row in the rowset returned by this query will have a Tag column with a value of 1 and a Parent column with a value of NULL.

To generate the required XML document, simply add the FOR XML EXPLICIT clause to the query. This action produces the following results:

```
<Item InvoiceNo="10248">11</Item>
<Item InvoiceNo="10248">42</Item>
<Item InvoiceNo="10248">72</Item>
```

> **Note** In Transact-SQL, the AS keyword is optional when you're assigning an alias. The query could have been written as *SELECT 1 Tag ...*, and so on.

Directives in EXPLICIT Mode Queries

The fourth part of the column name in a universal table is used to provide further control over how the data is represented. The directives supported by FOR XML EXPLICIT queries are the following:

- ***element***: Used to indicate that the data in this column should be encoded and represented as a subelement in the resulting XML fragment.
- ***xml***: Used to indicate that the column should be represented as a subelement in the resulting XML fragment. No encoding of data takes place.
- ***hide***: Used to indicate that a particular column should be present in the universal table but not in the XML fragment returned.
- ***xmltext***: Used to retrieve XML data from an overflow column and append it to the current element. This directive is customarily used when an overflow column has been used to store XML strings that don't belong elsewhere in the table.
- ***cdata***: Used to represent data in this column as a CDATA section in the resulting XML fragment.
- ***ID, IDREF,* and *IDREFS***: Used together with the XMLDATA option to return an inline schema with attributes of type *ID, IDREF,* or *IDREFS.* These directives can be used to create relationships between elements across multiple documents.

Retrieving Subelements with the *element* and *xml* Directives

The most commonly used directive is *element*. It specifies that the data in the column should be rendered as a subelement, rather than as an attribute. To see how this directive is used, let's extend our required XML result to the following format:

```
<Item InvoiceNo=OrderID>
    ProductID
    <Price>UnitPrice</Price>
</Item>
<Item InvoiceNo=OrderID>
    ProductID
    <Price>UnitPrice</Price>
</Item>
:
```

We've added an extra piece of data to the XML document, and therefore to the universal table, that needs to be implemented as a subelement of the *Item* element. The universal table required for this structure follows:

Tag	Parent	Item!1	Item!1!InvoiceNo	Item!1!Price!element
1	NULL	ProductID	OrderID	UnitPrice
1	NULL	ProductID	OrderID	UnitPrice
...	...	...	...	...

The Transact-SQL statement to produce an XML fragment based on this universal table is shown in the following example:

```
SELECT   1 AS Tag,
NULL AS Parent,
ProductID AS [Item!1],
OrderID AS [Item!1!InvoiceNo],
UnitPrice AS [Item!1!Price!element]
FROM [Order Details]
WHERE OrderID = 10248
FOR XML EXPLICIT
```

This code produces the following XML fragment containing an *Item* element with an *InvoiceNo* attribute, the ID of the product as a value, and a *Price* subelement:

```
<Item InvoiceNo="10248">
    11
    <Price>14</Price>
</Item>
<Item InvoiceNo="10248">
    42
    <Price>9.8</Price>
</Item>
<Item InvoiceNo="10248">
    72
    <Price>34.8</Price>
</Item>
```

You can execute this query by running EXPLICIT.vbs in the Demos\Chapter2 folder on the companion CD.

The *element* directive encodes the data in the column. For example, if we suppose a column contained the data *>5*, the *element* directive would encode this as *>5*. The *xml* directive performs the same function as *element* but doesn't encode the data.

The *element* and *xml* directives make it possible to retrieve XML fragments that contain a mixture of attribute-centric and element-centric mappings with EXPLICIT mode queries. The other directives are useful in certain specific circumstances, and we'll examine these shortly. But first let's see how we can use EXPLICIT mode to retrieve data from multiple tables.

Using EXPLICIT Mode to Retrieve Related Data

So far we've used EXPLICIT mode queries to retrieve data from a single table. What if you need data from more than one table? For example, let's suppose you want to retrieve an XML fragment containing the name of the products ordered. To do this, we can use a query joining the Order Details and Products tables, as shown here:

```
SELECT   1 AS Tag,
NULL AS Parent,
ProductName AS [Item!1],
OrderID AS [Item!1!InvoiceNo],
OD.UnitPrice AS [Item!1!Price!element]
FROM [Order Details] OD JOIN Products P
ON OD.ProductID = P.ProductID
WHERE OrderID = 10248
FOR XML EXPLICIT
```

The XML result for this query is shown here:

```
<Item InvoiceNo="10248">
    Queso Cabrales
    <Price>14</Price>
</Item>
<Item InvoiceNo="10248">
    Singaporean Hokkien Fried Mee
    <Price>9.8</Price>
</Item>
<Item InvoiceNo="10248">
    Mozzarella di Giovanni
    <Price>34.8</Price>
</Item>
```

In the preceding example, a JOIN operator was used to replace a foreign key column with data from the related table. This is relatively simple and is no different from how you would perform the same task in an AUTO or RAW mode query. However, suppose we wanted to retrieve the order header data for each order detail so that the XML produced contains a nested heirarchy in which each order is represented by an element that contains child elements representing the order details. To retrieve parent/child data in an EXPLICIT mode query is trickier than it first appears. You might imagine that you can retrieve related data. We'll do this simply by adding another table to the query like this:

```
SELECT   1 AS Tag,
NULL AS Parent,
ProductName AS [Item!1],
O.OrderID AS [Item!1!InvoiceNo],
OrderDate AS [Item!1!Date],
```

```
OD.UnitPrice AS [Item!1!Price!element]
FROM Orders O
JOIN [Order Details] OD ON O.OrderID = OD.OrderID
JOIN Products P ON OD.ProductID = P.ProductID
WHERE O.OrderID= 10248
FOR XML EXPLICIT
```

The results are shown here:

```
<Item InvoiceNo="10248" Date="1996-07-04T00:00:00">
    Queso Cabrales
    <Price>14</Price>
</Item>
<Item InvoiceNo="10248" Date="1996-07-04T00:00:00">
    Singaporean Hokkien Fried Mee
    <Price>9.8</Price>
</Item>
<Item InvoiceNo="10248" Date="1996-07-04T00:00:00">
    Mozzarella di Giovanni
    <Price>34.8</Price>
</Item>
```

You can execute this query by running EXPLICITJoin.vbs in the Demos\Chapter2 folder on the companion CD.

As you can see, this strategy does return a list of order items for a particular order. However, it's not the most efficient XML representation of the data. The order header information (the *OrderID* and *OrderDate* values) is repeated for each item. Ideally, we want to group all the order heading data under a single *Invoice* element, with a subelement containing the data relating to each item. A better XML structure for the data might look something like this:

```
<Invoice InvoiceNo="10248" Date="1996-07-04T00:00:00">
    <Item Product="Queso Cabrales">
        <Price>14</Price>
    </Item>
    <Item Product="Singaporean Hokkien Fried Mee">
        <Price>9.8</Price>
    </Item>
    <Item Product="Mozzarella di Giovanni">
        <Price>34.8</Price>
    </Item>
</Invoice>
```

To retrieve the data in this structure, we need to identify the required universal table. The first step is to identify the metadata column values we need, and this is where we encounter a major difference from the queries we have executed up to now. There are *two* tags that map to tables in the required fragment: *<Invoice>*, which maps to the Products table and *<Item>*, which maps to the Order Details table. The Tag and Parent values for these elements must be different; for example, we could assign the <*Invoice*> tag a value of 1 in the tag column and <*Item*> could be identified by the value 2. Notice also that the Parent values must be different as well. The *Invoice* element has no parent, and can therefore be assigned NULL in the Parent column, but the *Item* element is a child of the *Invoice* element, and so must have tag number 1 assigned in the Parent column.

Now, since the Tag and Parent values are explicitly assigned in the SELECT statement, we have a rather tricky problem: how do we assign two different sets of values in one query? The answer is we don't. The Transact-SQL UNION ALL keywords allow us to create multiple separate queries and collate the results. We can use the UNION ALL operator to build the universal table we need from two queries: one for the *Invoice* element and the other for the *Item* element.

> **Note** We use the UNION ALL operator rather than just UNION to eliminate any duplicate rows returned by any of the queries.

Here's the universal table we need to create. The first and fourth rows are returned by the *Invoice* element query. (Note that the Product and Price columns are NULL.) The other rows are returned by the *Item* element query.

Tag	Parent	Invoice!1!InvoiceNo	Invoice!1!Date	Item!2!Product	Item!2!Price!element
1	NULL	InvoiceNo	OrderDate	NULL	NULL
2	1	InvoiceNo	NULL	ProductName	UnitPrice
2	1	InvoiceNo	NULL	ProductName	UnitPrice
1	NULL	InvoiceNo	OrderDate	NULL	NULL
2	1	InvoiceNo	NULL	ProductName	UnitPrice
...	...	...	...	...	...

Let's first turn our attention to the *Invoice* element query. This query is fairly straightforward. The only difference from previous examples is that since the results are going to be combined with the *Item* element query using the UNION ALL operator, we need to specify the same columns in both queries. This means we need to specify a column for the Product and Price fields, even though the values aren't returned by this query. We get around this inconvenience by explicitly assigning a NULL in those columns.

```
SELECT   1 AS Tag,
         NULL AS Parent,
         OrderID AS [Invoice!1!InvoiceNo],
         OrderDate AS [Invoice!1!Date],
         NULL AS [Item!2!Product],
         NULL AS [Item!2!Price!element]
FROM Orders
WHERE OrderID = 10248
```

The *Item* element query is a little more complex. First, the Tag column needs to indicate that this data maps to tag number 2 in the hierarchy, and the Parent column needs to indicate that it's a child of tag number 1 (*Invoice*). Second, we need to return data from the Orders, Products, and Order Details tables so that we can match order details to their orders. This means that we have to use two joins. We must also use the same column layout as in the *Invoice* element query, so we include the *OrderID* column, which will be used to collate Orders with Order Details, and specify a NULL placeholder for the *OrderDate* columns.

```
SELECT   2,
         1,
         O.OrderID,
         NULL,
         P.ProductName,
         OD.UnitPrice
FROM Orders O JOIN [Order Details] OD
ON O.OrderID = OD.OrderID
JOIN Products P
ON OD.ProductID = P.ProductID
WHERE O.OrderID = 10248
```

The final task is to use the UNION ALL operator to combine the two queries and use an ORDER BY clause to ensure that the XML elements are collated properly, as shown here:

```
SELECT   1 AS Tag,
         NULL AS Parent,
         OrderID AS [Invoice!1!InvoiceNo],
         OrderDate AS [Invoice!1!Date],
         NULL AS [Item!2!Product],
         NULL AS [Item!2!Price!element]
FROM Orders
WHERE OrderID = 10248
UNION ALL
SELECT   2,
         1,
         O.OrderID,
         NULL,
```

(continued)

```
        P.ProductName,
        OD.UnitPrice
FROM Orders O JOIN [Order Details] OD
ON O.OrderID = OD.OrderID
JOIN Products P
ON OD.ProductID = P.ProductID
WHERE O.OrderID = 10248
ORDER BY [Invoice!1!InvoiceNo], [Item!2!Product]
FOR XML EXPLICIT
```

You can execute this query by running EXPLICITUnion.vbs in the Demos\Chapter2 folder on the companion CD.

You can use EXPLICIT mode to retrieve documents that contain data from multiple tables by simply using UNION ALL to add another query for each tag that maps to a table. Although the syntax seems complex at first, the key to building any EXPLICIT query is to start with the XML structure you want to retrieve and then count how many different tags there are that map to tables. Once you have done this, you can figure out the layout of the required universal table and work out the necessary Transact-SQL statement to generate the table.

Sorting Data with the *hide* Directive

You use the *hide* directive to retrieve columns you don't want to display in the resulting XML fragment. This might seem like a strange thing to want to do at first, but the practice is useful if you want to arrange the data in a specific order (using an ORDER BY clause) but don't need the sort column in the results. For ordinary queries, you don't need the *hide* directive to do this; any field can be used in an ORDER BY clause as long as it belongs to a table referenced in the FROM clause. However, when you're using the UNION ALL operator, all fields in the ORDER BY clause must appear in the SELECT list.

For example, the following query could be used to sort all invoices for a particular customer in order of date:

```
SELECT   1 AS Tag,
NULL AS Parent,
CustomerID AS [Invoice!1!Customer],
OrderID AS [Invoice!1!InvoiceNo],
OrderDate AS [Invoice!1!Date!hide],
NULL AS [Item!2!Product],
NULL AS [Item!2!Price!element]
FROM Orders
WHERE CustomerID = 'VINET'
UNION ALL
SELECT   2,
         1,
```

```
O.CustomerID,
O.OrderID,
O.OrderDate,
P.ProductName,
OD.UnitPrice
FROM Orders O JOIN [Order Details] OD
ON O.OrderID = OD.OrderID
JOIN Products P
ON OD.ProductID = P.ProductID
WHERE O.CustomerID = 'VINET'
ORDER BY [Invoice!1!InvoiceNo], [Item!2!Product], [Invoice!1!Date!hide]
FOR XML EXPLICIT
```

This code produces the following XML fragment in which the customer invoices are sorted by date but the date field isn't included in the results:

```
<Invoice Customer="VINET" InvoiceNo="10248">
    <Item Product="Mozzarella di Giovanni">
        <Price>34.8</Price>
    </Item>
    <Item Product="Queso Cabrales">
        <Price>14</Price>
    </Item>
    <Item Product="Singaporean Hokkien Fried Mee">
        <Price>9.8</Price>
    </Item>
</Invoice>
<Invoice Customer="VINET" InvoiceNo="10274">
    <Item Product="Flotemysost">
        <Price>17.2</Price>
    </Item>
    <Item Product="Mozzarella di Giovanni">
        <Price>27.8</Price>
    </Item>
</Invoice>
⋮
```

Using the *xmltext* Directive to Retrieve XML Values

One interesting problem facing developers of integration solutions is matching the data entities in one application with those in another. For example, let's suppose that when you're building the e-commerce solution for Northwind Traders, data from customers is received in XML documents. A customer might send the following customer details update document to the Northwind database:

```
<Customerdetails>
    <CustomerID>AROUT</CustomerID>
    <CompanyName>Around the Horn</CompanyName>
```

(continued)

```
    <ContactName>Thomas Hardy</ContactName>
    <ContactTitle>Sales Representative</ContactTitle>
    <Address>120 Hanover Sq.</Address>
    <City>London</City>
    <Region>Europe</Region>
    <PostalCode>WA1 1DP</PostalCode>
    <Country>UK</Country>
    <Phone>(171) 555-7788</Phone>
    <Fax>(171) 555-6750</Fax>
    <Web email="sales@aroundhorn.co.uk"
        site="www.aroundhorn.co.uk">
</Customerdetails>
```

The Customers table in the Northwind database has a matching column for each element in this document except for the *Web* element. Of course, customers could send much more data than is actually required by the Customers table. Rather than simply discard this data, you might create an overflow column in the Customers table and add the extra data as XML to this column. In the preceding example, we'd simply insert *<Web email="sales@aroundhorn.co.uk" site="www.aroundhorn.co.uk"/>* into the overflow column.

To retrieve XML data from the overflow column, we can use the *xmltext* directive. When you're using this directive, the position of the retrieved XML in the document depends on whether you specify an attribute name. If an attribute name is specified, the data is retrieved as a subelement with the specified name. If no attribute name is specified, the data is merged into the parent element. Let's see an example of each approach. First we'll specify an attribute name, as shown here:

```
SELECT  1 AS Tag,
        NULL AS Parent,
        companyname AS [customer!1!companyname],
        phone AS [customer!1!phone],
        overflow AS [customer!1!overflow!xmltext]
FROM Customers
WHERE CustomerID = 'AROUT'
FOR XML EXPLICIT
```

The results are shown here:

```
<customer companyname="Around the Horn" phone="(171) 555-7788">
    <overflow email="sales@aroundhorn.co.uk"
        site="www.aroundhorn.co.uk"/>
</customer>
```

The effect of not specifying an attribute name is shown here:

```
SELECT 1 AS Tag,
       NULL AS Parent,
       companyname AS [customer!1!companyname],
       phone AS [customer!1!phone],
       overflow AS [customer!1!!xmltext]
FROM Customers
WHERE CustomerID = 'AROUT'
FOR XML EXPLICIT
```

This code produces the following XML fragment:

```
<customer companyname="Around the Horn"
       phone="(171) 555-7788"
    email="sales@aroundhorn.co.uk"
    site="www.aroundhorn.co.uk"/>
```

This flexibility is a very powerful feature of the EXPLICIT statement. Entire XML documents can be stored in a single column and extracted using this statement.

Retrieving CDATA with the *cdata* Directive

XML documents often need to contain nonparsed character data. For example, you might want to include the text *Elements look like <this>* in an XML document, but if the text were parsed, the word *<this>* would be interpreted as an element. To avoid this problem, XML documents support the creation of CDATA sections. A CDATA section contains character data that isn't parsed by an XML parser.

To retrieve data from a table and place it in a CDATA section, you can use the *cdata* directive. The only rule you have to remember when using the *cdata* directive is that no attribute name can be specified.

In the following example, the telephone number of the Around the Horn customer is returned as CDATA:

```
SELECT 1 AS Tag,
       NULL AS Parent,
       companyname AS [customer!1!companyname],
       phone AS [customer!1!!cdata]
FROM customers
WHERE CustomerID = 'AROUT'
FOR XML EXPLICIT
```

The results are shown here:

```
<customer companyname="Around the Horn">
    <![CDATA[(171) 555-7788]]>
</customer>
```

Using the *ID*, *IDREF*, and *IDREFS* Directives and the XMLDATA Option

In Chapter 1, I described the use of the *ID, IDREF,* and *IDREFS* data types to represent relational data in an XML document. This can be a useful technique for exchanging complex data while minimizing the amount of data duplication in the document.

You can use the *ID, IDREF,* and *IDREFS* directives in EXPLICIT mode queries to specify relational fields in the resulting XML document. Of course, this approach is useful only if a schema is used to define the document and identify the fields employed to link one entity to another. The XMLDATA option provides a way to generate an inline schema for the XML document returned by a FOR XML query in RAW, AUTO, or EXPLICIT mode, and when used together with the *ID, IDREF,* or *IDREFS* directives in an EXPLICIT mode query, it can be used to identify relational fields in a document. For example, a list of all invoices for a particular customer might be required. Rather than duplicate product data for each invoice, you could include a separate list of products in the document and use an *ID/IDREF* relationship to link the products to the orders. You can see the query used to retrieve this data here:

```
SELECT 1 AS Tag,
       NULL AS Parent,
       ProductID AS [Product!1!ProductID!id],
       ProductName AS [Product!1!Name],
       NULL AS [Order!2!OrderID],
       NULL AS [Order!2!ProductNo!idref]
FROM Products
UNION ALL
SELECT 2,
       NULL,
       NULL,
       NULL,
       OrderID,
       ProductID
FROM [Order Details]
ORDER BY [Order!2!OrderID]
FOR XML EXPLICIT, XMLDATA
```

A partial result of this query appears here:

```
<Schema name="Schema1" xmlns="urn:schemas-microsoft-com:xml-data"
    xmlns:dt="urn:schemas-microsoft-com:datatypes">
    <ElementType name="Product" content="mixed" model="open">
        <AttributeType name="ProductID" dt:type="id"/>
        <AttributeType name="Name" dt:type="string"/>
```

```
        <attribute type="ProductID"/>
        <attribute type="Name"/>
    </ElementType>
    <ElementType name="Order" content="mixed" model="open">
        <AttributeType name="OrderID" dt:type="i4"/>
        <AttributeType name="ProductNo" dt:type="idref"/>
        <attribute type="OrderID"/>
        <attribute type="ProductNo"/>
    </ElementType>
</Schema>
<Product xmlns="x-schema:#Schema1" ProductID="1" Name="Chai"/>
<Product xmlns="x-schema:#Schema1" ProductID="2" Name="Chang"/>
<Product xmlns="x-schema:#Schema1" ProductID="3" Name="Aniseed Syrup"/>
⋮
<Order xmlns="x-schema:#Schema1" OrderID="10248" ProductNo="11"/>
<Order xmlns="x-schema:#Schema1" OrderID="10248" ProductNo="42"/>
<Order xmlns="x-schema:#Schema1" OrderID="10249" ProductNo="72"/>
```

The resulting XML fragment contains an inline schema, which defines the elements and attributes in the document. The fields specified as *ID* and *IDREF* in the EXPLICIT mode query are assigned to XML data types *ID* and *IDREF*. For the other fields, an appropriate data type has been selected based on the data returned by the query. The *ID* and *IDREF* fields create a relationship between the *ProductID* attribute in the *Product* element and the *ProductNo* attribute in the *Order* element.

Retrieving Binary Fields with the BINARY BASE64 Option

Binary data such as images can be retrieved in an XML document in BASE64-encoded format, which is useful if you need to send binary data to an application or trading partner. To retrieve binary BASE64 data, you must specify the BINARY BASE64 option in a FOR XML query, as shown here:

```
SELECT picture
FROM categories
WHERE categoryid = 1
FOR XML RAW, BINARY BASE64
```

This code returns an encoded image, as shown in the following partial XML fragment. (The binary data has been truncated.)

```
<row picture="FRwvAAIAAAANAA4AFAAhAP////9CaXRtYXAgSW1hZ2UAUGFpbnQu ... "/>
```

You can also retrieve a reference to binary data when using AUTO mode. This reference can be used to retrieve the data over HTTP through a SQL Server virtual root. (I'll talk about HTTP access to SQL Server in Chapter 4.) To retrieve a reference to binary data, you must include a primary key field in the query, as you can see here:

```
SELECT categoryid, picture
FROM categories
WHERE categoryid = 1
FOR XML AUTO
```

The resulting XML fragment contains an XPath reference to the record containing the binary data, as shown here:

```
<categories categoryid="1"
    picture="dbobject/categories[@CategoryID='1']/@Picture"/>
```

Summary

FOR XML queries give you a flexible way to extract data from SQL Server as XML. This technology enables you to generate complex business documents for exchange between applications and trading partners. Often, RAW or AUTO mode will be adequate for your needs, but for more complex XML formats, EXPLICIT mode makes it possible to extract data to your exact specification.

Of course, writing queries to extract XML is only part of the picture. You need to build software that can connect to the database server and consume the XML data produced. In the next chapter, we'll examine how the Microsoft ActiveX Data Objects 2.6 library can be used to build XML-aware client applications.

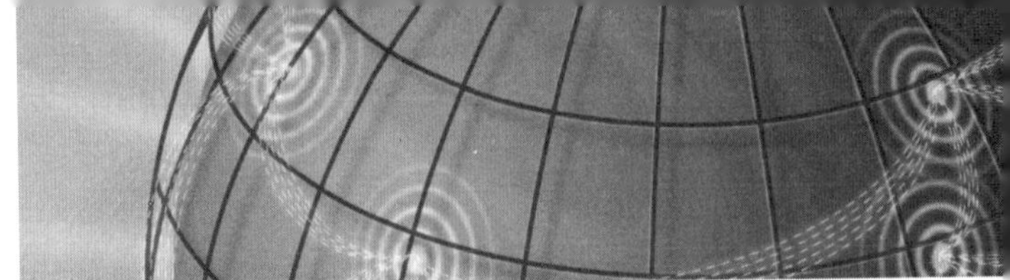

3

Using ADO for XML Data Access

In Chapter 2, we saw how data can be retrieved from Microsoft SQL Server as XML fragments. However, to build client applications or business components that retrieve XML data from SQL Server, we need a way to connect to the database server, submit FOR XML queries, and return the results.

Most Windows platform developers are familiar with the Microsoft ActiveX Data Objects (ADO) data access application programming interface (API). ADO is a COM-based library of components that can be used to access any kind of data in any kind of data source. It's built on top of the OLE-DB API, a standard interface for connecting to and interacting with data sources. ADO version 2.6 ships with SQL Server 2000.

> **Note** One of the frustrating parts of writing technical content is that the industry never seems to stand still. As I write this chapter, Microsoft is working on ADO.NET, a new, more XML-based data access API for the .NET platform. ADO.NET will introduce many new objects to enable more flexible data solutions. Even so, the functionality of ADO 2.6 will still be available in ADO.NET.

An ADO Refresher

The ADO library provides five main objects for use in accessing data: the *Connection, Command, Recordset, Record,* and *Stream* objects. Of these five, many developers are most familiar with the first three because these are commonly used to access data from relational databases, such as SQL Server and Microsoft Access.

The *Connection* object, required in any data access process, provides a network connection to the data source hosting the data. You don't need to create a *Connection* object explicitly; ADO implicitly produces one for any *Command, Recordset,* or *Record* objects accessing data.

You use a *Command* object to execute a command on the data source. For relational databases, the command might be a SQL statement or a stored procedure. ADO implicitly creates a *Command* object, such as the *Connection* object, for any *Connection, Recordset,* or *Record* object requiring a process on the data source if no explicit *Command* object exists.

You can use a *Recordset* object to retrieve and interact with sets of data. This data could be a rowset from a relational database, the contents of a file system folder, or any other collection of similar data entities.

The *Record* object represents a single row in a recordset. The *Record* object could be a row returned by a database query or a file in a file system folder. *Record* objects contain *Field* objects representing the columns in the row or properties of a file.

The *Stream* object represents a text or binary stream of data. This could be the contents of a file referenced by a *Record* object or any other stream of data.

XML Query Templates

As I just mentioned, a *Command* object is always used (explicitly or implicitly) when you use ADO to access data. The data returned is specified in some sort of query or command executed at the data source through the *Command* object. For example, you could use a Transact-SQL statement or a stored procedure to access rowset data in a SQL Server database. The underlying OLE-DB provider translates this statement if necessary before sending it to the data source.

To execute a FOR XML query by means of ADO, you must use a specific query syntax to instruct the SQL Server 2000 OLE-DB provider (SQLOLEDB) to execute a FOR XML query, and you must specify how the resulting XML fragment should be rendered as a well-formed XML document. The SQLOLEDB provider used to access data in SQL Server requires that FOR XML queries be submitted as XML documents known as *templates,* each containing a reference to the Microsoft XML-SQL namespace. The root element of the document used to submit a query serves as the root element in the resulting well-formed XML document. For example, the following XML root tags could enclose a query that would return an XML Invoice document:

```
<Invoice xmlns:sql='urn:schemas-microsoft-com:xml-sql'>
:
</Invoice>
```

Submitting a FOR XML Query

The XML-SQL namespace defines the *sql:query* tag, which is used to enclose one or more FOR XML queries in the query template. For example, the following query template could be used to generate an invoice from order data in the Northwind database:

```
<Invoice xmlns:sql='urn:schemas-microsoft-com:xml-sql'>
    <sql:query>
        SELECT SalesRecord.OrderID InvoiceNo,
               SalesRecord.OrderDate,
               LineItem.ProductID,
               LineItem.UnitPrice,
               LineItem.Quantity
        FROM Orders SalesRecord
        JOIN [Order Details] LineItem
        ON SalesRecord.OrderID = LineItem.OrderID
        WHERE SalesRecord.OrderID = 10248
        FOR XML AUTO
    </sql:query>
</Invoice>
```

If you use an ADO *Command* object to execute this query, you would get the following well-formed XML document. Later in this chapter, we'll discuss how to use a *Command* object to execute XML queries.

```
<?xml version='1.0'?>
<Invoice xmlns:sql="urn:schemas-microsoft-com:xml-sql">
    <SalesRecord InvoiceNo="10248" OrderDate="1996-07-04T00:00:00">
        <LineItem ProductID="11" UnitPrice="14" Quantity="12"/>
        <LineItem ProductID="42" UnitPrice="9.8" Quantity="10"/>
        <LineItem ProductID="72" UnitPrice="34.8" Quantity="5"/>
    </SalesRecord>
</Invoice>
```

A query template can contain multiple queries, the results of which are all enclosed in the root element. For example, the template on the following page could be used to return a list of items in a particular order and a total price.

```
<Invoice xmlns:sql='urn:schemas-microsoft-com:xml-sql'>
    <sql:query>
        SELECT SalesRecord.OrderID InvoiceNo,
               SalesRecord.OrderDate,
               LineItem.ProductID,
               LineItem.UnitPrice,
               LineItem.Quantity
        FROM Orders SalesRecord
        JOIN [Order Details] LineItem
        ON SalesRecord.OrderID = LineItem.OrderID
        WHERE SalesRecord.OrderID = 10248
        FOR XML AUTO
    </sql:query>
    <sql:query>
        SELECT Sum(UnitPrice) TotalPrice
        FROM [Order Details]
        WHERE OrderID = 10248
        FOR XML RAW
    </sql:query>
</Invoice>
```

The results from the two queries are combined in the following XML document:

```
<?xml version='1.0'?>
<Invoice xmlns:sql="urn:schemas-microsoft-com:xml-sql">
    <SalesRecord InvoiceNo="10248" OrderDate="1996-07-04T00:00:00">
        <LineItem ProductID="11" UnitPrice="14" Quantity="12"/>
        <LineItem ProductID="42" UnitPrice="9.8" Quantity="10"/>
        <LineItem ProductID="72" UnitPrice="34.8" Quantity="5"/>
    </SalesRecord>
    <row TotalPrice="58.6"/>
</Invoice>
```

> **Note** The second query calculates an aggregate value, and so AUTO mode can't be used.

Calling a Stored Procedure

Rather than include the FOR XML query in the query template itself, you could define a stored procedure in the database that contains the necessary FOR XML query. For example, the following Transact-SQL statements could be used to create a stored procedure that returns invoice data:

```
CREATE PROC GetInvoice @orderno int
AS
SELECT SalesRecord.OrderID InvoiceNo,
       SalesRecord.OrderDate,
       LineItem.ProductID,
       LineItem.UnitPrice,
       LineItem.Quantity
FROM Orders SalesRecord
JOIN [Order Details] LineItem
ON SalesRecord.OrderID = LineItem.OrderID
WHERE SalesRecord.OrderID = @orderno
FOR XML AUTO
```

The stored procedure could then be called in the *sql:query* element of a query template, as shown here:

```
<Invoice xmlns:sql='urn:schemas-microsoft-com:xml-sql'>
    <sql:query>EXEC GetInvoice 10248</sql:query>
</Invoice>
```

Using ADO to Execute XML Queries

To submit an XML query template, you need to use an ADO *Command* object connected to a SQL Server database using the SQLOLEDB provider. You can either create a *Connection* object explicitly and assign it to a *Command* object's *ActiveConnection* property, or you can simply construct an OLE DB connection string for the *ActiveConnection* property, for which a *Connection* object will be created implicitly. The following example uses an explicit connection:

```
Dim conDB 'AS ADODB.Connection
Dim cmdXML 'AS ADODB.Command
Set conDB = CreateObject("ADODB.Connection")

' Connect to the database using Integrated Security.
With conDB
    .Provider = "SQLOLEDB"
    .ConnectionString = "DATA SOURCE=myDBServer;" & _
        "INITIAL CATALOG=Northwind;" & _
        "INTEGRATED SECURITY=SSPI;"
    .Open
End With
Set cmdXML = CreateObject("ADODB.Command")

'Assign the Connection object to the Command object.
Set cmdXML.ActiveConnection = conDB
```

Submitting an XML Query Using the MSSQLXML Dialect

To ensure that the SQLOLEDB provider "knows" that the submitted query is an XML template query and not a conventional Transact-SQL command, we need to specify the *dialect* of the command. To do this, you need to set the *Dialect* property of the *Command* object to a globally unique identifier (GUID) representing the MSSQLXML dialect. This dialect indicates to the SQLOLEDB provider that the command is an XML query document. You then simply need to assign the XML query to the *CommandText* property, as shown in the following code:

```
'Create the query template.
Dim strQry 'As String
strQry = "<Invoice xmlns:sql='urn:schemas-microsoft-com:xml-sql'>"
strQry = strQry & "<sql:query>"
strQry = strQry & "SELECT OrderID, OrderDate FROM Orders "
strQry = strQry & "WHERE OrderID = 10248 FOR XML AUTO"
strQry = strQry & "</sql:query></Invoice>"

'Specify the MSSQLXML dialect.
cmdXML.Dialect = "{5D531CB2-E6Ed-11D2-B252-00C04F681B71}"
cmdXML.CommandText = strQry
```

SQL Server doesn't provide constants for the command dialect GUIDs, so you might want to declare your own constants to make your code more readable.

> **Note** The SQLOLEDB provider supports three dialect GUIDs: {C8B521FB-5CF3-11CE-ADE5-00AA0044773D}, which represents a Transact-SQL query and is the default; {5D531CB2-E6Ed-11D2-B252-00C04F681B71}, which represents an XML template query; and {EC2A4293-E898-11D2-B1B7-00C04F680C56}, which represents an XPath query. The SQL Server documentation refers to the first GUID as DBGUID_DEFAULT or DBGUID_SQL, the second as DBGUID_MSSQLXML, and the third as DBGUID_XPATH.

Finally, to receive the XML results, we need to use an ADO *Stream* object. This object must be opened and assigned to the *Command* object's *Output Stream* property, which is a provider-specific property (supported only by the SQLOLEDB provider) accessed through the *Properties* collection of the *Command* object. The following code shows this procedure:

```
'Create Stream object for results.
Dim stmXMLout 'AS ADODB.Stream
Set stmXMLout = CreateObject("ADODB.Stream")
```

```
'Assign the result stream.
stmXMLout.Open
cmdXML.Properties("Output Stream") = stmXMLout
```

> **Note** Visual Basic normally requires that you use the *Set* keyword to assign a value to an object variable. The *Output Stream* property is an exception to this rule. Although a stream is an object, an error will be raised if you try to assign a value using *Set*.

Now that the required configuration is in place, we can execute the query. We must specify the *adExecuteStream* option, which has a value of 1024, to ensure that the results are returned as a stream, as shown here:

```
'Execute the query.
cmdXML.Execute, , adExecuteStream
```

The query (or queries) in the XML template will then be executed and the resulting XML document will be written to the result stream. To process the results, simply read the contents of the result stream. In the following example, the results are displayed in a message box:

```
'Process the results.
Dim strXML 'AS String
strXML = Replace(stmXMLout.ReadText, ">", ">" & Chr(10) + Char(13))
MsgBox strXML, vbInformation, "XML Invoice"
```

For clarity, Listing 3-1 displays the full code listing. You can find the code listing in ADOQuery.vbs in the Demos\Chapter3 folder on the companion CD.

ADOQuery.vbs

```
Const adExecuteStream=1024
Const MSSQLXML_DIALECT = "{5D531CB2-E6Ed-11D2-B252-00C04F681B71}"
Dim conDB 'As ADODB.Connection
Dim cmdXML 'As ADODB.Command

Set conDB = CreateObject("ADODB.Connection")

' Connect to the database using Integrated Security.
With conDB
    .Provider = "SQLOLEDB"
    .ConnectionString = "DATA SOURCE=(local);" & _
        "INITIAL CATALOG=Northwind;" & _
        "INTEGRATED SECURITY=SSPI;"
    .Open
```

Listing 3-1. *(continued)*

Listing 3-1. *(continued)*

```
End With
Set cmdXML = CreateObject("ADODB.Command")

'Assign the Connection object to the Command object.
Set cmdXML.ActiveConnection = conDB

'Create the query template.
Dim strQry 'As String
strQry = "<Invoice xmlns:sql='urn:schemas-microsoft-com:xml-sql'>"
strQry = strQry & "<sql:query>"
strQry = strQry & "SELECT OrderID, OrderDate FROM Orders "
strQry = strQry & "WHERE OrderID = 10248 FOR XML AUTO"
strQry = strQry & "</sql:query></Invoice>"

'Specify the MSSQLXML dialect and assign the query.
cmdXML.Dialect = MSSQLXML_DIALECT
cmdXML.CommandText = strQry

'Create Stream object for results.
Dim stmXMLout 'AS ADODB.Stream
Set stmXMLout = CreateObject("ADODB.Stream")

'Assign the result stream.
stmXMLout.Open
cmdXML.Properties("Output Stream") = stmXMLout

'Execute the query.
cmdXML.Execute , , adExecuteStream

'Process the results.
Dim strXML 'As String
strXML = Replace(stmXMLout.ReadText, ">", ">" & Chr(10) + Char(13))
MsgBox strXML, vbInformation, "XML Invoice"
```

Submitting an XML Query as a Stream Object

The procedure I just demonstrated is similar to that used to execute any other database query. However, you'll encounter some limitations using the *CommandText* property for XML queries. First, for very large query documents (particularly when they're read from a file), you incur a cost by reading the document and then writing it to the *CommandText* property. Second, the *CommandText* property supports only UNICODE encoding, which might not be the format of an XML template stored in a file.

An alternative approach is to use a *Stream* object for the inbound query. The SQLOLEDB provider supports a *CommandStream* property of the *Command* object that can be used to submit a command as a stream in a similar way that the *CommandText* property can be used to submit a command as a string.

To use this technique, you create a *Stream* object for the inbound query, as shown here:

```
Dim stmXMLin 'AS ADODB.Stream

'Create Stream object for inbound query.
Set stmXMLin = CreateObject("ADODB.Stream")
```

Next we need to write the XML query template into the inbound stream and then reposition the current character marker in the stream to the beginning, ready to be read by the SQLOLEDB provider, as shown here:

```
'Write query to inbound stream.
stmXMLin.Open
stmXMLin.WriteText strQry, adWriteChar

'Set Stream object position to the beginning of the stream.
stmXMLin.Position = 0
```

To assign the inbound stream to the *Command* object, we need to use the *CommandStream* property:

```
'Assign Stream object to Command object.
Set cmdXML.CommandStream = stmXMLin
```

For clarity, Listing 3-2 shows the complete code listing necessary to submit a query as a stream. You can also find the code listing in ADOQueryStream.vbs in the Demos\Chapter3 folder on the companion CD.

ADOQueryStream.vbs

```
Dim conDB 'AS ADODB.Connection
Dim cmdXML 'AS ADODB.Command

Set conDB = CreateObject("ADODB.Connection")

' Connect to the database using Integrated Security.
With conDB
    .Provider = "SQLOLEDB"
    .ConnectionString = "DATA SOURCE=(local);" & _
        "INITIAL CATALOG=Northwind;" & _
        "INTEGRATED SECURITY=SSPI;"
    .Open
End With
```

Listing 3-2. *(continued)*

Listing 3-2. *(continued)*

```
Set cmdXML = CreateObject("ADODB.Command")

'Assign the Connection object to the Command object.
Set cmdXML.ActiveConnection = conDB

'Create Stream object for inbound query.
Dim stmXMLin 'AS ADODB.Stream
Set stmXMLin = CreateObject("ADODB.Stream")

'Create the query template.
Dim strQry 'AS String
strQry = "<Invoice xmlns:sql='urn:schemas-microsoft-com:xml-sql'>"
strQry = strQry & "<sql:query>
strQry = strQry & "SELECT OrderID, OrderDate FROM Orders "
strQry = strQry & "WHERE OrderID = 10248 FOR XML AUTO"
strQry = strQry & "</sql:query></Invoice>"

'Write query to inbound stream.
stmXMLin.Open
stmXMLin.WriteText strQry, adWriteChar

'Set Stream object position to the beginning of the stream.
stmXMLin.Position = 0

'Assign Stream object to Command object.
Set cmdXML.CommandStream = stmXMLin

'Create stream for outbound result.
Dim stmXMLout 'AS ADODB.Stream
Set stmXMLout = CreateObject("ADODB.Stream")

'Assign the result stream.
stmXMLout.Open
cmdXML.Properties("Output Stream") = stmXMLout

'Execute the query.
cmdXML.Execute, , adExecuteStream

'Process the results.
Dim strXML 'AS String
strXML = Replace(stmXMLout.ReadText, ">", ">" & Chr(10) + Char(13))
MsgBox strXML, vbInformation, "XML Invoice"
```

This approach overcomes the limitations associated with using the *CommandText* property for XML queries. First, using a stream to read and write large amounts of text is more efficient than using strings. Second, the *CommandStream* property supports not just UNICODE but any encoding format understood by the XML parser. For these reasons, using the *CommandStream* property is nearly always preferable to using *CommandText*.

XML-Related SQLOLEDB Provider Properties

The SQLOLEDB provider makes many properties available through the ADO *Command* object to make working with XML easier. These properties are discussed in the following sections.

Applying a Style Sheet with the *XSL* Property

You could encounter many situations in which you'll want to apply an XSL style sheet to the XML data as you retrieve it. For example, the Northwind Traders invoice might need to be rendered as HTML or transformed into a different XML grammar before being sent to the customer.

To apply a style sheet to XML data retrieved over ADO, the *XSL* property of the *Command* object can be set to the file path of the XSL file that you need to apply. For example, the following Microsoft Visual Basic code applies a style sheet named *invoice.xsl,* which is stored in the directory where the application is located.

```
cmdXML.Properties("xsl") = App.Path & "\invoice.xsl"
```

The results returned through the output stream will now reflect the XML data after it has been transformed by the style sheet. The specified path can also be a URL, allowing you to store your style sheets on a remote Web server, as shown in the following sample code:

```
cmdXML.Properties("xsl") = "http://myWebserver/invoice.xsl"
```

To perform the same task in a Microsoft Active Server Page (ASP), you can use the *Server.MapPath* method to access a style sheet, which you store in the same virtual directory as the ASP.

Using Relative Paths and the *Base Path* Property

Instead of using absolute paths to reference files, you can set the *Base Path* property of the *Command* object. Once this property has been set, all other files, such as style sheets, can be referenced using a relative path.

In the following example, the application directory is specified as the *Base Path*; all subsequent file references can then be relative:

```
cmdXML.Properties("Base Path") = App.Path
cmdXML.Properties("xsl") = "invoice.xsl"
```

As with the *XSL* property, the *Base Path* property can be used to reference a virtual root or a Web folder using a URL:

```
cmdXML.Properties("Base Path") = "http://myWebserver"
cmdXML.Properties("xsl") = "invoice.xsl"
```

Controlling File References with the *SS Stream Flags* Property

The *SS Stream Flags* property is used to configure the way ADO accesses files such as style sheets. This property can be used as a security measure to allow files such as style sheets to be selected dynamically at run time while restricting the locations in which those files can be accessed.

A number of constant values can be assigned to the *SS Stream Flags* property. For example, the STREAM_FLAGS_DISALLOW_URL constant, which has a value of 1, can be used to prevent a URL from being used for the *XSL* or *Base Path* property, as shown here:

```
cmdXML.Properties("SS STREAM FLAGS")= STREAM_FLAGS_DISALLOW_URL
```

You can specify multiple constants by using the OR operator. For example, the following code disallows URLs and absolute paths, ensuring that all file references are relative to the directory where the application is located.

```
cmdXML.Properties("Base Path") = App.Path
cmdXML.Properties("SS STREAM FLAGS")= _
    STREAM_FLAGS_DISALLOW_URL Or STREAM_FLAGS_DISALLOW_ABSOLUTE_PATH
```

The full list of constants and their uses appears here:

- **STREAM_FLAGS_DISALLOW_URL** Prevents the use of a URL for the *Base Path*, *XSL*, or *Mapping Schema* property. The value for this constant is 1.
- **STREAM_FLAGS_DISALLOW_ABSOLUTE_PATH** Prevents the use of an absolute path reference. All files must be relative to the *Base Path* property. The value for this constant is 2.
- **STREAM_FLAGS_DISALLOW_QUERY** Prevents a query from being passed to SQL Server. (Use this constant to restrict access so that only mapping schemas can be used to access data.) The value for this constant is 4.
- **STREAM_FLAGS_DONTCACHEMAPPINGSCHEMA** Prevents a mapping schema from being cached. The value for this constant is 8.
- **STREAM_FLAGS_DONTCACHETEMPLATE** Prevents a query template from being cached. The value for this constant is 16.
- **STREAM_FLAGS_DONTCACHEXSL** Prevents a style sheet from being cached. The value for this constant is 32.

> **Note** Many of the constants relate to the use of the *Mapping Schema* property. I'll talk about this property in the "Mapping Schemas" section of Chapter 6.

Managing the Output Format with the *Output Encoding* Property

Until now, we've processed the retrieved XML data by reading the text from the output stream. You can also send the stream to a browser through the *Response* object in an ASP script. In fact, if you're retrieving XML data using ADO from an ASP, you can simply specify the *Response* object as the output stream, as shown here:

```
<% cmdXML.Properties("Output Stream") = Response %>
```

This code causes the results of the query to be sent straight to the browser when the query is executed.

The way the data is displayed in the browser depends on the encoding used in the stream. You can control this encoding by setting the *Output Encoding* property to a valid encoding string, such as *UTF-8* or *Unicode*. For example, the following code explicitly sets the encoding to Unicode:

```
cmdXML.Properties("Output Encoding") = "Unicode"
```

Summary

In this chapter, we've discussed the use of ADO to access XML data in a SQL Server database. The key to retrieving XML is to submit queries in the form of an XML document based on the Microsoft XML-SQL namespace. The inbound document should include one or more *sql:query* elements containing a FOR XML query (or a call to a stored procedure containing a FOR XML query).

In most circumstances, you should use a *Stream* object for both the inbound query document and the outbound results, although you can set the *Dialect* property to the MSSQLXML_DIALECT GUID and use the *CommandText* property for the inbound query.

You can apply a style sheet to the results by setting the *XSL* property of the *Command* object and using this object's *Base Path* and *SS Stream Flags* properties to control how the style sheet file is accessed.

Finally, you can return the results directly to a browser through the ASP *Response* object, and you can control the encoding used by setting the *Output Encoding* property.

In the next chapter, we'll discuss HTTP database publishing, an alternative approach to retrieving XML data from SQL Server 2000.

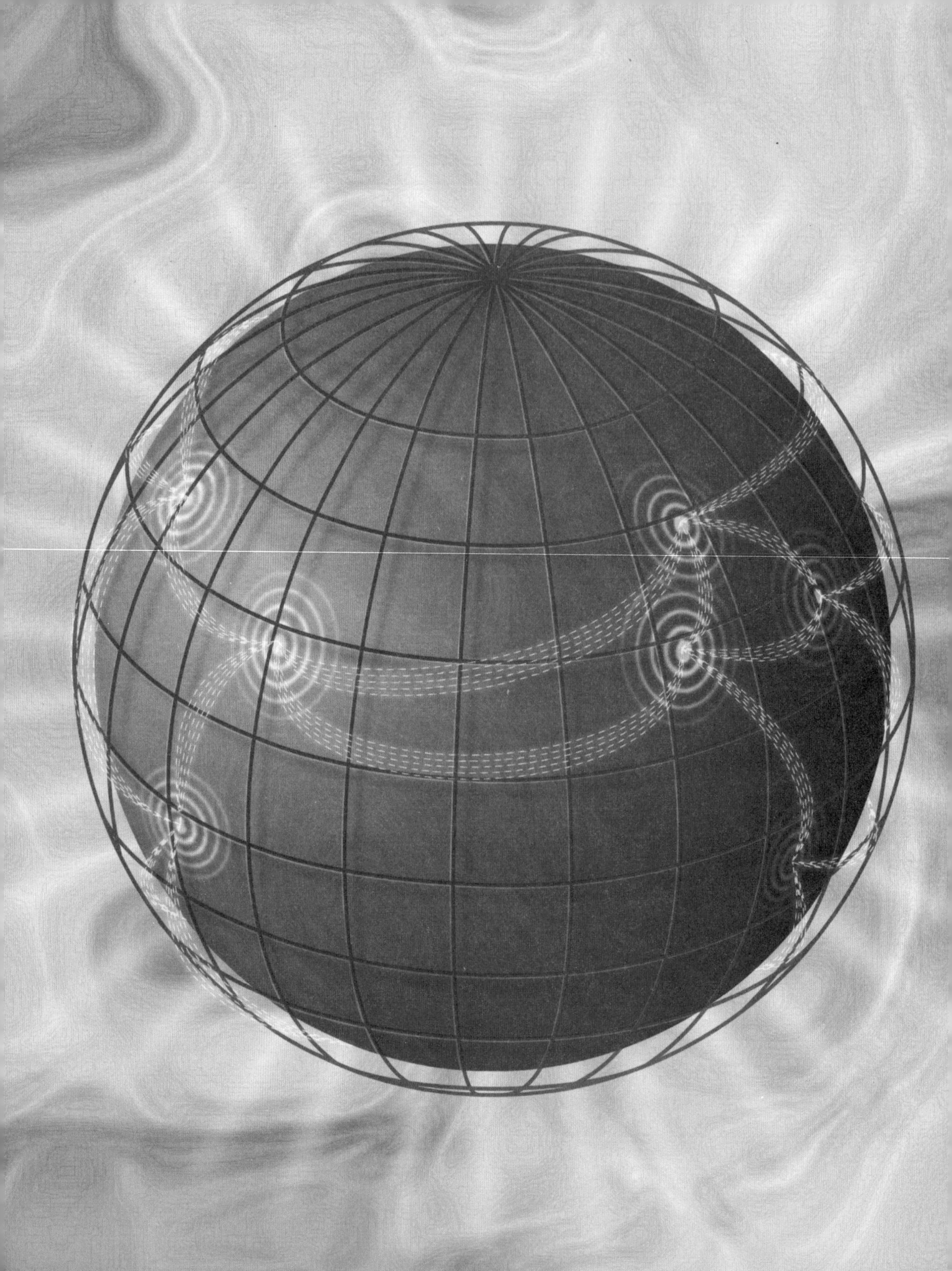

4

Using HTTP for Data Access

In Chapter 3, I explained how you can use ADO to access XML data in Microsoft SQL Server 2000. This approach is useful when you're building business components that need to retrieve data in XML format while providing additional business processing services. You can make data available through an ASP-based Web site by calling these components from the ASP files themselves.

An alternative approach to publishing data for intranet- and Internet-based applications is to use the HTTP publishing functionality provided in SQL Server 2000. This way, you can make XML data available through a Microsoft Internet Information Services (IIS) virtual directory in the same way a conventional Web site is published. The ability to publish data over HTTP allows you to build highly data-centric Web sites easily and quickly, with much less code than an ASP application would require. XSL style sheets can be applied to the XML data to transform it to HTML for browser-based clients or into other formats such as Wireless Markup Language (WML) for Wireless Application Protocol (WAP)–enabled cell phones. Alternatively, both internal applications and trading partners could simply retrieve the data as XML by making an HTTP request.

Northwind Traders could take advantage of this capability by publishing product data on the Internet. Customers could then browse the catalog in HTML format or even download it as XML to import into their own systems. In addition, Northwind Traders employees could use an intranet-based application to view order data by simply browsing the database virtual directory.

SQL Server HTTP Publishing Architecture

SQL Server HTTP publishing is made possible through an ISAPI application named SQLISAPI, which ships with SQL Server. Creating an IIS virtual root based on this application makes a specified SQL Server database available through an HTTP

URL address, such as *http://mywebserver/mydatabase*. The SQLISAPI application itself uses the SQL Server 2000 OLE-DB provider (SQLOLEDB) to access the database and returns XML or HTML to the HTTP client. You can see this architecture in Figure 4-1.

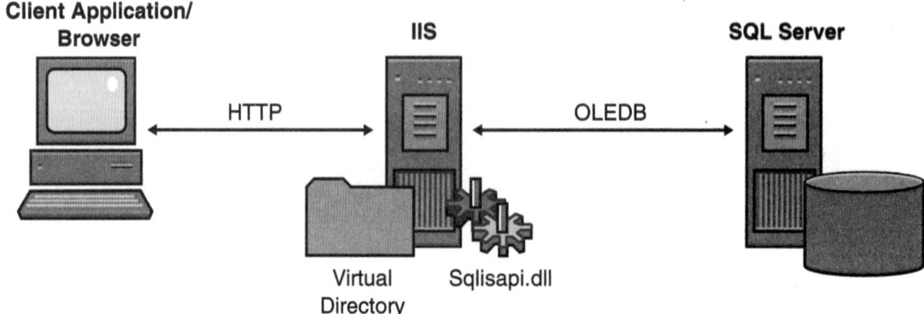

Figure 4-1 SQL Server 2000 HTTP data access architecture

Client applications can request data in one of the following four ways:

- By sending a FOR XML query as a query string in the URL
- By posting an XML query template to the ISAPI application
- By specifying an XML query template in a virtual root on the Web server
- By specifying an XML schema in a virtual root on the Web server

> **Note** Because the first two of these options allow the client application to send any query to the server, they're unlikely to be used in most production environments for security reasons, particularly on the Internet. Most Internet-based applications use server-side templates or schemas to publish data in a more controlled fashion. I'll talk about using XML templates to publish data in Chapter 5 and using schemas to publish data in Chapter 6.

Publishing a Database Through an IIS Virtual Directory

The tool used to manage SQL Server HTTP publishing is a Microsoft Management Console (MMC) snap-in named Configure SQL XML Support In IIS. This tool can be found in the Microsoft SQL Server program group on the Start menu. The unimaginative (and cumbersome) name does at least manage to accurately describe what the tool does. With this snap-in, you can create and manage IIS virtual directories that use the SQLISAPI application to publish XML data from SQL Server.

After you launch the snap-in and expand the server, each of the Web sites configured in IIS on the local computer appears in the left-hand pane. You can manage remote servers by selecting IIS Virtual Directory Management For SQL Server at the root of the tree and choosing Connect from the Action menu. Figure 4-2 shows the Configure SQL XML Support In IIS tool.

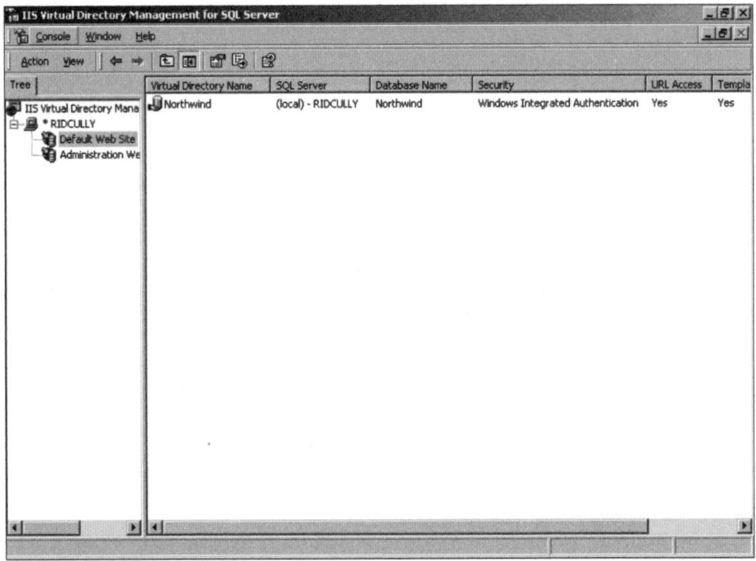

Figure 4-2 The Configure SQL XML Support In IIS MMC snap-in tool

To publish a new virtual directory, you need to select the Web site on which you want to publish the directory, choose New, and then choose Virtual Directory from the Action menu to open the New Virtual Directory Properties dialog box. (Or right-click the Web site and use the shortcut menu.) Then you use this dialog box to configure the properties of the new virtual directory.

Specifying a Name and a Path for the Virtual Directory

The General tab of the New Virtual Directory Properties dialog box is shown in Figure 4-3. You use this tab to configure the name and location of the virtual directory.

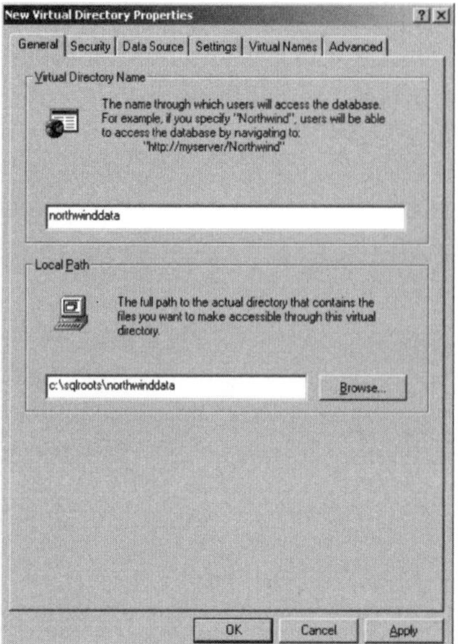

Figure 4-3 Specifying a name and a path for the virtual directory

In the Virtual Directory Name section, specify the name of the virtual directory that will be used as part of the URL to access the data it publishes. The URL takes the form *http://domain/virtualdirectory*. In intranet environments, the name of the IIS server hosting the virtual directory is usually specified in the *domain* part of the URL, so, for example, a virtual directory named *northwinddata* on an IIS server named *webserver1* would be accessed using the URL *http://webserver1/northwinddata*. On the Internet, it's customary to use the fully qualified DNS domain name to identify a particular Web server, so you're likely to see a URL like *http://www.northwindtraders.com/northwinddata*. In either case, you use the name of the virtual directory to access the application, so you should choose a meaningful name that reflects the data being published.

In the Local Path section, you can specify the full path to the physical folder on the file system that the virtual directory relates to. In a conventional Web application, the HTML and ASP files used by the application would be stored here. In a SQLISAPI application, however, the folder doesn't need to contain anything (although it must still be specified). If the folder is stored on an NTFS volume, you must ensure that any Microsoft Windows user accounts used to access the application (as configured on the Security tab of the dialog box) have been granted read permission.

Securing the Virtual Directory

You make your choices on the Security tab in the New Virtual Directory Properties dialog box to specify the type of security you want to use for the virtual directory, or more specifically, the authentication mechanism you want to use. This tab is shown in Figure 4-4.

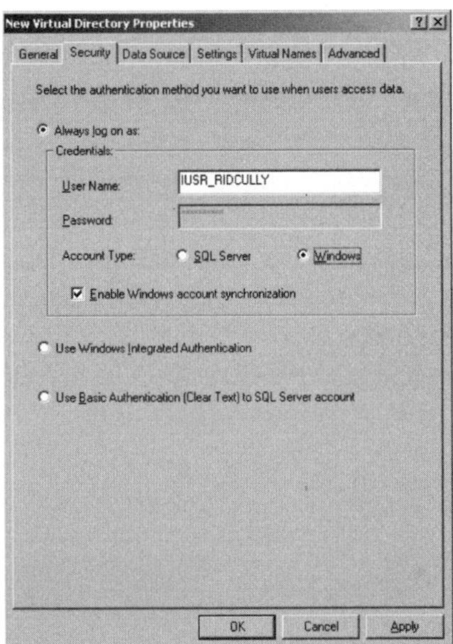

Figure 4-4 Specifying virtual directory security

Choosing an Authentication Model

You can choose from a number of ways to authenticate users when they're accessing SQL Server. In a three-tier application (such as a SQL Server IIS application), you can use one of two basic models: the trusted server model or the impersonation/delegation model. In the trusted server model, the end users are anonymous to SQL Server and a specified account is used by the Web server to connect to the database on the user's behalf. In the impersonation/delegation model, the user supplies a user name and password and the Web server uses the supplied credentials to "impersonate" the user when the Web server is accessing the database.

> **Note** Strictly speaking, you use the term *impersonation* when the Web server uses the user's credentials to access resources on the *local* server. You use the term *delegation* when the Web server accesses resources on a *remote* server using the user's credentials. Whichever term is used, the basic principle is the same.

Of these two models, the trusted server model is the most scalable because it allows every end user to use the same credentials (and therefore the same connection settings) to access the database, making connection pooling more effective and minimizing the amount of security management that needs to be performed in the database itself. However, the impersonation/delegation model allows much more granular database permissions to be granted and enables much finer control of auditing. The approach you choose depends on the security and scalability requirements in your particular circumstances.

Figure 4-5 shows a comparison of these security models:

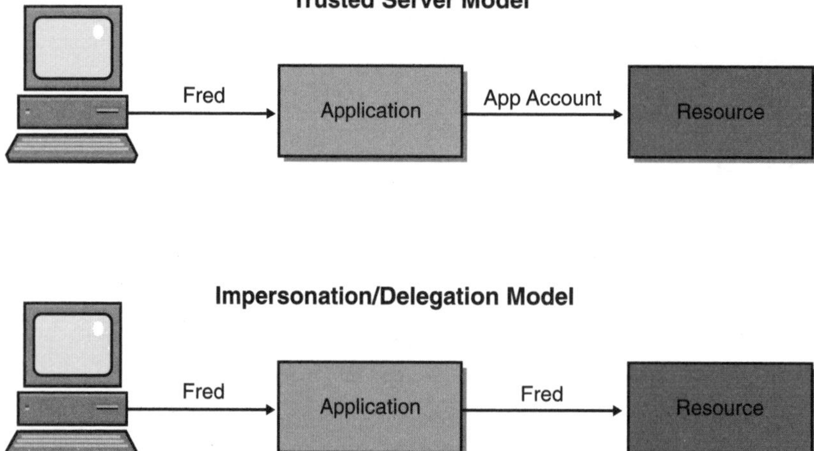

Figure 4-5 Trusted server vs. impersonation/delegation authentication

For each of these models, you can choose from two possible configurations when you're publishing a SQL Server virtual directory. SQL Server supports both integrated security based on a Windows 2000 user account and SQL Server security based on a separate SQL Server login. Because SQL Server authentication isn't selected in a default installation of SQL Server 2000, you might have to use SQL Server Enterprise Manager to enable SQL Server authentication if you want to allow access through a SQL Server login.

> **Note** Generally, Microsoft advises you to use Windows integrated security wherever possible because it's more secure and manageable. You should use SQL Server logins only when the user can't be authenticated by Windows, such as when you're using the impersonation/delegation model with a browser that doesn't support Windows integrated authentication.

Using the Trusted Server Model

You can use the trusted server model by selecting the Always Logon As option and specifying the security credentials to be used. You can specify a Windows user account or a SQL Server login to be used for database access on behalf of all HTTP clients.

If a Windows account is specified, you can use any local or domain account. (The default is the local IUSR_*computername* account used by IIS for anonymous access.) You can specify the password here or allow IIS to synchronize the password automatically. By default, Enable Windows Account Synchronization is selected. You must, of course, ensure that the specified Windows account has access to the database and appropriate permissions for such database objects as tables, views, and stored procedures.

Using the Impersonation/Delegation Model

You can use the impersonation/delegation model by selecting either the Use Windows Integrated Authentication option or Use Basic Authentication (Clear Text) To SQL Server Account option.

To use Windows integrated authentication, the user must be accessing the virtual directory through an application or browser that supports Windows authentication (such as Microsoft Internet Explorer). If the user is already logged on to Windows, her credentials are encrypted and sent in the HTTP request header. If the user isn't currently logged on to Windows or her account has insufficient permissions, she'll be prompted to log on and her credentials will be sent in an encrypted fashion.

Using a SQL Server account for the impersonation/delegation security model involves sending the security credentials in plain text (unencrypted) from the browser to the Web server. This approach should rarely, if ever, be used in a production system without some other form of encryption, such as the Secure Sockets Layer (SSL) protocol.

Encrypting Data using SSL

You'll encounter many occasions, particularly when building partner integration solutions, for which the data being accessed must remain confidential. To facilitate privacy, you can use the SSL protocol to encrypt the network traffic passed between the Web server and the client application or browser. To take advantage of SSL security, you must use the Internet Services Manager administration tool to install a certificate on the Web server and configure the virtual directory. Users will then be able to access the data in a secure manner using an HTTPS URL.

Specifying the Data Source

You specify the SQL Server database providing data to the SQLISAPI application on the Data Source tab of the New Virtual Directory Properties dialog box. Figure 4-6 shows the Data Source tab.

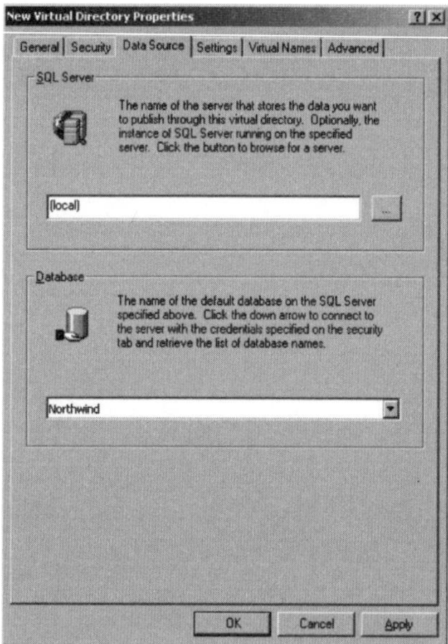

Figure 4-6 Specifying the data source

You must specify the server on which the data is stored and the name of the database you want to publish data from. You use this configuration together with the security settings to construct the OLEDB connection string that the SQLISAPI application will use to connect to the database.

Specifying Data Access Settings

You use the Settings tab of the New Virtual Directory Properties dialog box to govern how data can be accessed through the virtual directory. This tab is shown in Figure 4-7.

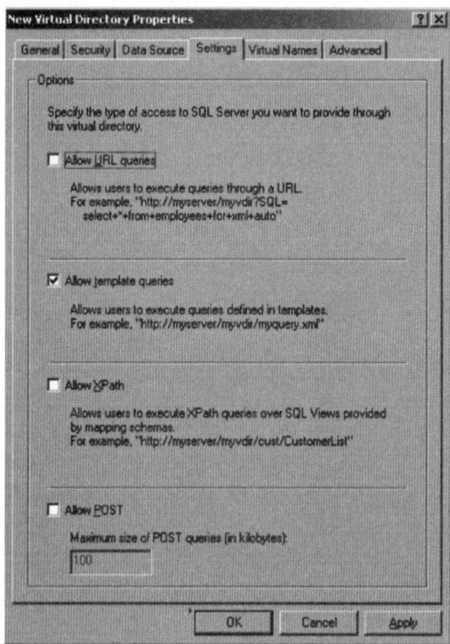

Figure 4-7 Specifying settings

Allowing URL Queries

URL queries are Transact-SQL statements specified as query strings in the URL used to access the virtual directory. If URL queries are allowed, the SQL statement is executed and the results are returned to the HTTP client. (I'll talk about the syntax used to execute URL queries in the section "Using URL Queries to Test a Virtual Directory" later in this chapter.) URL queries give you a convenient way to develop and test a SQL Server application that uses a virtual directory, but because the client application can use a query string to send any Transact-SQL statement to the server, URL queries aren't generally recommended for production systems for security reasons.

Allowing Template Queries

Template queries are the most commonly used way to publish data in an application through the virtual directory. The templates are stored as XML files on the Web server and encapsulate Transact-SQL queries. When you use a server-side template to execute a query, only the query results are returned to the client application or browser. The details of the actual query are hidden from the caller, making this a more secure approach to publishing data.

I'll talk about the use of templates for database access over HTTP in Chapter 5, "Using XML Templates to Retrieve Data over HTTP."

Allowing XPath Queries

The XPath language is defined by the World Wide Web Consortium (W3C) as a standard navigation language. XPath queries enable you to use a subset of the XPath language to retrieve data based on an *annotated schema*. (You'll learn all about the use of annotated schemas in Chapter 6, "Mapping Data with Annotated Schemas.") The schema is stored on the Web server as an XML file and maps XML elements and attributes to data in the database. You can use XPath to specify which data defined in the schema should be returned.

Allowing POST Queries

A query template can be sent to the Web server as an HTTP POST query. The query will then be executed, and the results will be sent back to the client. The template itself is usually implemented as a hidden form field on an HTML page.

Using the POST method to send templates requires that both the Allow POST and Allow URL Queries options be enabled and raises the same security issues that allowing URL queries does.

> **Note** If you have installed the XML For SQL Server 2000 tool, the Settings tab will contain an additional option to allow posting of updategrams. I'll talk about XML For SQL Server 2000 in Chapter 8, "Additional Tools."

Creating Virtual Names

You configure the *virtual names* defined for the directory on the Virtual Names tab of the New Virtual Directory Properties dialog box. Virtual names are used in URLs to specify templates, schemas or database objects. The Virtual Names tab is shown in Figure 4-8.

You can create virtual names of type template, schema, and dbobject by clicking New on the Virtual Names tab to open the Virtual Name Configuration dialog box, where you can define the virtual name, type, and path for a virtual name.

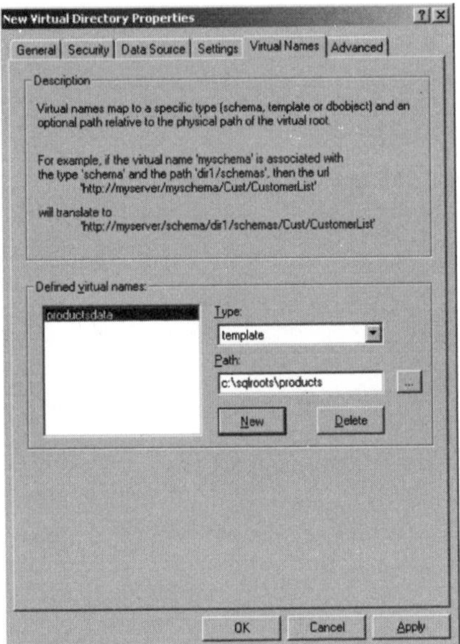

Figure 4-8 Creating virtual names

Using Virtual Names for Templates and Schemas

For templates and schemas, you can use virtual names to represent folders containing the XML template or schema files. For example, in our northwinddata virtual directory application, you can assign the virtual name *productsdata* to a folder that contains a template named *catalog.xml*. This template would then be accessed using the URL *http://webserver1/northwinddata/productsdata/catalog.xml*. When you specify a folder or a file as a virtual name, you must ensure that the appropriate NTFS permissions are set to allow the necessary accounts read access.

Using Virtual Names for Database Objects

For database objects, such as binary images, you can create a virtual name with no associated file or folder. This strategy allows you to use a URL to retrieve binary data. For example, you could use the virtual name *dbobject* to access the Picture field in the Categories table for a particular category in the Northwind database. The XPath necessary to retrieve the data would be included in a URL such as this one: *http://webserver1/northwinddata/dbobject/categories[@CategoryID='1']/@picture*.

> **Note** Although you can specify any name for a database object virtual name, naming it *dbobject* is a particularly sensible choice because this is the name that binary field references returned by AUTO mode queries include by default.

Specifying Advanced Options

The Advanced tab in the New Virtual Directory Properties dialog box allows you to specify advanced options. You can see the Advanced tab in Figure 4-9.

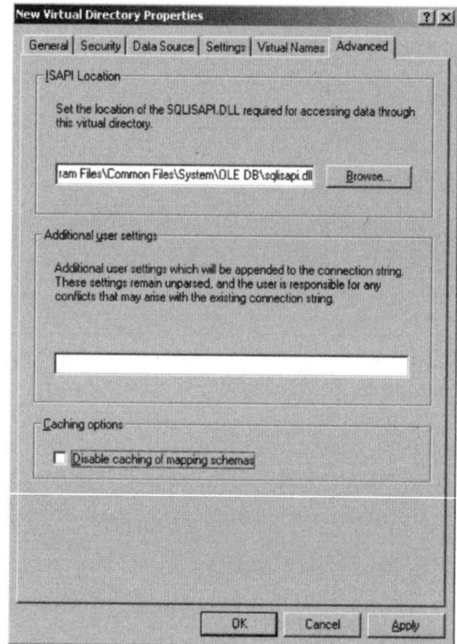

Figure 4-9 Setting advanced options

The first option on the Advanced tab allows you to set the location of the SQLISAPI application DLL. Should you move this DLL, you should update the location here.

The Advanced tab also enables you to append custom settings to the OLEDB connection string used to connect to the database and to disable caching of annotated schemas. By default, schemas are cached in memory the first time they're used to access data. While you're developing the schema, you might want to disable caching, which forces the schema to be reloaded with each request.

Scripting Virtual Directory Configuration

Although you would normally use the MMC snap-in to configure SQL Server virtual directories, it's worth pointing out that you can manage every aspect of HTTP publishing programmatically by writing scripts that use the automation objects provided by SQL Server. This strategy is particularly useful if you need to create reusable scripts to install your applications that use SQL Server virtual directory.

SQL Server provides a hierarchical object model of automation objects for virtual directory management. Figure 4-10 shows a graphical representation of the objects.

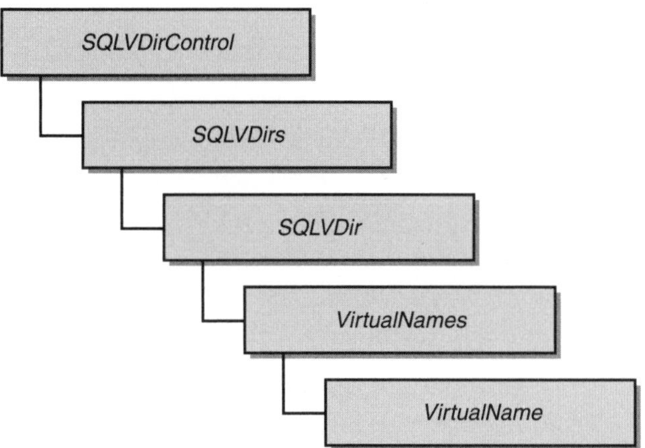

Figure 4-10 The SQL Server Virtual Directory Management objects

The *SQLVDirControl* Object

At the root of the hierarchy is the *SQLVDirControl* object, which is used to manage an IIS Web site. The *SQLVDirControl* object provides the *Connect* method, which you can use to connect to a local or remote IIS Web site. The *Connect* method accepts two parameters: the server to connect to and the ordinal number of the Web site on the server that you wish to manage. If you don't specify the parameters, they default to the local server and the first Web site, respectively. The object also provides a matching *Disconnect* method and a collection of SQL Server virtual directories in the specified site through its *SQLVDirs* property.

The following code sample shows how to connect to the first Web site on a server named *webserver* and access its collection of virtual directories:

```
Dim objSQLIIS
Dim objVDirCol
Set objSQLIIS = CreateObject("SQLVDir.SQLVDirControl")
objSQLIIS.Connect "webserver", "1"
Set objVDirCol = objSQLIIS.SQLVDirs
'Process virtual directories
:
objSQLIIS.Disconnect
```

The *SQLVDirs* Collection Object

You can use the *SQLVDirs* collection object to access existing virtual directories, create a new virtual directory, or remove an existing virtual directory. This object provides the *Item* property for accessing a specific virtual directory. Items can be accessed by name or ordinal position. The following code accesses the virtual directory *northwinddata*:

```
Dim objVDir
Set objVDir = objVDirCol.Item("northwinddata")
```

To create a new virtual directory, you can use the *AddVirtualDirectory* method of the *SQLVDirs* collection object this way:

```
Dim objVDirNW
Set objVDirNW = objVDirCol.AddVirtualDirectory("Nwind2")
```

You can also delete virtual directories by using the *RemoveVirtualDirectory* method of the *SQLVDirs* collection object.

The *SQLVDir* Object

The *SQLVDir* object is used to manage an individual virtual directory. It has a number of properties and methods related to the configuration options available in the New Virtual Directory Properties dialog box described earlier in this chapter. The most commonly used properties of this object are *Name*, *PhysicalPath*, *ServerName*, *DatabaseName*, *SecurityMode*, *UserName*, *Password*, and *AllowFlags*.

The *Name* property is used to configure the name of the virtual directory.

The *PhysicalPath* property is used to specify the physical path to the directory associated with the virtual directory.

The *ServerName* property enables you to specify the name of the server that has Microsoft SQL Server 2000 installed.

The *DatabaseName* property allows you to specify the name of the database on the specified server.

The *SecurityMode* property enables you to configure the login authentication model used with the virtual directory. You can set it to a numerical value: 1 for trusted server SQL Server security, 2 for trusted server Windows integrated security, 4 for impersonation/delegation using basic authentication to a SQL Server account, and 8 for impersonation/delegation with Windows integrated authentication.

The *UserName* and *Password* properties enable you to configure the credentials used to access the database. You need to specify these two properties if you choose either trusted server Windows integrated security or trusted server SQL Server security.

The *AllowFlags* property is used to configure the types of access allowed through the virtual directory. Numerical values are used to represent the possible types of access as shown in this table:

Value	Type of Access Allowed
1	URL queries
8	Templates
64	XPath queries

The values can be combined to allow multiple types of access. For example, specifying 72 (8 + 64) allows both templates (value 8) and XPath queries (value 64).

The following code sample shows how a virtual directory can be configured using script:

```
With objVDirNW
    .Name = "Nwind2"
    .PhysicalPath = "C:\Nwind2"
    .ServerName = "DBServer1"
    .DatabaseName = "Northwind"
    .SecurityMode = 2
    .UserName = "webuseraccount"
    .Password = "password"
    .AllowFlags = 64
End With
```

The *VirtualNames* Collection Object

You use the *VirtualNames* collection object to manage the virtual names belonging to a virtual directory. Just as the *SQLVDirs* collection, the *VirtualNames* collection object provides an *Item* property to access existing virtual names and an *AddVirtualName* method to create new virtual names. The *AddVirtualName* method includes parameters for the name, type, and location of the virtual name being created. The virtual name type can be specified as 1 for dbobject, 2 for schema, or 4 for template. The following code sample shows a virtual name for templates being added to a virtual directory:

```
objVDirNW.VirtualNames.AddVirtualName "TemplateFiles", 4, _
    "C:\nwind2\templates"
```

The *VirtualName* Object

You can use the *VirtualName* object to read or change the properties of an existing virtual name using the *Name*, *Type*, and *Path* properties. For example, you could use the following code to change the path of the *TemplateFiles* virtual name created in the previous example:

```
Set objVName = objVDirNW.VirtualNames.Item("TemplateFiles")
objVName.Path = "D:\nwind2\templates"
```

The CreateVRoot.vbs file used to set up the demos on the companion CD contains code to script the creation of a virtual directory.

Using URL Queries to Test a Virtual Directory

The easiest way to test that a virtual directory has been correctly configured is to enable URL queries and test the application by submitting queries using an XML-aware browser such as Internet Explorer. To ensure that your security configuration is working correctly, you should test the application using a remote client machine.

When you retrieve data from a URL, you use parameters to specify the query to be executed and other formatting settings. These parameters are passed using the standard format for URL query strings. To separate the parameters from the URL, use a question mark character (?). When you must pass a number of parameters, use an ampersand character (&) to separate them. For example, the following URL format would be used to access data from a URL using two parameters:

```
http://webserver1/northwinddata?param1=value&param2=value
```

Retrieving XML Documents Using a URL Query

An XML document can be retrieved using a URL query by specifying a *sql* parameter containing a FOR XML query. Because FOR XML queries return XML fragments rather than well-formed XML documents, a root element must be specified in the URL. You accomplish this by selecting the root element explicitly or by specifying a *root* parameter.

The following example shows a URL query that could be used to retrieve data from the Products table in the Northwind database. The root element is included as part of the *sql* parameter.

```
http://webserver1/northwinddata?sql=SELECT+'<catalog>';SELECT+*+FROM
    +products+FOR+XML+AUTO;SELECT+'</catalog>'
```

You can execute this query by opening the shortcut named Explicit Root in the Demos\Chapter4 folder on the companion CD. This query could also be performed by specifying a *root* parameter, as shown in this example:

```
http://webserver1/northwinddata?sql=SELECT+*+FROM+products
    +FOR+XML+AUTO&root=catalog
```

Encoding Special Characters in a URL Query

Some characters that could appear in a Transact-SQL query have a special meaning in a URL and must be encoded. For example, consider the following query:

```
SELECT * FROM products
WHERE productname LIKE 'G%'
FOR XML AUTO
```

Although this is a perfectly legal Transact-SQL query, it would return an error if executed through a URL because the percentage symbol, used in Transact-SQL as a wildcard, has a special meaning in a URL, where it is used to specify an encoded character. To execute the query in a URL, the percentage symbol should be encoded in hexadecimal as *%25*. A URL query containing the encoded symbol appears here:

```
http://webserver1/northwinddata?sql=SELECT+*+FROM+products
    +WHERE+productname+LIKE+'G%25'+FOR+XML+AUTO&root=catalog
```

You can execute this query by opening the shortcut named Encode Characters in the Demos\Chapter4 folder on the companion CD. The following table shows the characters that must be encoded when you use them in a URL query:

Character	Meaning	Hexadecimal Encoding
+	Space	%20
/	Directory separator	%2F
?	Parameter marker	%3F
%	Encoded character marker	%25
#	Bookmark indicator	%23
&	Parameter separator	%26

Note Spaces aren't allowed in URLs and should be encoded using a plus (+) symbol or its hexadecimal equivalent (%20). For example, a URL might contain the parameter *sql=SELECT+*+FROM+products+FOR+XML*. Internet Explorer automatically replaces spaces with hexadecimal-encoded plus symbols.

Specifying a Style Sheet in a URL Query

Say that you want to specify that an XSL style sheet should be applied to the XML data returned by a URL query. You can accomplish this task by storing the style sheet in the virtual directory referenced by the SQLISAPI application and adding an *xsl* parameter to the URL. The SQLOLEDB provider applies the style sheet to the XML data, and the IIS server returns the resulting document to the browser. You can use this technique to retrieve the data as HTML using a non-XML–aware browser.

To see how this technique could be useful, let's assume you want to retrieve the ProductID and ProductName fields from each record in the Products table and display them in an HTML table. You could create the following style sheet and save it as *catalog.xsl* in the SQL Server virtual directory:

```
<?xml version="1.0"?>
<xsl:stylesheet xmlns:xsl="http://www.w3.org/1999/XSL/Transform" version="1.0">
    <xsl:template match="/">
        <HTML>
            <BODY>
                <TABLE border="1">
                    <TR>
                        <TD><B>Product ID</B></TD>
                        <TD><B>Product Name</B></TD>
                    </TR>
                    <xsl:for-each select="catalog/products">
                        <TR>
                            <TD>
                            <xsl:value-of select="@productid"/>
                            </TD>
                            <TD>
                            <xsl:value-of select="@productname"/>
                            </TD>
                        </TR>
                    </xsl:for-each>
                </TABLE>
            </BODY>
        </HTML>
    </xsl:template>
</xsl:stylesheet>
```

This style sheet is also available in the Demos\Chapter4 folder on the companion CD. You could then specify the style sheet using the *xsl* parameter in a URL query, as shown here:

```
http://webserver1/northwinddata?sql=SELECT+productid,+productname
    +FROM+products+FOR+XML+AUTO&root=catalog&xsl=catalog.xsl
```

You can execute this query by opening the shortcut named Apply Style Sheet in the Demos\Chapter4 folder on the companion CD. The data would be returned to the browser as HTML and rendered in a table, similar to the one shown here (which has been truncated for clarity):

Product ID	Product Name
17	Alice Mutton
3	Aniseed Syrup
40	Boston Crab Meat
60	Camembert Pierrot
18	Carnarvon Tigers

Specifying a Content Type

The SQLISAPI application returns the data with an appropriate content type specified in the header so that the client application or browser can properly render the results. For most queries, the data is returned with text/xml as its default content type, unless a style sheet that formats the data as HTML is used, in which case the content type defaults to text/html. You can override the default content type by adding a *contenttype* parameter to the URL, as shown in the following example:

```
http://webserver1/northwinddata?sql=SELECT+productid,+productname
    +FROM products+FOR+XML+AUTO&root=catalog&xsl=catalog.xsl
    +&contenttype=text/xml
```

In this example, the HTML produced by the style sheet is displayed by an XML-aware browser as an XML document rather than rendered, as shown here:

```
<HTML>
    <BODY>
        <TABLE border="1">
            <TR>
                <TD><B>Product ID</B></TD>
                <TD><B>Product Name</B></TD>
            </TR>
            <TR>
                <TD>17</TD>
                <TD>Alice Mutton</TD>
            </TR>
            <TR>
                <TD>3</TD>
                <TD>Aniseed Syrup</TD>
            </TR>
            ⋮
        </TABLE>
    </BODY>
</HTML>
```

You can execute this query by opening the shortcut named Content Type in the Demos\Chapter4 folder on the companion CD.

Returning Non-XML Query Results

The ability to specify the content type is particularly useful when you're using an XML-aware browser, such as Internet Explorer, to retrieve data that isn't a fully well-formed XML document. If you execute a Transact-SQL query with no FOR XML clause, your data is simply returned as a character stream; if you execute a FOR XML query with no root element specified, your data will come back as one or more XML fragments. Returning either of these sets of data to an XML-aware browser without specifying a content type other than XML would result in a parsing error.

You can use HTTP to execute queries with no FOR XML clause to return a single column from a table or a view, as shown in the following example:

```
http://webserver1/northwinddata?sql=SELECT+productname
    +FROM+products&contenttype=text/html
```

You can execute this query by opening the shortcut named Non XML Query in the Demos\Chapter4 folder on the companion CD. This code returns a stream containing the *Productname* field for each row, as shown here:

```
Alice MuttonAniseed SyrupBoston Crab MeatCamembert PierrotCarnarvon
    TigersChaiChang ...
```

Because the data is returned in a nondelimited stream, this approach is probably most useful for fixed-width columns.

XML fragments can be returned with no root element, allowing you to use custom client logic to build a well-formed XML document. For example, you could execute the following URL query:

```
http://webserver1/northwinddata?sql=SELECT+productid,+productname
    +FROM+products+FOR+XML+AUTO&contenttype=text/html
```

Data returned to an XML-aware browser using this approach results in a blank Web page because browsers don't render the contents of a tag. If you look at the source of the page, you can see the actual XML fragments returned to the browser, as shown here:

```
<products productid="17" productname="Alice Mutton"/>
<products productid="3" productname="Aniseed Syrup"/>
<products productid="40" productname="Boston Crab Meat"/>
<products productid="60" productname="Camembert Pierrot"/>
<products productid="18" productname="Carnarvon Tigers"/>
⋮
```

If you also specify the ELEMENTS option in the URL query, the element values in the element-centric XML fragments will be rendered as a character stream and returned to the browser.

Executing Stored Procedures in a URL Query

You can execute a stored procedure using either the Transact-SQL EXECUTE syntax or the Open Database Connectivity (ODBC) CALL syntax. In either case, you can specify parameters by position or by name with the value. For example, you can create a stored procedure in the Northwind database using the following Transact-SQL script:

```
CREATE PROC getpricelist @category integer
AS
SELECT productname, unitprice
FROM products
WHERE categoryid = @category
FOR XML AUTO
```

To call this stored procedure in a URL query, you can use the EXECUTE syntax and specify the parameter by position, as shown here:

```
http://webserver1/northwinddata?sql=EXECUTE+getpricelist+2
    +&root=pricelist
```

You can execute this query by opening the shortcut named Execute Proc in the Demos\Chapter4 folder on the companion CD. You could also specify the parameter by name with the value, as shown here:

```
http://webserver1/northwinddata?sql=EXECUTE+getpricelist
    +@category=2&root=pricelist
```

Another option is to use ODBC CALL syntax to execute the stored procedure:

```
http://webserver1/northwinddata?sql={CALL+getpricelist}+2
    +&root=pricelist
```

Again, the parameter could be passed by name with the value:

```
http://webserver1/northwinddata?sql={CALL+getpricelist}
    +@category=2&root=pricelist
```

You can execute this query by opening the shortcut named Call Proc in the Demos\Chapter4 folder on the companion CD. Because one syntax isn't really better than another, most developers use the format most familiar to them.

Summary

In this chapter, you've seen how to publish a virtual directory for XML data access, either using the Configure SQL XML Support In IIS MMC snap-in or by writing a script that uses the automation objects for virtual directory management.

You've also learned how to execute queries in a URL and retrieve the results over HTTP. Although this is a valid way to retrieve data in a test or development environment, in most production solutions, you need to create templates or schemas that encapsulate the data you want to publish.

In the next chapter, we'll examine how XML templates can be created and published using a virtual name.

5

Using XML Templates to Retrieve Data over HTTP

In Chapter 4, I described how a Microsoft SQL Server virtual directory can be published to allow users access to a database over HTTP. In this chapter, I'll explain how you can publish XML templates to encapsulate the data you want to make available. Using XML templates gives you a more controlled security environment than simply allowing users to send queries in a URL to a server for data retrieval.

Templates contain one or more queries that retrieve data from the database. The results are then sent to the calling browser or client application. Because the client receives only the query results and not the source code for the query, the data access logic is encapsulated like the source code of an ASP file. This arrangement allows you to publish data securely over the Internet. For example, Northwind Traders could make the product catalog available over the Internet by creating a template that retrieves the necessary data from the database. Customers could then simply access the template using a browser. Customers would never see the SQL used to access the data; they would see only the resulting product list.

What Is a Template?

I described XML templates in Chapter 3. A template is an XML document based on the Microsoft XML-SQL namespace. When you use templates with HTTP, you can store the template file in a virtual name of template type and access the file by specifying the template name in a URL. For example, a template named products.xml saved in a virtual name known as *onlinesales* could be accessed using a URL similar to this one:

```
http://webserver1/northwinddata/onlinesales/products.xml
```

You create the virtual name of template type by using the Configure SQL XML Support In IIS MMC snap-in tool or the automation objects for virtual directory management, as described in Chapter 4. A single virtual directory can contain many virtual names, so it's up to you to decide how to arrange your templates. You might want to create multiple virtual names to reflect different types of data. For example, in an intranet application, you might choose to create a set of templates that deal with employees and place the templates in one virtual name while you store templates relating to customers in a different virtual name. You can also store templates in subdirectories of virtual names and extend the URL used to access the templates accordingly.

To use templates, you must configure the virtual directory to allow template queries. You accomplish this by selecting Allow Template Queries on the Settings tab of the Virtual Directory Properties dialog box in the Configure SQL XML Support In IIS MMC snap-in tool or by setting the *AllowFlags* property of the *SQLVDir* object to 8.

Creating Templates

As I mentioned, a template is an XML file containing a document based on the Microsoft XML-SQL namespace. The template usually contains at least one query. Let's assume that Northwind Traders wants to publish its catalog on the Web. A sensible approach might be to allow customers to browse the catalog by product category. The first stage in building this solution would be to create a template that retrieves a list of categories, as shown in the following sample code:

```
<?xml version='1.0' ?>
<categorylist xmlns:sql='urn:schemas-microsoft-com:xml-sql'>
    <sql:query>
        SELECT categoryid, categoryname
        FROM categories
        FOR XML AUTO, ELEMENTS
    </sql:query>
</categorylist>
```

You can save this category list template as categories.xml in the *onlinesales* virtual name. From this code, you can see that the templates used with HTTP have the same format as the query templates used with ADO. When the template is accessed, the *query* tags are resolved into the XML fragments they return and the template containing the resolved query results is returned to the caller.

Creating Parameterized Templates

To make your templates more flexible, you can add parameters. This strategy allows users to request data based on one or more variable values. For example, a template containing a parameter would allow users to supply a category ID and return a list of the products in the specified category.

Parameters are placed in the header of the template, which is defined using the *header* tag. Each parameter is then defined using the *param* tag, with an optional default value. You could use the following template to retrieve products by category:

```
<?xml version='1.0' ?>
<productlist xmlns:sql='urn:schemas-microsoft-com:xml-sql'>
    <sql:header>
        <sql:param name='categoryid'>1</sql:param>
    </sql:header>
    <sql:query>
        SELECT productid, productname, unitprice
        FROM products
        WHERE categoryid = @categoryid
        FOR XML AUTO, ELEMENTS
    </sql:query>
</productlist>
```

This template is saved as Products.xml in the Demos\Chapter5\Templates folder on the companion CD. This template includes a single parameter with a default value of 1. Notice that the *param* tag includes a *name* attribute used to identify the parameter; you use this name in the SQL query by prefixing it with the @ symbol.

To access data using a parameterized template, you specify the parameters in the URL as a query string. For example, the products in category number 2 could be retrieved from the products.xml template using the following URL:

```
http://webserver1/northwinddata/onlinesales/products.xml?categoryid=2
```

You can execute this query by opening the shortcut named Product List in the Demos\Chapter5 folder on the companion CD.

Applying Style Sheets with Templates

When you use a template to retrieve data, you might need to apply an XSL style sheet to the XML returned. An XSL style sheet contains instructions for presenting the XML data in a different format such as HTML or WML, or it might be used to transform the data from one XML grammar to another.

The most common use of an XSL style sheet is to render the data as HTML for display in a browser. For example, the Northwind Traders catalog could be published on a Web site by applying XSL style sheets to the XML data retrieved by the queries in the templates. The style sheet used with the categories.xml template would need to display the list of categories and provide hyperlinks to the products.xml template that includes the *categoryid* parameter. You could use the following style sheet to render the category list as an HTML table:

```
<?xml version='1.0'?>
<xsl:stylesheet xmlns:xsl=
    'http://www.w3.org/1999/XSL/Transform' version='1.0'>
    <xsl:template match='/'>
        <BODY>
            <TABLE>
                <TR>
                    <TD><B>Click a Product Category</B></TD>
                </TR>
                <xsl:for-each select='categorylist/categories'>
                    <TR>
                        <TD>
                            <A>
                                <xsl:attribute name='HREF'>
                                    products.xml?categoryid=
                                    <xsl:value-of select='categoryid'/>
                                </xsl:attribute>
                                <xsl:value-of select='categoryname'/>
                            </A>
                        </TD>
                    </TR>
                </xsl:for-each>
            </TABLE>
        </BODY>
    </xsl:template>
</xsl:stylesheet>
```

This style sheet is also available in the Demos\Chapter5\Templates folder on the companion CD in the file named categories.xsl. Notice that the code uses the *categoryid* parameter in the construction of the hyperlink to the products.xml template. This tactic enables the appropriate parameter to be passed to the products.xml template when the user clicks the desired category name.

The product list itself could be rendered as HTML using a style sheet similar to the following example:

```
<?xml version='1.0' ?>
<xsl:stylesheet xmlns:xsl=
    'http://www.w3.org/1999/XSL/Transform' version='1.0'>
    <xsl:template match='/'>
        <HTML>
            <BODY>
                <H2>Product List</H2>
                <TABLE>
                    <TR>
```

```
                    <TD><B>Product</B></TD>
                    <TD><B>Price</B></TD>
                </TR>
                <xsl:for-each select='productlist/products'>
                <TR>
                    <TD><xsl:value-of select='productname'/></TD>
                    <TD><xsl:value-of select='unitprice'/></TD>
                </TR>
                </xsl:for-each>
            </TABLE>
        </BODY>
    </HTML>
  </xsl:template>
</xsl:stylesheet>
```

You can also find this style sheet in the Demos\Chapter5\Templates folder on the companion CD in the file named products.xsl.

Applying a Style Sheet on the Server

Creating the appropriate style sheets is only a part of the solution. You must also provide a way for the application to apply the correct style sheet when the data from a template has been retrieved. For Web pages on an Internet site, it is usually best to apply the style sheet on the server and return HTML to the browser, as shown in Figure 5-1.

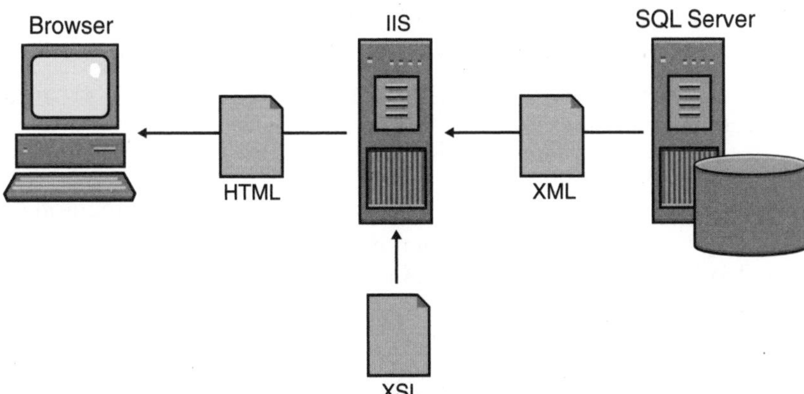

Figure 5-1 Server-side XSL processing

Using the *XSL* Attribute

To apply the products.xsl style sheet to the data returned by the products.xml template, you could save the style sheet in the template virtual name (or a subfolder) and reference it in the template using an *xsl* attribute in the root element, as shown in the example at the top of the next page.

```
<?xml version='1.0' ?>
<productlist xmlns:sql='urn:schemas-microsoft-com:xml-sql'
    sql:xsl='products.xsl'>
    <sql:header>
        <sql:param name='categoryid'>1</sql:param>
    </sql:header>
    <sql:query>
        SELECT productid, productname, unitprice
        FROM products
        WHERE categoryid = @categoryid
        FOR XML AUTO, ELEMENTS
    </sql:query>
</productlist>
```

This template is saved as ProductListServerXSL.xml in the Demos\Chapter5\Templates folder on the companion CD. The addition of the *xsl* attribute causes the OLE-DB provider to apply the style sheet and return the transformed data to the client. In this case, the result is an HTML document. However, you should be particularly aware of one issue when you're using the *xsl* attribute: the problem of content types. By default, templates return documents with a content type of text/xml. An XML-aware browser treats any document of this type as an XML document and attempts to parse and display it. Because an HTML document generated from a style sheet can, in fact, be a valid XML document, the browser parses and displays the document instead of rendering the HTML. To overcome this obstacle, you must specify a *contenttype* parameter of text/html in a query string when using a URL to access a template. For example, the URL used to retrieve the category list in HTML format would be:

```
http://webserver1/northwinddata/onlinesales/CategoryListServerXSL.xml
    ?contenttype=text/html
```

You can execute this query by opening the shortcut named Category List (ServerSideXSL) in the Demos\Chapter5 folder on the companion CD. Because the categories.xsl style sheet contains hyperlinks to the products.xml template, you also need to modify the links in the categories.xsl style sheet to include the *contenttype* parameter, as shown here:

```
<A>
    <xsl:attribute name='HREF'>
        ProductListServerXSL.xml?categoryid=<xsl:value-of
            select='categoryid'/>
        &amp;contenttype=text/html
    </xsl:attribute>
    <xsl:value-of select='categoryname'/>
</A>
```

You can find the complete style sheet in the file named CategoryListServer.xsl in the Demos\Chapter5\Templates folder.

> **Note** Because the ampersand has a particular meaning in an HTML document, any query strings containing multiple parameters must use *&* in place of *&*.

Figure 5-2 shows the output after the URL executed the categories.xml template.

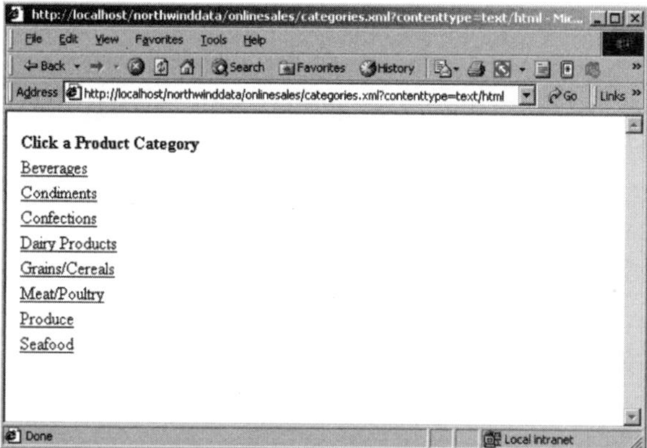

Figure 5-2 The category list page

If you click the category name you want on the category list page, the product list page will open, as shown in Figure 5-3.

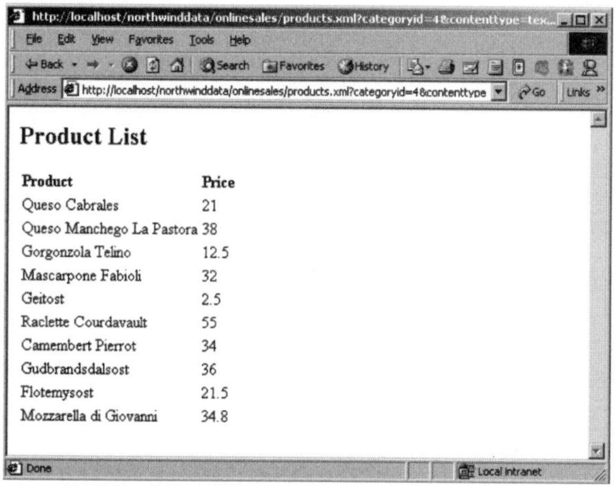

http://localhost/northwinddata/onlinesales/products.xml?categoryid=4&contenttype=tex...

Address http://localhost/northwinddata/onlinesales/products.xml?categoryid=4&contenttype

Product List

Product	Price
Queso Cabrales	21
Queso Manchego La Pastora	38
Gorgonzola Telino	12.5
Mascarpone Fabioli	32
Geitost	2.5
Raclette Courdavault	55
Camembert Pierrot	34
Gudbrandsdalsost	36
Flotemysost	21.5
Mozzarella di Giovanni	34.8

Figure 5-3 The product list page

Specifying a Style Sheet in the URL

You can also apply a style sheet on the server by specifying an *xsl* parameter in the URL that you're using to access the template. In this case, you must save the style sheet in the virtual root directory or in one of its subdirectories. You must specify the relative path if you store the style sheet in a subdirectory of the virtual directory. For example, you could make use of the following URL to retrieve data from the categories.xml template and apply the categories.xsl style sheet:

```
http://webserver1/northwinddata/onlinesales/categories.xml
    ?xsl=CategoryListServer.xsl
```

You can execute this query by opening the shortcut named Category List (Style Sheet in URL) in the Demos\Chapter5 folder on the companion CD. Because the categories.xsl style sheet formats the data as HTML, the content type defaults to text/html so that the browser can display the HTML page properly. If a template includes an *xsl* attribute and a different style sheet is specified in the URL, the style sheet referenced by the *xsl* attribute in the template is applied first; the style sheet specified in the URL is then applied to the resulting document.

Applying a Style Sheet on the Client Side

You can take a different approach if the client supports XML. By referencing the style sheet in a processing instruction, you can download the XML data to the client and the style sheet can then be accessed and applied. The processing instruction declares the location of the style sheet in the template. Figure 5-4 illustrates this approach.

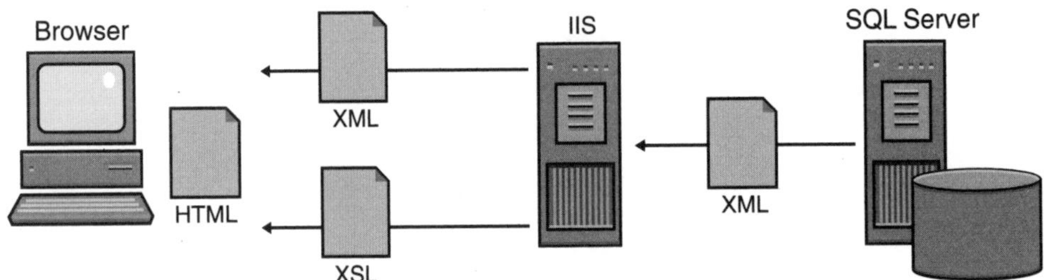

Figure 5-4 Client-side XSL processing

To apply the products.xsl style sheet to the XML data retrieved by the products.xml template, you need to add a processing instruction to the top of the template after the XML declaration, as shown in the following example:

```
<?xml version='1.0' ?>
<?xml-stylesheet type='text/xsl' href='products.xsl'?>
    <productlist xmlns:sql='urn:schemas-microsoft-com:xml-sql'>
    <sql:header>
```

```
        <sql:param name='categoryid'>1</sql:param>
    </sql:header>
    <sql:query>
        SELECT productid, productname, unitprice
        FROM products
        WHERE categoryid = @categoryid
        FOR XML AUTO, ELEMENTS
    </sql:query>
</productlist>
```

This template is saved as ProductListClientXSL.xml in the Demos\Chapter5\Templates folder on the companion CD. If you're equipped with Microsoft Internet Explorer 5, you could access the product list using this template. In this case, the XML parser on the client interprets the processing instruction and the style sheet is then downloaded and processed. This approach has the advantage of removing some of the processing load from the server but requires an additional network trip to download the style sheet. Of course, you also need to consider that the client must be XML-enabled or the style sheet will never be applied, which makes this approach most suitable for internal applications or intranet sites. For Internet-based applications, you're more likely to find that server-side XSL processing is the best option.

Posting a Template

The templates we've considered so far in this chapter are stored on the server. Keeping your templates on the server is a good way to control the data that users can access because only the queries defined in your server-side templates can be used. However, you might on occasion want to allow the template to be defined dynamically on the client and submitted to the SQL Server virtual directory. You would typically use this approach to avoid the necessity of creating a template virtual name and defining the server-side templates.

Templates can be posted to the server over HTTP, which allows you to design Web pages or client applications on which you construct a template dynamically before you submit it via the virtual directory. The results of the queries in the template are then returned to the client as an HTTP response. To enable this kind of database access, you must select both the Allow URL Queries and Allow POST options on the Settings tab of the Virtual Directory Properties dialog box in the Configure SQL XML Support In IIS MMC snap-in tool.

Posting a Template from an HTML Form

To post a template from a Web page, the easiest approach is to use a hidden form field to contain the template. For example, Northwind Traders might choose to use client-side templates in an intranet application that allows employees to retrieve customer data. You could use an HTML page similar to the following sample to retrieve details about a specific customer:

```
<HTML>
    <HEAD>
        <TITLE>Customer Details</TITLE>
    </HEAD>
    <BODY>
        <FORM action='http://webserver1/northwinddata' method='POST'>
            <B>Employee ID Number</B>
            <INPUT type=text name=EmployeeID value='1'>
            <INPUT type=hidden name=xsl value=employee.xsl>
            <INPUT type=hidden name=template value='
            <employeedata xmlns:sql="urn:schemas-microsoft-com:xml-sql">
                <sql:header>
                    <sql:param name="EmployeeID">1</sql:param>
                </sql:header>
                <sql:query>
                    SELECT FirstName, LastName
                    FROM Employees
                    WHERE EmployeeID=@EmployeeID
                    FOR XML AUTO
                </sql:query>
            </employeedata>
            '>
            <P><input type='submit'>
        </FORM>
    </BODY>
</HTML>
```

You could also find this sample in the Demos\Chapter5 folder on the companion CD in a file named employee.html. In this code sample, you can see how the template is implemented as a hidden form field named *template*. This field is assigned a string value containing the XML template. Any parameters are automatically reconciled with HTML *input* elements of the same name, so in this example, the value posted to the server in the Employee ID Number text box will be used as the *EmployeeID* parameter in the template.

You can also see how you can apply an XSL style sheet to the data by including an HTML *input* element named *xsl*. The value for this *input* element should be a reference to an XSL file. The style sheet is processed on the server, and the HTML response is sent back to the browser.

> **Note** If you want to return XML to the browser, simply include a hidden HTML *input* element named *contenttype* with a value of text/xml.

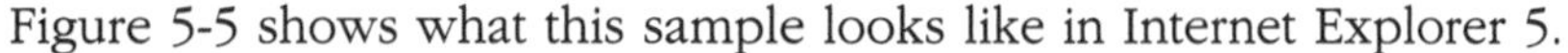

Figure 5-5 shows what this sample looks like in Internet Explorer 5.

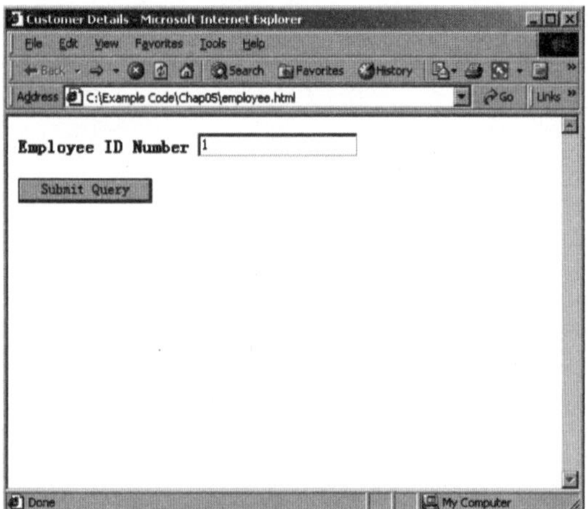

Figure 5-5 The Customer Details page

The advantage of posting templates from HTML pages is that you can allow users to access HTML pages in a conventional Web site without having to manage a set of template files in a SQL Server virtual name. You will, however, still need to create a SQL Server virtual directory to post the templates to. The main disadvantage is that the SQL used to retrieve the data is no longer encapsulated and can be viewed in the source code of the HTML page containing the template.

Posting Templates from Non-HTML Clients

You can also post templates from non-HTML client applications, such as COM+ components or Microsoft Windows applications. This procedure allows you to define queries on the client application without using ADO to communicate with the database server, thus forcing all requests to be routed through a Web server and potentially a firewall.

For example, you could use a COM+ component containing the following method to retrieve data from the Orders table in the Northwind database:

```
Public Function getOrderData(intOrderNo As Integer)
Dim xmlHttp As MSXML2.xmlHttp
Dim doc As MSXML2.DOMDocument
Dim strQry As String

' Construct the template.
strQry = "<?xml version='1.0' ?>"
strQry = strQry & "<orderdetails>"
strQry = strQry & "<sql:query "
strQry = strQry & "xmlns:sql='urn:schemas-microsoft-com:xml-sql'>"
strQry = strQry & " SELECT orderid, orderdate, shipname FROM orders "
strQry = strQry & " WHERE orderid = " & intOrderNo
strQry = strQry & "FOR XML AUTO"
strQry = strQry & "</sql:query>"
strQry = strQry & "</orderdetails>"

' Load the template into the MSXML parser.
Set doc = New MSXML2.DOMDocument
doc.loadXML strQry

' Post the template.
Set xmlHttp = New MSXML2.xmlHttp
xmlHttp.Open "POST", "http://webserver1/northwinddata", False
xmlHttp.setRequestHeader "Content-Type", "application/xml"
xmlHttp.send doc

' Retrieve the results.
getOrderData = xmlHttp.responseText
End Function
```

Code similar to this is saved as post.vbs in the Demos\Chapter5 folder on the companion CD. In this example, the template is constructed as a string and then loaded into the MSXML parser, which allows your code to validate the XML template before sending it to the server. Next the template is posted to the server using the *XMLHTTP* object provided in the MSXML library. Notice that the *Content-Type* parameter in the request header is set to *application/xml* so that the data retrieved by the template will be returned to the client as an XML document. Finally the query results are read from the *responseText* property of the *XMLHTTP* object.

This approach to using templates means that most of the development effort is focused on the client application or business components. However, because posting templates requires that the virtual directory allow URL queries, you're relying solely on database security permissions to restrict access to data. You should therefore carefully consider the design of your application and use server-side templates where possible because of the greater security they offer.

Summary

In this chapter, I've discussed the use of templates over HTTP to retrieve XML data from SQL Server. Templates are probably the most common way to develop Web-based applications that allow users to browse data. When you're designing a template-based application, you should consider carefully whether style sheets should be processed on the server or the client, remembering that most Internet-based applications use server-side processing. You might also consider building applications that post templates to the server, although this approach can add some security risks.

In the next chapter, I'll describe how to use annotated schemas to map business documents to database tables.

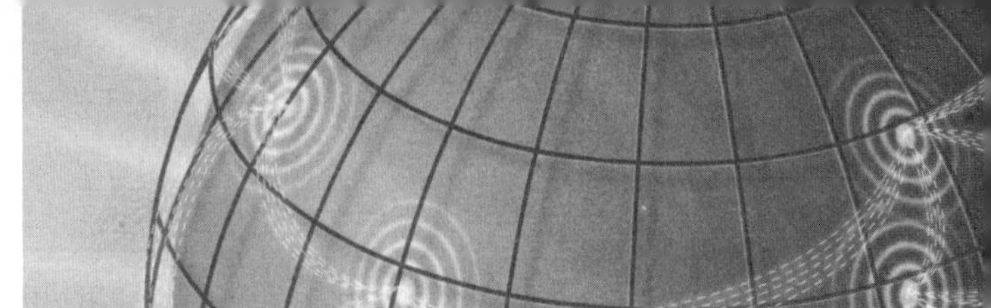

6

Retrieving Data with Mapping Schemas

So far we've seen how templates can be used to retrieve XML data from Microsoft SQL Server, over both ADO and HTTP connections. In this chapter, we'll examine another approach: mapping schemas.

XML Schemas—An Overview

When two organizations agree to exchange business documents using XML, one of the issues they need to resolve is the definition of the documents they'll exchange. For example, because Northwind Traders is a supplier to many businesses, Northwind Traders and its customers would have to establish the definition of and rules for working with a catalog document listing the goods available for order before they could build a working instance of a catalog. Among the questions they would need to ask are the following:

- What information does a catalog need to contain?
- In what order does that information appear in the catalog?
- Is there any information that can be considered optional?

Defining an XML Document with a Schema

Of course, once the application developers had decided to use XML, they'd need to consider some more specific questions:

- What elements and attributes are used in an XML representation of a catalog?
- Which elements contain which attributes and subelements?
- Can some elements be repeated several times in a single catalog? If so, how many times?
- What data types are valid for specific elements or attributes?

The answers to these sorts of questions form a *schema,* the purpose of which is to provide to developers a shared definition of what a particular type of XML document should look like. In this way, different organizations can all exchange documents that adhere to the same schema, allowing them to build XML-enabled applications to validate their documents and process them in a consistent fashion.

> **Note** Schemas are the intended replacement for the older Document Type Definition (DTD). DTDs define XML documents in much the same way that schemas do but have limited support for data types and are written using non-XML syntax, which means that XML developers need to learn two different syntaxes and that XML parsers need to be able to parse DTDs as well as XML.

XML-Data Reduced (XDR) Schemas

The World Wide Web Consortium (W3C) is the governing body responsible for controlling standards on the Internet. In fact, XML itself is a W3C standard. As I'm writing this chapter, the standard for the syntax to be used in XML schemas is in the process of being approved. In the meantime, Microsoft and other companies have proposed to the W3C that XML-Data syntax be used to define schemas for use in document exchange scenarios today.

XML-Data Reduced (XDR) is a subset of the XML-Data syntax that can be used to define XML schemas. Microsoft XML-aware products, including SQL Server and the Microsoft XML parser, support the XDR specification for schemas.

Note It's not clear when the final XML schema standard will be approved by the W3C, and when it is, the standard is likely to be semantically different from the XML-Data proposal. Microsoft has committed to supporting the eventual W3C standard in all its XML-based products and technologies, including SQL Server. In the meantime, Microsoft products use the XDR for schema definitions, and it's expected that any support added for the XML schema standard will be complemented by backward-compatibility for XDR.

An Example Schema

So what does an XDR schema look like? Let's take a simple example. Suppose a catalog schema must be defined for Northwind Traders. It might look something like the following example:

```
<?xml version="1.0"?>
<Schema name="NWCatalogSchema"
    xmlns="urn:schemas-microsoft-com:xml-data"
    xmlns:dt="urn:schemas-microsoft-com:datatypes">

    <ElementType name="Description" dt:type="string"/>
    <ElementType name="Price" dt:type="fixed.14.4"/>

    <ElementType name="Product" model="closed">
        <AttributeType name="ProductCode" dt:type="string"/>
        <attribute type="ProductCode" required="yes"/>
        <element type="Description" minOccurs="1" maxOccurs="1"/>
        <element type="Price" minOccurs="1" maxOccurs="1"/>
    </ElementType>

    <ElementType name="Category" model="closed">
        <AttributeType name="CategoryID" dt:type="string"/>
        <AttributeType name="CategoryName" dt:type="string"/>
        <attribute type="CategoryID" required="yes"/>
        <attribute type="CategoryName" required="yes"/>
        <element type="Product" minOccurs="1" maxOccurs="*"/>
    </ElementType>

    <ElementType name="Catalog" model="closed">
        <element type="Category" minOccurs="1" maxOccurs="1"/>
    </ElementType>

</Schema>
```

You can also find this schema in the Demos\Chapter6\Schemas folder on the companion CD in a file named CatalogSchema.xml. This schema answers the questions posed earlier by defining the elements and attributes that you can use in a catalog document. It also uses the *datatypes* namespace to define the data types of the elements and attributes. Finally, by specifying a *closed model* for the elements, the schema ensures that only the elements defined in the schema can be used in a catalog document. Northwind Traders and its trading partners could use this schema to validate documents, such as the one shown here:

```
<?xml version="1.0"?>
<Catalog xmlns=
    "x-schema:http://www.northwindtraders.com/schemas/CatalogSchema.xml">
    <Category CategoryID="1" CategoryName="Beverages">
        <Product ProductCode="1">
            <Description>Chai</Description>
            <Price>18</Price>
        </Product>
        <Product ProductCode="2">
            <Description>Chang</Description>
            <Price>19</Price>
        </Product>
    </Category>
    <Category CategoryID="2" CategoryName="Condiments">
        <Product ProductCode="3">
            <Description>Aniseed Syrup</Description>
            <Price>10</Price>
        </Product>
    </Category>
</Catalog>
```

> **Note** For more information about XDR schemas, visit the XDR Schema Developer's Guide section of the MSDN Web site at *http://msdn.microsoft.com/library/psdk/xmlsdk/xmlp7k6d.htm.*

Mapping Schemas

In most organizations, the business data that needs to be included in documents such as catalogs, invoices, or purchase orders is stored in a database. One of the challenges in building an integrated system that uses XML to exchange business data is extracting the data from the database in the required XML format. Of course, we've already seen that SQL Server 2000 gives you a number of ways to extract data as XML, and we could use any of these ways to create an XML document. However, if we have an XML schema already defined for our business document, wouldn't it be simpler just to map the elements and attributes in the schema to tables and columns in the database?

To help you accomplish this task, SQL Server supports the use of *mapping schemas*. A mapping schema is simply an XML schema with which you retrieve an XML fragment containing the appropriate data from the database. You can make use of *default mapping*, in which elements in your XDR schema map to same-name tables and attributes map to same-name columns, or you can add annotations to your schema to indicate the data in the database that each element or attribute in the schema corresponds to.

Using Default Mappings

The simplest way to use a schema to retrieve XML data is to use the default mapping assumed by SQL Server. When you specify a mapping schema from a client application, SQL Server assumes that each element maps to a table of the same name and that each attribute or subelement maps to a column of that name in the table. For example, consider the Products table in the Northwind database. The table contains several columns, including ProductID, ProductName, and UnitPrice. You could use the following schema to retrieve an XML fragment representing the data in those columns. (For simplicity, no data types are defined in this schema.) Later in this chapter, I'll explain how to use a schema to retrieve XML data from a database.

```
<?xml version="1.0"?>
<Schema name="NWProductSchema"
    xmlns="urn:schemas-microsoft-com:xml-data">
    <ElementType name="Products">
        <AttributeType name="ProductID"/>
        <AttributeType name="ProductName"/>
        <AttributeType name="UnitPrice"/>
        <attribute type="ProductID"/>
        <attribute type="ProductName"/>
        <attribute type="UnitPrice"/>
    </ElementType>
</Schema>
```

This schema is saved as NWProductSchema.xml in the Demos\Chaper6\Schemas folder on the companion CD. The XML fragment returned using this schema would resemble the following XML:

```
<Products ProductID="1" ProductName="Chai" UnitPrice="18"/>
<Products ProductID="2" ProductName="Chang" UnitPrice="19"/>
<Products ProductID="3" ProductName="Aniseed Syrup" UnitPrice="10"/>
⋮
```

As you can see, each column is mapped in an attribute-centric fashion. You can use an element-centric mapping for one or more columns by declaring the *content* attribute for an element in the schema with the *textOnly* value, as shown in this example:

```
<?xml version="1.0"?>
<Schema name="NWProductSchemaElts"
    xmlns="urn:schemas-microsoft-com:xml-data">
    <ElementType name="ProductName" content="textOnly"/>
    <ElementType name="UnitPrice" content="textOnly"/>
    <ElementType name="Products">
        <AttributeType name="ProductID"/>
        <attribute type="ProductID"/>
        <element type="ProductName"/>
        <element type="UnitPrice"/>
    </ElementType>
</Schema>
```

This schema is saved as NWProductSchemaElts in the Demos\Chapter6\Schemas folder on the companion CD. This schema would produce an XML fragment with the following format:

```
<Products ProductID="1">
    <ProductName>Chai</ProductName>
    <UnitPrice>18</UnitPrice>
</Products>
<Products ProductID="2">
    <ProductName>Chang</ProductName>
    <UnitPrice>19</UnitPrice>
</Products>
<Products ProductID="3">
    <ProductName>Aniseed Syrup</ProductName>
    <UnitPrice>10</UnitPrice>
</Products>
⋮
```

The default mapping requires no special changes to XDR schemas, but it can be used only when all the elements and attributes in a schema map exactly to tables and columns in the database. In most real business scenarios, you won't find this precision. To map more complex business documents to database entities, you need to explicitly define a custom mapping.

Using Annotations to Map Data

To create custom mappings between elements or attributes in a schema and tables or columns in a database, you must add annotations to the schema. The annotations themselves are defined in the XML-SQL namespace, and so a reference to that namespace must be included in the schema.

Mapping an XML Document to a Single Table

Once you've referenced the namespace, you can use the *relation* attribute to map an element to a table and the *field* attribute to map an attribute or element to a column. For example, you could use the following schema to create custom mappings to the Products table in the Northwind database:

```
<?xml version="1.0"?>
<Schema name="NWProductSchemaAnn"
    xmlns="urn:schemas-microsoft-com:xml-data"
    xmlns:sql="urn:schemas-microsoft-com:xml-sql">

    <ElementType name="Description"/>
    <ElementType name="Price"/>

    <ElementType name="Product" sql:relation="Products">
        <AttributeType name="ProductCode"/>
        <attribute type="ProductCode" sql:field="ProductID"/>
        <element type="Description" sql:field="ProductName"/>
        <element type="Price" sql:field="UnitPrice"/>
    </ElementType>

</Schema>
```

You can find this schema file in the Demos\Chapter6\Schemas folder on the companion CD in a file named ProductsSchemaAnn.xml. In this schema, the *Product* element is mapped to the *Products* table. The *ProductCode* attribute, the *Description* element, and the *Price* element are mapped to the *ProductID*, *ProductName*, and *UnitPrice* columns, respectively. This schema would return the following XML fragment:

```
<Product ProductCode="1">
    <Description>Chai</Description>
    <Price>18</Price>
</Product>
<Product ProductCode="2">
    <Description>Chang</Description>
    <Price>19</Price>
</Product>
<Product ProductCode="3">
    <Description>Aniseed Syrup</Description>
    <Price>10</Price>
</Product>
⋮
```

Mapping XML Data to Multiple Tables

In reality, most schemas need to be more complex than the examples we've seen so far because most business data is stored in multiple tables. So the mappings in our schema need to reflect that. For example, the Northwind catalog schema needs to include data from the Categories table as well as the Products table.

> **Note** You could use a SQL Server view to consolidate the data from multiple tables and map the schema to the view. However, this approach adds an unnecessary layer of abstraction and, more seriously, could prevent us from using the schema with tools such as the Bulk Load component or updategrams to insert or update data.

You can use a *relationship* element to create a mapping schema that references data in multiple tables. This annotation can be used to return elements containing attributes from multiple tables or to create a hierarchical representation of the relationships in the database. The *relationship* element contains four attributes with which you create a link between database tables; this mechanism works in a similar way to a JOIN clause in a Transact-SQL SELECT statement. You use the *key-relation* attribute to identify the table in the relationship in which the primary key used to join the tables is defined. The *key* attribute identifies the actual primary key field. You use the *foreign-relation* attribute to identify the table in the relationship containing the foreign key, and you use the *foreign-key* attribute to identify the foreign key field.

In the case of the Northwind catalog, the Categories and Products tables can be joined using the CategoryID field. Each row in the Categories table has a unique CategoryID field that is defined as a foreign key in the Products table to identify the category of each product. You could use the following annotated schema to define an XML catalog document in which the products are arranged hierarchically by category:

```
<?xml version="1.0"?>
<Schema name="NWCatalogSchemaAnn"
    xmlns="urn:schemas-microsoft-com:xml-data"
    xmlns:sql="urn:schemas-microsoft-com:xml-sql">

    <ElementType name="Description"/>
    <ElementType name="Price"/>

    <ElementType name="Product" sql:relation="Products">
        <AttributeType name="ProductCode"/>
        <attribute type="ProductCode" sql:field="ProductID"/>
        <element type="Description" sql:field="ProductName"/>
```

```
        <element type="Price" sql:field="UnitPrice"/>
    </ElementType>

    <ElementType name="Category" sql:relation="Categories">
        <AttributeType name="CategoryID"/>
        <AttributeType name="CategoryName"/>
        <attribute type="CategoryID" sql:field="CategoryID"/>
        <attribute type="CategoryName" sql:field="CategoryName"/>
        <element type="Product">
            <sql:relationship key-relation="Categories"
                key="CategoryID"
                foreign-relation="Products"
                foreign-key="CategoryID"/>
        </element>
    </ElementType>
</Schema>
```

This schema file is also available in the Demos\Chapter6\Schemas folder on the companion CD in a file named CatalogSchemaAnn.xml. In this schema, the *relationship* element joins the *Categories* and *Products* tables, creating an XML hierarchy of *Category* elements containing *Product* elements, as shown in the following XML fragment:

```
<Category CategoryID="1" CategoryName="Beverages">
    <Product ProductCode="1">
        <Description>Chai</Description>
        <Price>18</Price>
    </Product>
    <Product ProductCode="2">
        <Description>Chang</Description>
        <Price>19</Price>
    </Product>
    ⋮
</Category>
<Category CategoryID="2" CategoryName="Condiments">
    <Product ProductCode="3">
        <Description>Aniseed Syrup</Description>
        <Price>10</Price>
    </Product>
    ⋮
</Category>
⋮
```

As you can see, this code is much closer to the catalog schema we defined at the beginning of this chapter. The only difference is that the root element (*Catalog*) hasn't been defined in the annotated schema because it doesn't map to any fields or tables in the database. We'll see how this problem can be overcome later in the chapter, but now we need to see how we might use a mapping schema from a client application.

Using a Mapping Schema to Retrieve Data

Schemas can be used to retrieve data over ADO or HTTP connections. The client application merely needs to specify the schema to be used, the name of the root element used to contain the resulting XML fragment, and an XPath expression determining which rows should actually be returned. XPath expressions are used with schemas to specify the following:

- The location in the XML hierarchy to begin retrieving data
- Criteria to determine the rows that should be returned

Using an XPath Expression with a Schema

The most straightforward XPath is simply the name of the top-level element defined in the schema. Using this expression returns an XML fragment containing all the mapped elements and attributes in the schema. For example, you could use the following XPath expression to retrieve all the data mapped in the catalog schema described earlier:

```
Category
```

The XML fragment returned by this XPath expression is shown here. Later in this chapter, I'll explain how to use XPath expressions to retrieve XML data from a database.

```
<Category CategoryID="1" CategoryName="Beverages">
    <Product ProductCode="1">
        <Description>Chai</Description>
        <Price>18</Price>
    </Product>
    <Product ProductCode="2">
        <Description>Chang</Description>
        <Price>19</Price>
    </Product>
    ⋮
</Category>
<Category CategoryID="2" CategoryName="Condiments">
    <Product ProductCode="3">
        <Description>Aniseed Syrup</Description>
        <Price>10</Price>
    </Product>
    ⋮
</Category>
⋮
```

If you want to retrieve an XML fragment listing all the products without any category information, you could use the following XPath expression to retrieve data in the Northwind catalog schema:

```
Category/Product
```

This expression would return the following XML fragment:

```
<Product ProductCode="1">
    <Description>Chai</Description>
    <Price>18</Price>
</Product>
<Product ProductCode="2">
    <Description>Chang</Description>
    <Price>19</Price>
</Product>
⋮
```

You could also specify an XPath expression that contains criteria to limit the rows returned. For example, the following XPath expression could be used to access the catalog schema and retrieve only the products in category 2:

```
Category[@CategoryID='2']
```

This expression returns the following XML fragment:

```
<Category CategoryID="2" CategoryName="Condiments">
    <Product ProductCode="3">
        <Description>Aniseed Syrup</Description>
        <Price>10</Price>
    </Product>
    <Product ProductCode="4">
        <Description>Chef Anton's Cajun Seasoning</Description>
        <Price>22</Price>
    </Product>
    ⋮
</Category>
```

Using Mapping Schemas with ADO

ADO 2.6 supports the use of mapping schemas to retrieve XML data. To use a mapping schema with ADO, you instantiate a *Command* object to submit the query and a *Stream* object to receive the results. Your code must also specify the schema to be used, the root element for the resulting XML, and an XPath expression determining the data returned.

Creating the *Command* and *Stream* Objects

The code to create the *Command* and *Stream* objects and prepare them for use appears here:

```
Dim objCmd
Dim objStrm

Set objCmd = CreateObject("ADODB.Command")
Set objStrm = CreateObject("ADODB.Stream")
objCmd.ActiveConnection = "PROVIDER=SQLOLEDB;" & _
    "DATA SOURCE=server1;" & _
    "INITIAL CATALOG=Northwind;" & _
    "INTEGRATED SECURITY=SSPI;"
objStrm.Open
objCmd.Properties("Output Stream") = objStrm
```

Specifying the Schema

You use the *Mapping Schema* property of the *Command* object to specify your schema. This property is supported by the SQLOLEDB provider and accessed through the *Properties* collection, as you can see in this example code:

```
objCmd.Properties("Mapping Schema") = _
    "c:\schemas\CatalogSchemaAnn.xml"
```

Or you could set the *Base Path* property to the directory containing the schema file and the *Mapping Schema* property to the relative path to the schema file, as you see here:

```
objCmd.Properties("Base Path") = "c:\schemas"
objCmd.Properties("Mapping Schema") = "CatalogSchemaAnn.xml"
```

This approach is particularly useful if you want to apply a style sheet to the results and the style sheet is stored in a relative location to the schema.

Specifying the Root Element

If the schema returns an XML fragment, you must add a root element to create a well-formed XML document. This requirement can be met by setting the *Xml Root* property through the *Command* object's *Properties* collection, as shown in this sample code:

```
objCmd.Properties("Xml Root") = "Catalog"
```

This action results in an XML document that has a root element *Catalog* and contains the data mapped through the schema.

You can also add a root element to the results simply by concatenating a literal string, which can be useful if you want to include a custom namespace reference in the root element of the document.

```
strXMLRoot = "<Catalog xmlns="x-schema:CatalogSchemaAnn.xml">
strXMLEnd = "</Catalog">
strXML = strXMLRoot & strXMLResults & strXMLEnd
```

In this sample, the results of the query are stored in *strXMLResults* and the appropriate root and end tags are added to produce a well-formed XML document with a reference to the *CatalogSchemaAnn.xml* schema.

Using an XPath Expression with a *Command* Object

You assign the XPath expression that determines the data returned through the schema to the *CommandText* property of the *Command* object. For the XPath expression to be processed as such, and not as the default Transact-SQL expression, the *Dialect* property of the *Command* object must be set to the GUID identifying the DBGUID_XPATH dialect:

```
objCmd.Dialect = "{ec2a4293-e898-11d2-b1b7-00c04f680c56}"
objCmd.CommandText = "Category"
```

This code fragment uses an XPath expression to retrieve all of the data mapped in the schema. The SQLOLEDB provider will interpret the XPath and use the annotations in the schema to construct the corresponding FOR XML EXPLICIT query. This query will then be executed, and the resulting XML will be returned in the output stream.

Receiving XML Results from a Mapping Schema

To receive and process the results from the mapping schema, you simply need to read the data from the output stream by using the *ReadText* method of the *Stream* object. The following code sample shows the entire process of retrieving XML using a mapping schema with ADO:

```
Dim objCmd
Dim objStrm
Const adExecuteStream = 1024
Const DBGUID_XPATH = "{ec2a4293-e898-11d2-b1b7-00c04f680c56}"

'Set up Command and Stream objects.
Set objCmd = CreateObject("ADODB.Command")
Set objStrm = CreateObject("ADODB.Stream")
objCmd.ActiveConnection = "PROVIDER=SQLOLEDB;" & _
    "DATA SOURCE=Server1;" & _
    "INITIAL CATALOG=Northwind;" & _
    "INTEGRATED SECURITY=SSPI;"
objStrm.Open

With objCMD
    .Properties("Output Stream") = objStrm
```

(continued)

```
    'Specify the schema.
    .Properties("Base Path") = "C:\schemas"
    .Properties("Mapping Schema") = "CatalogSchemaAnn.xml"

    'Specify the root element.
    .Properties("Xml Root") = "Catalog"

    'Specify the XPath expression.
    .Dialect = DBGUID_XPATH
    .CommandText = "Category"
End With

'Execute the query and process the results.
objCmd.Execute, , adExecuteStream
msgbox objStrm.ReadText
```

You can also find code similar to this in the Demos\Chapter6 folder on the companion CD in a file named getCatalog.vbs.

Applying a Style Sheet with ADO

You might occasionally want to apply an XSL style sheet to the XML that's returned through a schema. For example, you might be using an ASP to retrieve data from the database and display that data in a Web page. In that case, you might want to transform the data into HTML before sending it to the browser.

As with XML templates, you can use ADO to apply a style sheet by setting the *Xsl* property through the *Command* object's *Properties* collection. In the following code example for an ASP, a mapping schema named *CatalogSchemaAnn.xml* in the *XMLFiles* subfolder of the virtual root is used to retrieve the products in the category passed to the page as a query string. You make use of an XSL style sheet named *Catalog.xsl* in the same location to transform the data to HTML, as you see here:

```
<%
Dim objCmd
Dim objStrm
Dim strXPath
Const adExecuteStream = 1024
Const DBGUID_XPATH = "{ec2a4293-e898-11d2-b1b7-00c04f680c56}"

'Create an XPath for the specified category.
strXPath = "Category[@CategoryID='" & _
    Request.QueryString("CategoryID") & _
    "']"

'Set up Command and Stream objects.
Set objCmd = CreateObject("ADODB.Command")
Set objStrm = CreateObject("ADODB.Stream")
```

```
objCmd.ActiveConnection = "PROVIDER=SQLOLEDB;" & _
    "DATA SOURCE=server1;" & _
    "INITIAL CATALOG=Northwind;" & _
    "INTEGRATED SECURITY=SSPI;"
objStrm.Open

With objCmd
    .Properties("Output Stream") = objStrm

    'Specify the schema.
    .Properties("Base Path") = Server.MapPath("XMLFiles")
    .Properties("Mapping Schema") = "CatalogSchemaAnn.xml"

    'Specify the style sheet.
    .Properties("Xsl") = "Catalog.xsl"

    'Specify the root element.
    .Properties("Xml Root") = "Catalog"

    'Specify the XPath expression.
    .Dialect = DBGUID_XPATH
    .CommandText = strXPath
End With

'Execute the query and process the results.
objCmd.Execute, , adExecuteStream
Response.Write objStrm.ReadText
%>
```

Using Mapping Schemas over HTTP

You can use mapping schemas with SQLISAPI virtual directory applications to retrieve XML data over HTTP. You can take one of two approaches: you can publish a schema in a virtual name and access it directly through a URL, or you can reference a mapping schema in an XML template.

Using a Schema Virtual Name

You can publish schemas in a virtual name of type *schema*. This practice allows users to access the schema directly using a URL, in the same way they would access templates in a template virtual name. To enable access to schemas in a URL, you must create a schema virtual name and select the *Allow XPath* option for the SQL Server virtual directory application. Both of these tasks can be accomplished using the Configure SQL XML Support In IIS tool.

Once the virtual root has been configured appropriately, schemas can be accessed using a URL of the following form:

```
http://servername/virtualroot/virtualname/schemafile/xpath?root=rootelement
```

As you can see, the URL contains the name of the schema, the XPath expression, and the root element. For example, you could use the following URL to define an XPath query against the CatalogSchemaAnn.xml schema to retrieve data from the Northwind database:

```
http://server1/northwinddata/schemas/CatalogSchemaAnn.xml/
    Category?root=Catalog
```

You can navigate to this URL by opening the shortcut named CatalogSchemaAnn in the Demos\Chapter6 folder on the companion CD.

Referencing a Schema in a Template

You can reference a schema in an XML template by using the *xpath-query* element and specifying the schema with this element's *mapping-schema* attribute. As with all templates, you use the root element of the template itself as the root of the results.

You indicate the XPath expression that you plan to use in the *xpath-query* element, as shown in the following sample code:

```
<Catalog xmlns:sql="urn:schemas-microsoft-com:xml-sql">
    <sql:xpath-query mapping-schema="..\Schemas\CatalogSchemaAnn.xml">
        Category
    </sql:xpath-query>
</Catalog>
```

You can find this template in the Demos\Chapter6\Templates folder on the companion CD in a file named NWCatalogSchema.xml. This template could be published in a virtual name and accessed over HTTP like any other template.

You can use parameters in a template to customize the XPath expression. This procedure is similar to using parameters in a template that contains a SQL query, except that you use the *$* symbol rather than the @ symbol to indicate a parameter in the query:

```
<Catalog xmlns:sql="urn:schemas-microsoft-com:xml-sql">
    <sql:header>
        <sql:param name="CategoryID">1</sql:param>
    </sql:header>
    <sql:xpath-query mapping-schema="..\Schemas\CatalogSchemaAnn.xml">
        Category[@CategoryID=$CategoryID]
    </sql:xpath-query>
</Catalog>
```

This template is saved as CatalogParam.xml in the Demos\Chapter6\Templates folder on the companion CD. You can view the results by opening the shortcut named Template With Param in the Demos\Chapter6 folder. This template returns the data relating to a particular category. The category number is passed as a parameter in the template.

You can also define the schema in the template itself by using an *inline* schema. You use the *id* attribute to uniquely identify the element in which this attribute is contained and the *is-mapping-schema* attribute to indicate an inline schema in the *Schema* element. The value of the *id* attribute will then be used to reference the inline schema in the *xpath-query* element. The *is-mapping-schema* attribute takes a Boolean type value. Here's an example of a template with an inline schema:

```
<?xml version="1.0" ?>
<ProductList xmlns:sql="urn:schemas-microsoft-com:xml-sql">

    <Schema
        xmlns="urn:schemas-microsoft-com:xml-data"
        sql:is-mapping-schema="1"
           sql:id="ProductSchema">
        <ElementType name="Products">
            <AttributeType name="ProductID"/>
            <AttributeType name="ProductName"/>
               <AttributeType name="UnitPrice"/>
            <attribute type="ProductID"/>
            <attribute type="ProductName"/>
            <attribute type="UnitPrice"/>
        </ElementType>
    </Schema>

    <sql:xpath-query mapping-schema="#ProductSchema">
        Products
    </sql:xpath-query>
</ProductList>
```

This code is also available in the Demos\Chapter6\Templates folder on the companion CD in a file named InlineSchema.xml. Inline schemas can be a useful way to keep all the data access logic together, but because the schema isn't published as a separate document, you can't share it with other applications.

Caching Schemas

By default, SQL Server caches schemas to improve performance on subsequent data requests. While this strategy is certainly desirable in most production scenarios, you might want to disable schema caching during development because changes made to the schema might not be immediately reflected in query results.

When you use schemas to retrieve data over ADO, you can prevent a schema from being cached by setting the *SS Stream Flags* property to 8 (which is represented by the constant STREAM_FLAGS_DONTCACHEMAPPINGSCHEMA), as shown in this code sample:

```
objCmd.Properties("SS_STREAM_FLAGS")=STREAM_FLAGS_DONTCACHEMAPPINGSCHEMA
```

When you use HTTP to access schemas, you can prevent schema caching by using the Configure SQL XML Support In IIS tool; check the Disable Caching Of Mapping Schemas check box on the Advanced tab of the Virtual Directory Properties dialog box.

Advanced Annotations

The *relation*, *field*, and *relationship* annotations allow you to map data in an XML schema to data in your SQL Server database. However, you can use advanced annotations such as *is-constant*, *map-field*, and *target-namespace* in a schema to help further define the relationship between the schema and the database. These annotations can be particularly useful when you need to map an existing XML schema to data in your database. In this section, we'll examine these advanced annotations.

Defining Constants in a Schema

One of the common issues that developers face when trying to map XML schemas to data in a database is what to do about XML elements or attributes that have no corresponding table or column in the database. For example, suppose Northwind Traders and other suppliers decided to agree on a standard XML schema representing an invoice document. This document could be sent to customers as a request for payment when an order has been shipped. The suppliers could use the following XML schema to define an invoice:

```
<?xml version="1.0" ?>
<Schema name="NWInvoiceSchema"
    xmlns="urn:schemas-microsoft-com:xml-data">

    <ElementType name="Item">
        <AttributeType name="ProductID"/>
        <AttributeType name="Quantity"/>
        <AttributeType name="Price"/>
        <AttributeType name="Discount"/>
        <attribute type="ProductID" required="yes"/>
        <attribute type="Quantity" required="yes"/>
        <attribute type="Price" required="yes"/>
        <attribute type="Discount" required="no"/>
    </ElementType>
```

```
    <ElementType name="LineItems">
        <element type="Item" minOccurs="1" maxOccurs="*"/>
    </ElementType>

    <ElementType name="InvoiceNo"/>
    <ElementType name="InvoiceDate"/>
    <ElementType name="ShippingCharge"/>
    <ElementType name="CustomerID"/>

    <ElementType name="Invoice">
        <element type="InvoiceNo" minOccurs="1" maxOccurs="1"/>
        <element type="InvoiceDate" minOccurs="1" maxOccurs="1"/>
        <element type="CustomerID" minOccurs="1" maxOccurs="1"/>
        <element type="LineItems" minOccurs="1" maxOccurs="1"/>
        <element type="ShippingCharge" minOccurs="1" maxOccurs="1"/>
    </ElementType>
</Schema>
```

(This code is also available in the Demos\Chapter6\Schemas folder on the companion CD in a file named InvoiceSchema.xml.) This schema contains elements and attributes that correspond to data in the Northwind database, but it also contains some data that can't be mapped. The following XML document shows what Northwind Traders invoices should look like based on this schema:

```
<?xml version="1.0"?>
<Invoice xmlns="x-schema:InvoiceSchema.xml">
    <InvoiceNo>10952</InvoiceNo>
    <InvoiceDate>16/03/1998</InvoiceDate>
    <CustomerID>ALFKI</CustomerID>
    <LineItems>
        <Item ProductID="6"
            Quantity="16"
            Price="25"
            Discount="5"/>
        <Item ProductID="28"
            Quantity="2"
            Price="45.60"/>
    </LineItems>
    <ShippingCharge>40.42</ShippingCharge>
</Invoice>
```

Mapping data in the Northwind database using the schema above presents a challenge. It is clear that the *Invoice* element can be mapped to the *Orders* table and that the *Items* element can be mapped to the *Order Details* table. However, there's no matching database entity for the *LineItems* element used to contain the items in the invoice.

To handle this situation, you can specify *LineItems* as a constant element. Constant elements appear in the XML fragments retrieved using the schema but don't map to data in the database. You can declare a constant element in a schema using the *is-constant* annotation. This annotation takes a Boolean value. The invoice schema with the necessary annotations to map data to the Northwind database is shown here:

```
<?xml version="1.0" ?>
<Schema name="NWInvoiceSchemaAnn"
    xmlns="urn:schemas-microsoft-com:xml-data"
    xmlns:sql="urn:schemas-microsoft-com:xml-sql">

    <ElementType name="Item" sql:relation="[Order Details]">
        <AttributeType name="ProductID"/>
        <AttributeType name="Quantity"/>
        <AttributeType name="Price"/>
        <AttributeType name="Discount"/>
        <attribute type="ProductID" required="yes" sql:field="ProductID"/>
        <attribute type="Quantity" required="yes" sql:field="Quantity"/>
        <attribute type="Price" required="yes" sql:field="UnitPrice"/>
        <attribute type="Discount" required="no" sql:field="Discount"/>
    </ElementType>

    <ElementType name="LineItems" sql:is-constant="1">
        <element type="Item" minOccurs="1" maxOccurs="*">
            <sql:relationship key-relation="Orders"
                key="OrderID"
                foreign-relation="[Order Details]"
                foreign-key="OrderID"/>
        </element>
    </ElementType>

    <ElementType name="InvoiceNo"/>
    <ElementType name="InvoiceDate"/>
    <ElementType name="ShippingCharge"/>
    <ElementType name="CustomerID"/>

    <ElementType name="Invoice" sql:relation="Orders">
        <element type="InvoiceNo" minOccurs="1" maxOccurs="1"
            sql:field="OrderID"/>
        <element type="InvoiceDate" minOccurs="1" maxOccurs="1"
            sql:field="OrderDate"/>
        <element type="CustomerID" minOccurs="1" maxOccurs="1"
            sql:field="CustomerID"/>
        <element type="LineItems" minOccurs="1" maxOccurs="1"/>
        <element type="ShippingCharge" minOccurs="1" maxOccurs="1"
            sql:field="Freight"/>
    </ElementType>
</Schema>
```

This schema is also available in the Demos\Chapter6\Schemas folder on the companion CD in a file named InvoiceSchemaAnn.xml. You can view the data it returns by opening the shortcut named Invoice Schema in the Demos\Chapter 6 folder. Notice in this example that the *is-constant* annotation is used to denote the *LineItems* element as a constant, thus allowing it to appear in the XML document without mapping it to data in the database. You could now use this schema to retrieve an invoice for a specific order by including the order ID in the XPath expression used to extract the data. For example, you could use the XPath *Invoice[InvoiceNo='10952']* to generate the invoice for order number 10952.

An interesting side-effect of this approach is that since only a single invoice is returned, the XML fragment returned is in fact a well-formed XML document and no root element needs to be specified by the client application. Of course, the root element for most business documents is actually defined in the schema. For example, the CatalogSchema.xml schema described earlier in the chapter contained this declaration:

```
<ElementType name="Catalog" model="closed">
    <element type="Category" minOccurs="1" maxOccurs="1"/>
</ElementType>
```

You can use the *is-constant* annotation to return the root element declared in the schema with the XML fragment, as shown here:

```
<ElementType name="Catalog" sql:is-constant="1">
    <element type="Category" minOccurs="1" maxOccurs="1"/>
</ElementType>
```

You can find this schema in the Demos\Chapter6\Schemas folder on the companion CD in a file named NWCatalogZncRoot.xml. This schema would allow the entire catalog document to be returned to a client application if you use the XPath expression *Catalog* in your query. No root element would need to be supplied by the client application because the root is returned with the data.

Excluding Fields

Sometimes an element exists in the schema that you don't want to appear in the resulting XML document. For example, suppose the suppliers agree to include an optional field in the invoice schema to specify the particular branch an item was bought from. This might be a perfectly sensible piece of information for suppliers who have branches in multiple locations, but Northwind Traders doesn't need it.

You can use the *map-field* annotation with a value of *0* to indicate that an optional element or attribute shouldn't be retrieved. This strategy allows you to continue to use the same schema as your trading partners without having to map irrelevant data. The *map-field* annotation can be used with any attribute, or any element declared with a *content* attribute with the value of *textOnly*. For example, you could make the following modifications to the invoice schema, allowing suppliers with branches to specify a branch but also allowing Northwind invoices to omit the branch data:

```
<ElementType name="Branch" content="textOnly"/>

<ElementType name="Invoice" sql:relation="Orders">
    <element type="InvoiceNo" minOccurs="1" maxOccurs="1"
        sql:field="OrderID"/>
    <element type="InvoiceDate" minOccurs="1" maxOccurs="1"
        sql:field="OrderDate"/>
    <element type="Branch" minOccurs="0" maxOccurs="1"
        sql:map-field="0"/>
    <element type="CustomerID" minOccurs="1" maxOccurs="1"
        sql:field="CustomerID"/>
    <element type="LineItems" minOccurs="1" maxOccurs="1"/>
    <element type="ShippingCharge" minOccurs="1" maxOccurs="1"
        sql:field="Freight"/>
</ElementType>
```

This schema is saved as InvoiceSchemaUnmapped.xml in the Demos\Chapter6\Schemas folder. You can view the data it returns by opening the shortcut named Invoice With Unmapped Field in the Demos\Chapter6 folder on the companion CD.

Specifying Key Fields

So far, we've used the *relationship* annotation to produce nested XML hierarchies that represent the relationships between primary keys and foreign keys. We've assumed in all of the examples so far that the element on the primary key side of the relationship will contain the elements on the foreign key side of the relationship. For example, the *Category* element contains the *Product* element.

While this arrangement is certainly the more usual way to represent data, we sometimes might want to show a foreign key element that contains a primary key element. For example, suppose we wanted to create a product list schema in which each product is listed with a subelement showing the category that the product belongs to. In this case, the relationship is reversed and the foreign key element (*Product*) contains the primary key element (*Category*).

You might imagine that the following schema would produce the list we're looking for:

```
<?xml version="1.0" ?>
<Schema xmlns="urn:schemas-microsoft-com:xml-data"
```

```
    xmlns:dt="urn:schemas-microsoft-com:datatypes"
    xmlns:sql="urn:schemas-microsoft-com:xml-sql">

    <ElementType name="Category" sql:relation="Categories">
        <AttributeType name="CategoryName"/>
        <attribute type="CategoryName" sql:field="CategoryName"/>
    </ElementType>

    <ElementType name="Product" sql:relation="Products">
        <AttributeType name="ProductID"/>
        <AttributeType name="ProductName"/>
        <attribute type="ProductID" sql:field="ProductID"/>
        <attribute type="ProductName" sql:field="ProductName"/>
        <element type="Category">
            <sql:relationship
                key-relation="Products"
                key="CategoryID"
                foreign-relation="Categories"
                foreign-key="CategoryID"/>
        </element>
    </ElementType>
</Schema>
```

This code is also available in the Demos\Chapter6\Schemas folder on the companion CD in a file named CatalogSchemaAnnRev.xml. If you use this schema to retrieve the product data, the XML fragment returned from the schema looks like this:

```
<Product ProductID="1" ProductName="Chai"/>
<Product ProductID="2" ProductName="Chang"/>
<Product ProductID="24" ProductName="Guaraná Fantástica"/>
<Product ProductID="34" ProductName="Sasquatch Ale"/>
<Product ProductID="35" ProductName="Steeleye Stout"/>
<Product ProductID="38" ProductName="Côte de Blaye"/>
<Product ProductID="39" ProductName="Chartreuse verte"/>
<Product ProductID="43" ProductName="Ipoh Coffee"/>
<Product ProductID="67" ProductName="Laughing Lumberjack Lager"/>
<Product ProductID="70" ProductName="Outback Lager"/>
<Product ProductID="75" ProductName="Rhönbräu Klosterbier"/>
<Product ProductID="76" ProductName="Lakkalikööri">
    <Category CategoryName="Beverages"/>
    <Category CategoryName="Beverages"/>
    <Category CategoryName="Beverages"/>
    <Category CategoryName="Beverages"/>
    <Category CategoryName="Beverages"/>
    <Category CategoryName="Beverages"/>
    <Category CategoryName="Beverages"/>
    <Category CategoryName="Beverages"/>
```

(continued)

```
    <Category CategoryName="Beverages"/>
    <Category CategoryName="Beverages"/>
    <Category CategoryName="Beverages"/>
    <Category CategoryName="Beverages"/>
</Product>
:
```

As you can see, the nesting in the resulting XML fragment is incorrect. We have the wrong result because the *CategoryID* field has been interpreted as being the primary key of the Products table due to the *relationship* annotation in the *Product* element. To fix this problem, you must use the *key-fields* annotation to explicitly specify the primary key field of the Products table. For tables with composite primary keys, you list and separate with a space each field in the key. The *key-fields* annotation can be used to produce proper nesting in the results. You could make the following modification to the preceding schema to specify the *key-fields* annotation:

```
<?xml version="1.0" ?>
<Schema xmlns="urn:schemas-microsoft-com:xml-data"
    xmlns:dt="urn:schemas-microsoft-com:datatypes"
    xmlns:sql="urn:schemas-microsoft-com:xml-sql">

    <ElementType name="Category" sql:relation="Categories">
        <AttributeType name="CategoryName"/>
        <attribute type="CategoryName" sql:field="CategoryName"/>
    </ElementType>

    <ElementType name="Product" sql:relation="Products"
        sql:key-fields="ProductID">
        <AttributeType name="ProductID"/>
        <AttributeType name="ProductName"/>
        <attribute type="ProductID" sql:field="ProductID"/>
        <attribute type="ProductName" sql:field="ProductName"/>
        <element type="Category">
            <sql:relationship
                key-relation="Products"
                key="CategoryID"
                foreign-relation="Categories"
                foreign-key="CategoryID"/>
        </element>
    </ElementType>
</Schema>
```

This schema is saved as ProductListSchema.xml in the Demos\Chapter6\Schemas folder on the companion CD. You can view the data it returns by opening the shortcut named Product List in the Demos\Chapter6 folder. This schema returns an XML document with the correct nesting, as you see here:

```
<Product ProductID="1" ProductName="Chai">
    <Category CategoryName="Beverages"/>
</Product>
<Product ProductID="2" ProductName="Chang">
    <Category CategoryName="Beverages"/>
</Product>
<Product ProductID="3" ProductName="Aniseed Syrup">
    <Category CategoryName="Condiments"/>
</Product>
⋮
```

Although you don't always need the *key-fields* annotation, it's good practice to specify the primary key fields explicitly whenever you create schemas that contain relationships. Keeping to this discipline can help prevent hours of frustration trying to explain some unexpected results.

Filtering Values

You can use the *limit-field* and *limit-value* annotations to filter your results based on a particular column value in a related table. You might find this tactic useful for generating documents containing a subset of the data in your database tables. You must use *limit-field* on an element or attribute that has *relationship* specified. For example, suppose you required a product list that contained the category name and product name of each product. You could use the following schema:

```
<?xml version="1.0" ?>
<Schema xmlns="urn:schemas-microsoft-com:xml-data"
    xmlns:sql="urn:schemas-microsoft-com:xml-sql">
    <ElementType name="StockItem" sql:relation="Categories"
        sql:key-fields="CategoryID">
        <AttributeType name="CategoryName"/>
        <AttributeType name="ProductName"/>
        <attribute type="CategoryName" sql:field="CategoryName"/>
        <attribute type="ProductName" sql:relation="Products"
             sql:field="ProductName">
             <sql:relationship key-relation="Categories"
                 key="CategoryID"
                 foreign-relation="Products"
                 foreign-key="CategoryID"/>
        </attribute>
    </ElementType>
</Schema>
```

This schema returns a list of all the products in the database. However, suppose you wanted to list only the products that haven't been discontinued. To do this, you need to filter the result set to show only products with a *Discontinued* value of *0*. You can achieve your properly filtered result set by adding the *limit-field* and *limit-value* annotations, as shown in this example:

```
<?xml version="1.0" ?>
<Schema xmlns="urn:schemas-microsoft-com:xml-data"
    xmlns:sql="urn:schemas-microsoft-com:xml-sql">

    <ElementType name="StockItem" sql:relation="Categories"
        sql:key-fields="CategoryID">
        <AttributeType name="CategoryName"/>
        <AttributeType name="ProductName"/>
        <attribute type="CategoryName" sql:field="CategoryName"/>
        <attribute type="ProductName" sql:relation="Products"
            sql:field="ProductName"
            sql:limit-field="Discontinued"
            sql:limit-value="0">
            <sql:relationship key-relation="Categories"
                key="CategoryID"
                foreign-relation="Products"
                foreign-key="CategoryID"/>
        </attribute>
    </ElementType>
</Schema>
```

This schema is saved as NonDiscontinued.xml in the Demos\Chaper6\Schemas folder on the companion CD. In this example, you use the *limit-field* annotation to define the name of the column in the foreign key table that you're using to filter the results. The *limit-value* annotation defines the required value. The preceding schema will return only products with a *Discontinued* value of *0*.

Using ID, IDREF, and IDREFS Annotations

You can use the XDR data types *ID*, *IDREF*, and *IDREFS* to create a relational schema using XML. For example, suppose the warehouse employees at Northwind Traders require a picking list document. This document should list an order with details of the products that the supplier needs to dispatch. It's probably easier to retrieve the items in order if the stock in the warehouse is arranged physically by category, so the picking list needs to contain category information for each product.

Rather than repeat category information for each product in the picking list, the application developer decides that it's more efficient to list all the categories, assign a unique ID to each one, and then use the ID to reference the appropriate category for each product. This procedure resembles the way you use primary and foreign keys in a relational database with one (fairly major) deviation: ID values in an XML document must be completely unique within the document. Unlike a database in which two primary key fields (for example ProductID and OrderID) potentially have the same value, you can't have two identical ID fields in an XML document, even if they're associated with different attributes. To help solve this problem, you can employ the *id-prefix* annotation to add a unique prefix to an ID field. By this means, you can use ID fields even in a document containing two or more elements with identical values.

For example, you could use the following schema to define the picking list document:

```
<?xml version="1.0" ?>
<Schema xmlns="urn:schemas-microsoft-com:xml-data"
    xmlns:dt="urn:schemas-microsoft-com:datatypes"
    xmlns:sql="urn:schemas-microsoft-com:xml-sql">

    <ElementType name="Category" sql:relation="Categories">
        <AttributeType name="CategoryID" dt:type="id"
            sql:id-prefix="Ctgy-"/>
        <AttributeType name="CategoryName"/>
        <attribute type="CategoryID" sql:field="CategoryID"/>
        <attribute type="CategoryName" sql:field="CategoryName"/>
    </ElementType>

    <ElementType name="CategoryList" sql:is-constant="1">
        <element type="Category"/>
    </ElementType>

    <ElementType name="Item" sql:relation="[Order Details]"
        sql:key-fields="OrderID ProductID">
        <AttributeType name="OrderID"/>
        <AttributeType name="ProductID"/>
        <AttributeType name="Quantity"/>
        <AttributeType name="CategoryID" dt:type="idref"
            sql:id-prefix="Ctgy-"/>
        <attribute type="OrderID" sql:field="OrderID"/>
        <attribute type="ProductID" sql:field="ProductID"/>
        <attribute type="Quantity" sql:field="Quantity"/>
        <attribute type="CategoryID" sql:relation="Products"
            sql:field="CategoryID">
            <sql:relationship key-relation="[Order Details]"
                key="ProductID"
                foreign-relation="Products"
                foreign-key="ProductID"/>
        </attribute>
    </ElementType>
```

(continued)

```
    <ElementType name="ItemList" sql:is-constant="1">
        <element type="Item"/>
    </ElementType>

    <ElementType name="PickList" sql:is-constant="1">
        <element type="CategoryList"/>
        <element type="ItemList"/>
    </ElementType>
</Schema>
```

This schema is also available in the Demos\Chapter6\Schemas folder on the companion CD in a file named PickListSchema.xml. It returns an XML document such as this one:

```
<PickList>
    <CategoryList>
        <Category CategoryID="Ctgy-1" CategoryName="Beverages"/>
        <Category CategoryID="Ctgy-2" CategoryName="Condiments"/>
        <Category CategoryID="Ctgy-3" CategoryName="Confections"/>
        <Category CategoryID="Ctgy-4" CategoryName="Dairy Products"/>
        <Category CategoryID="Ctgy-5" CategoryName="Grains/Cereals"/>
        <Category CategoryID="Ctgy-6" CategoryName="Meat/Poultry"/>
        <Category CategoryID="Ctgy-7" CategoryName="Produce"/>
        <Category CategoryID="Ctgy-8" CategoryName="Seafood"/>
    </CategoryList>
    <ItemList>
        <Item OrderID="10248" ProductID="11" Quantity="12"
            CategoryID="Ctgy-4"/>
        <Item OrderID="10248" ProductID="42" Quantity="10"
            CategoryID="Ctgy-5"/>
        <Item OrderID="10248" ProductID="72" Quantity="5"
            CategoryID="Ctgy-4"/>
        <Item OrderID="10249" ProductID="14" Quantity="9"
            CategoryID="Ctgy-7"/>
        <Item OrderID="10249" ProductID="51" Quantity="40"
            CategoryID="Ctgy-7"/>
        ⋮
    </ItemList>
</PickList>
```

You can view this data by opening the shortcut named Pick List in the Demos\Chapter6 folder on the companion CD. You can find the category information for a particular item in this XML document by locating the *Category* element with the corresponding *CategoryID* attribute.

Note The primary reason for using ID, IDREF, and IDREFS attributes to create a relational schema is to allow programmatic navigation of the document. For example, the Microsoft implementation of the XML Document Object Model (DOM) provides the *nodeFromID* method, which you can use to retrieve data from the appropriate ID element based on an IDREF attribute in the current element. The use of ID, IDREF, and IDREFS attributes to navigate a document requires an XML parser that supports XDR schemas. If your parser doesn't support XDR, you might want to consider an alternative approach, such as XSLT *key* attributes. For more information about XSLT, refer to the XSLT Reference in the MSDN library at *msdn.microsoft.com/library*.

Specifying a Target Namespace

You might occasionally want elements in your XML document to be in a specific namespace. Perhaps you want to include a namespace that specifically identifies your XML schema file so that client applications can validate the document against the published schema. To accomplish this aim, you can include the *target-namespace* annotation in the *Schema* element of your schema, which causes each element or attribute retrieved by the schema to be assigned the namespace specified in the *target-namespace* annotation.

Consider the following schema in which a target namespace is specified:

```
<?xml version="1.0"?>
<Schema xmlns="urn:schemas-microsoft-com:xml-data"
    xmlns:dt="urn:schemas-microsoft-com:datatypes"
    xmlns:sql="urn:schemas-microsoft-com:xml-sql"
    sql:target-namespace=
      "x-schema:http://www.northwindtraders.com/schemas/Products.xml">
    <ElementType name="Description"/>
    <ElementType name="Price"/>
    <ElementType name="Product" sql:relation="Products">
        <AttributeType name="ProductCode"/>
        <attribute type="ProductCode" sql:field="ProductID"/>
        <element type="Description" sql:field="ProductName"/>
        <element type="Price" sql:field="UnitPrice"/>
    </ElementType>
    <ElementType name="ProductList" sql:is-constant="1">
        <element type="Product"/>
    </ElementType>
</Schema>
```

The schema is saved as Products.xml in the Demos\Chapter6\Schemas folder on the companion CD. In this example, the schema is published in an Internet site, allowing users to access it and validate XML documents based on it. The XML document produced by this mapping schema contains a reference to the namespace with an arbitrarily assigned prefix, as shown in this XML document:

```
<y0:ProductList
    xmlns:y0=
    "x-schema:http://www.northwindtraders.com/schemas/Products.xml">
    <y0:Product ProductCode="1">
        <y0:Description>Chai</y0:Description>
        <y0:Price>18</y0:Price>
    </y0:Product>
    <y0:Product ProductCode="2">
        <y0:Description>Chang</y0:Description>
        <y0:Price>19</y0:Price>
    </y0:Product>
    ⋮
</y0:ProductList>
```

I'll explain how to get this XML document later in this section. One major issue needs to be addressed when you're building a client application that uses a mapping schema with *target-namespace* annotation. Because SQL Server generates the namespace prefix automatically, you'll find it difficult to specify an appropriate XPath expression. The only way around this problem is to use a template to access the schema and include a reference to the same namespace in the template. This way, you can use the prefix declared in the template to specify the XPath. For example, you could use the following template file to access the product list schema:

```
<?xml version="1.0"?>
<ProductData xmlns:sql="urn:schemas-microsoft-com:xml-sql">
    <sql:xpath-query
     xmlns:prd=
     "x-schema:http://www.northwindtraders.com/schemas/Products.xml"
        mapping-schema = "..\Schemas\Products.xml">
        prd:ProductList
    </sql:xpath-query>
</ProductData>
```

This template is saved as ProductList.xml in the Demos\Chapter6\Templates folder on the companion CD. It will return a product list document based on the Products.xml schema namespace. The document will be contained within a *ProductData* root element, as shown here:

```
<?xml version="1.0"?>
<ProductData xmlns:sql="urn:schemas-microsoft-com:xml-sql">
```

```
        <y0:ProductList xmlns:y0=
            "x-schema:http://www.northwindtraders.com/schemas/Products.xml">
            <y0:Product ProductCode="1">
                <y0:Description>Chai</y0:Description>
                <y0:Price>18</y0:Price>
            </y0:Product>
            <y0:Product ProductCode="2">
                <y0:Description>Chang</y0:Description>
                <y0:Price>19</y0:Price>
            </y0:Product>
            ⋮
        </y0:ProductList>
</ProductData>
```

You can view this data by opening the shortcut named ProductListNS in the Demos\Chapter6 folder.

> **Note** The namespace prefix used in the resulting XML is still generated by SQL Server and isn't related to the prefix used in the template. This means that the client application must be able either to process the document without requiring the namespace prefix or to read from within the document itself the namespace prefix used. You can use the XML DOM to read the document and ascertain the prefix used.

Retrieving Binary Data

You can retrieve binary data, such as images or text, by using a mapping schema. The XML *bin.base64* data type maps to such SQL Server data types as *binary*, *image*, and *varbinary*. To map the *bin.base64* data type to a specific SQL Server data type, you should use XML-SQL *datatype* annotation. This annotation can be used in a schema to declare an element or attribute that maps to a text, ntext, image, or binary column. The following example shows how to use the *datatype* annotation in a schema:

```
<?xml version="1.0"?>
<Schema name="NWCatalog"
    xmlns="urn:schemas-microsoft-com:xml-data"
    xmlns:sql="urn:schemas-microsoft-com:xml-sql">
   <ElementType name="Category" sql:relation="Categories">
      <AttributeType name="CategoryID"/>
      <AttributeType name="CategoryName"/>
      <AttributeType name="Picture"/>
```

(continued)

```
        <attribute type="CategoryID" sql:field="CategoryID"/>
        <attribute type="CategoryName" sql:field="CategoryName"/>
        <attribute type="Picture" sql:field="Picture"
            sql:datatype="image"/>
    </ElementType>
</Schema>
```

This schema is saved as CatalogImagesBin.xml in the Demos\Chapter6\Schemas folder on the companion CD. It returns the *Picture* attribute as a binary BASE64-encoded string. If you would prefer to receive a URL that could be used to retrieve the image through a dbobject virtual name, you can use the *url-encode* annotation. This annotation takes a Boolean type value. When you're using the *url-encode* annotation, you must provide a way to uniquely identify each row returned by the query, either by specifying a relationship or by including the *key-fields* annotation. The following modified example shows how a URL for binary data can be retrieved:

```
<?xml version="1.0"?>
<Schema xmlns="urn:schemas-microsoft-com:xml-data"
    xmlns:sql="urn:schemas-microsoft-com:xml-sql">

    <ElementType name="Category" sql:relation="Categories"
        sql:key-fields="CategoryID">
        <AttributeType name="CategoryID"/>
        <AttributeType name="CategoryName"/>
        <AttributeType name="Picture"/>
        <attribute type="CategoryID" sql:field="CategoryID"/>
        <attribute type="CategoryName" sql:field="CategoryName"/>
        <attribute type="Picture" sql:field="Picture" sql:url-encode="1"/>
    </ElementType>
</Schema>
```

This schema is saved as CatalogImagesURL.xml in the Demos\Chapter6\Schemas folder on the companion CD. It returns each picture attribute as a URL:

```
Picture="dbobject/Categories[@CategoryID='1']/@Picture"
```

Retrieving CDATA Sections

Because database fields can often contain data including markup characters, you can specify that the field mapped by an element or attribute in a schema should be retrieved as a CDATA section by using the *use-cdata* annotation. This annotation takes a Boolean type value. You can use this annotation with any element node other than elements that have the *ID*, *IDREF*, *IDREFS*, *NMTOKEN*, *NMTOKENS*, or *url-encode* annotation specified.

The following example shows a schema that maps a product name to a CDATA section:

```
<?xml version="1.0" ?>
<Schema xmlns="urn:schemas-microsoft-com:xml-data"
    xmlns:sql="urn:schemas-microsoft-com:xml-sql">

    <ElementType name="ProductName"/>
    <ElementType name="Product" sql:relation="Products">
        <AttributeType name="ProductID"/>
        <attribute type="ProductID" sql:field="ProductID"/>
        <element type="ProductName" sql:field="ProductName"
            sql:use-cdata="1"/>
    </ElementType>
</Schema>
```

This schema is saved as ProductCData.xml in the Demos\Chapter6\Schemas folder on the companion CD. It returns *Product* elements containing CDATA sections, as shown here:

```
<Product ProductID="1">
    <ProductName><![CDATA[Chai]]></ProductName>
</Product>
<Product ProductID="2">
    <ProductName><![CDATA[Chang]]></ProductName>
</Product>
<Product ProductID="18">
    <ProductName><![CDATA[Chartreuse verte]]></ProductName>
</Product>
⋮
```

You can view this data by opening the shortcut named ProductsCData in the Demos\Chapter6 folder on the companion CD.

Retrieving Overflow Columns

As I explained in Chapter 3, some database solutions use an overflow column for unconsumed XML data. You can use the *overflow-field* annotation with any element mapped to a table to retrieve the unconsumed XML from the overflow column in the table. You can assume that the data in the overflow column consists of a well-formed XML document, and any attributes of the root element of the XML document stored in the overflow column are returned as attributes of the element mapped to the table. Any subelements stored in the overflow column are returned as subelements of the element mapped to the table.

For example, suppose an overflow column named *extradata* was added to the Products table in the Northwind Traders database. The *extradata* fields for product number 1 might contain the XML string *<extradata imported="yes"><Origin>China</Origin></extradata>*. You can use the following schema to retrieve product data:

```
<?xml version="1.0" ?>
<Schema xmlns="urn:schemas-microsoft-com:xml-data"
    xmlns:sql="urn:schemas-microsoft-com:xml-sql">
    <ElementType name="Product" sql:relation="Products"
        sql:overflow-field="extradata">
        <AttributeType name="ProductID"/>
        <AttributeType name="ProductName"/>
        <attribute type="ProductID" sql:field="ProductID"/>
        <attribute type="ProductName" sql:field="ProductName"/>
    </ElementType>
</Schema>
```

The XML for product number 1 returned by this schema would look like this:

```
<Product ProductID="1"
    ProductName="Chai"
       imported="yes">
    <Origin>China</Origin>
</Product>
```

Summary

In this chapter, you've seen how XDR schemas can be annotated and used as mapping schemas to retrieve XML data from SQL Server. This can be an extremely useful approach in building business-to-business (B2B) applications in which schemas are used to define the business documents exchanged by trading partners. By simply adding annotations to the XDR schemas that you and your trading partners have agreed to use, you can transparently map the data in the XML documents to the tables and columns in your database.

7

Inserting XML Data Using *OpenXML*

In the previous chapters, we've examined many ways of extracting XML data from Microsoft SQL Server. This process is, of course, a vital aspect of building an integration solution and one that deserves the amount of attention we have given it. However, another equally important issue is the task of inserting XML data into the database. In this chapter, we'll turn our attention to the *OpenXML* function, which is used primarily to insert data from an XML document into tables in the database.

A Model for Receiving XML Documents

Suppose that the Northwind Traders company allows customers to place orders by sending an XML purchase order over the Web. The order might be posted to an HTTP application, sent in an e-mail, or transmitted in some other fashion. However the document gets there, software at Northwind Traders needs to receive the incoming order and insert the details into the database.

A possible approach to this task would be to have the receiving application pass the XML document to a stored procedure in the database that inserts the order data into the appropriate tables. Figure 7-1 shows this model.

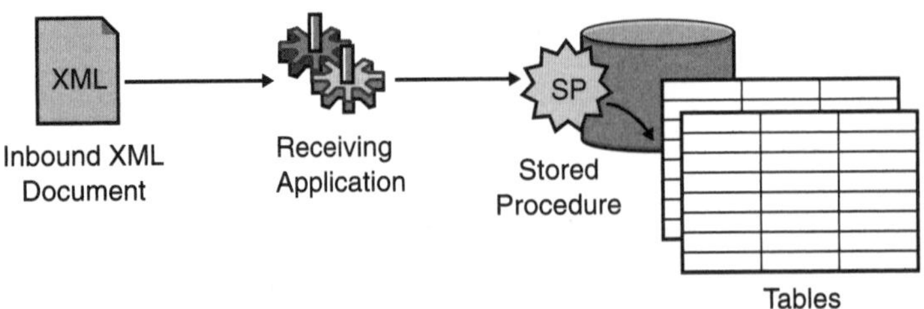

Figure 7-1 Receiving and inserting an XML document

Passing XML Data to a Stored Procedure

When you write a stored procedure for inserting data from an XML document into the database, you must ensure that the parameter you plan to use to pass the XML data to the procedure is large enough to handle the maximum size of documents you'll be receiving. The following table shows the relevant data types that you can specify for parameters receiving XML documents:

Data Type	Maximum Size
Char	8000 characters (fixed length)
Varchar	8000 characters (variable length)
nChar	4000 characters (fixed-length Unicode)
nVarchar	4000 characters (variable-length Unicode)
Text	2,147,483,647 characters
nText	1,073,741,823 characters (Unicode)

In most scenarios, you should use *Varchar* or *nVarchar* parameters because they're adequate for most business documents, such as purchase orders or invoices. If you're developing applications for a business that might exchange multilingual documents, including characters that don't appear in the installed character set for SQL Server, you should use a Unicode data type, which will help minimize any character conversion issues.

Parsing and Shredding an XML Document

Before you can use the *OpenXML* function to insert data, the XML document needs to be parsed and mapped to an in-memory tree structure that represents the nodes in the document. You use the *sp_xml_preparedocument* stored procedure, which reads the document and verifies that it's a valid XML document. The stored procedure then returns a handle to a node tree that can be used to retrieve data from the elements and attributes in the document.

After the node tree has been created, you can use the *OpenXML* function to return a rowset containing data in the XML document. The primary use of this functionality is to get XML data into a relational format so that it can be inserted into a table. This process is known as *shredding* the document. Because most XML documents contain data that maps to multiple tables, the document might need to be shredded several times to insert all of the data.

Figure 7-2 shows the process of parsing and shredding an XML document.

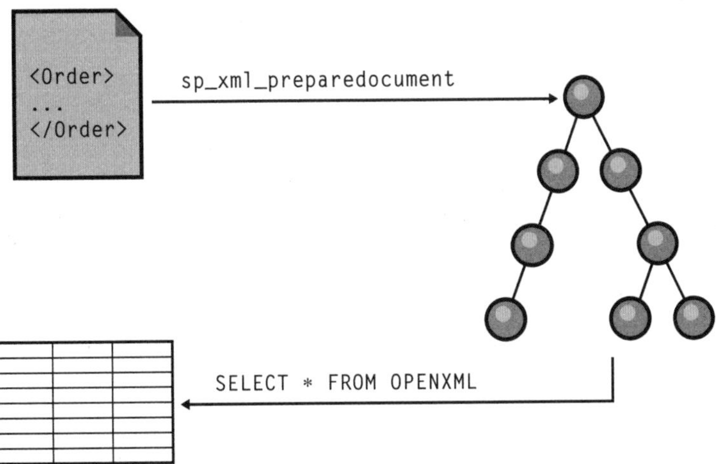

Figure 7-2 Parsing and shredding an XML document

Cleaning Up

Once a document has been fully processed, you should use the *sp_xml_removedocument* stored procedure to reclaim the memory used by the node tree. Getting into the habit of deleting the document tree can help prevent memory shortage problems in your SQL Server application.

The following example shows a stored procedure that inserts data from an XML document into a table. Note the use of *sp_xml_preparedocument*, *OpenXML*, and *sp_xml_removedocument*.

```
CREATE PROCEDURE InsertOrder @xmlOrder VARCHAR(2000)
AS
DECLARE @iTree INTEGER
EXEC sp_xml_preparedocument @iTree OUTPUT, @xmlOrder
INSERT orders (OrderID, CustomerID, EmployeeID, OrderDate)
SELECT * FROM
    OPENXML(@iTree, 'Order', 1)
    WITH (OrderID INTEGER,
```

(continued)

```
        CustomerID nCHAR(5),
        EmployeeID INTEGER,
        OrderDate DATETIME)
EXEC sp_xml_removedocument @iTree
```

In this procedure, you can see that the syntax for the *OpenXML* statement includes a number of parameters and clauses. We'll examine these in detail throughout the rest of this chapter.

Generating Rowsets with the *OpenXML* Function

The *OpenXML* function returns a rowset containing data from an XML document. The rows and columns in the rowset are determined by parameter values that you can specify in Transact-SQL. Here's the full syntax of the *OpenXML* function:

```
OPENXML(iDoc, rowpattern, flags)
[WITH (rowsetschema [colpatterns] | tablename)]
```

The use of some of these parameters is immediately obvious, but the use of others is a little more complex. Let's examine the *OpenXML* function syntax in the sample code I showed you earlier more closely.

```
OPENXML(@iTree, 'Order', 1)
WITH (OrderID INTEGER,
      CustomerID nCHAR(5),
      EmployeeID INTEGER,
      OrderDate DATETIME)
```

You can view this Transact-SQL code in the SimpleOrder.sql script in the Demos\Chapter7 folder on the companion CD. First we use the *iDoc* parameter (named *@iTree* in our code sample) to specify the internal node tree representing the XML document. This parameter contains the value returned by the *sp_xml_preparedocument* stored procedure.

Next we use the *rowpattern* parameter to define the elements in the XML document that should be returned. The value itself, in this case *Order*, is an XPath expression determining the point in the XML tree at which the search should begin and can include a criteria expression to limit the rows returned. Conceptually, the *rowpattern* parameter is the equivalent of the FROM and WHERE clauses in a Transact-SQL query.

The *flags* parameter tells SQL Server to search for attributes, subelements, or both. This value can be 0 (the default, which is attributes), 1 (attributes), or 2 (elements). To search for both attributes and elements, you need to combine the values to produce 3. In the sample code, the *OpenXML* function returns rowsets containing the attributes of the *Order* elements in the XML document.

We use the WITH clause to define the structure of the rowset. Essentially, the WITH clause specifies the columns that will be returned. In this respect, the WITH clause is conceptually similar to the SELECT clause in a Transact-SQL query. You can take one of two approaches to defining the rowset structure. You can declare the columns in the rowset schema explicitly, the way you would do in a CREATE TABLE statement, or you can specify the name of an existing table that has the required structure. The WITH clause provides the necessary column mapping information to create a rowset from the XML data. The columns in the rowset will map to the XML attributes or subelements (depending on the *flags* value) of the elements specified in the *rowpattern* parameter, with matching names and compatible data types. If you choose to define the columns explicitly, you can return columns from other parts of the document, or with nonmatching names, by specifying a *colpattern* parameter. This parameter is an XPath expression, relative to each element returned by the *rowpattern* parameter, which is used to navigate the tree and retrieve a specified attribute or element value.

The rowset schema in the sample code is declared explicitly, with no *colpattern* parameters specified, so the *OpenXML* function returns the *OrderID*, *CustomerID*, *EmployeeID*, and *OrderDate* attributes from each *Order* element in the XML document. For a clearer understanding of the function's behavior, suppose the following XML document is passed to our *InsertOrder* stored procedure:

```
<?xml version="1.0"?>
<Order OrderID="1001" CustomerID="ALFKI"
   OrderDate="01/01/2001" EmployeeID="2"/>
```

The *OpenXML* function in the procedure would return the following rowset:

OrderID	CustomerID	EmployeeID	OrderDate
1001	ALFKI	2	2001-01-01 00:00:00.000

In the following sections, we'll examine the details of the *OpenXML* function more closely.

Specifying the Row Pattern

Let's suppose that we receive a more complex document. For example, a purchase order would probably contain a hierarchy of order information, as shown in this example:

```
<?xml version="1.0"?>
<Order OrderID="1001" CustomerID="ALFKI"
   EmployeeID="2" OrderDate="01/01/2001">
```

(continued)

```
    <Items>
        <Item ProductID="11" Qty="1" UnitPrice="12.99">
            <Discount>0</Discount>
        </Item>
        <Item ProductID="17" Qty="2" UnitPrice="4.99">
            <Discount>0.5</Discount>
        </Item>
        <Item ProductID="21" Qty="1" UnitPrice="11.99">
            <Discount>0</Discount>
        </Item>
    </Items>
</Order>
```

This document contains multiple hierarchical levels from which rows could be returned.

When represented as a tree structure, this document would create the following nodes of elements and attributes. (Attributes are prefixed with the @ symbol.)

- / (root)
    - *Order (@OrderID, @CustomerID, @EmployeeID, @OrderDate)*
        - *Items*
            - *Item (@ProductID, @Qty, @UnitPrice)*
                - *Discount*
            - *Item (@ProductID, @Qty, @UnitPrice)*
                - *Discount*
            - *Item (@ProductID, @Qty, @UnitPrice)*
                - *Discount*

You can use the *rowpattern* parameter in an *OpenXML* function to do two things: It can specify the level of the hierarchy you want to search, and it can limit the rows returned by specifying criteria based on the values of elements and attributes in the document.

The simplest XPath expression you can specify in the *rowpattern* parameter is the root of the document (/), which isn't a particularly useful row pattern because it allows you to retrieve only the root of the document. The rowset generated by *OpenXML* will then have a single column based on the root element—in this case *Order*—containing the values of all elements in the document in the form of a space-delimited string. For example, the following Transact-SQL statement would return a single column named *Order* with the value 0 0.5 0 if you used it to retrieve data from the preceding XML sample code.

```
SELECT * FROM
OPENXML(@iTree, '/', 2)
WITH
([Order] VARCHAR(10))
```

To retrieve a more useful rowset, the *rowpattern* parameter should specify the path to the level in the document from which you require data. You define the path as an XPath expression in which the nodes in the tree, separated by / delimiters, are identified. For example, to retrieve data from the *Order* element, you should specify the XPath expression */Order*; if you want to drill down to the *Item* level, you need to use the XPath expression */Order/Items/Item*. The initial /, which represents the root, can be omitted, allowing you to specify simply *Order* as the XPath expression for the *Order* element. You could use the following sample code to retrieve the attributes of the *Item* elements in the preceding purchase order document:

```
SELECT * FROM
OPENXML(@iTree, 'Order/Items/Item', 1)
WITH
(ProductID INTEGER,
 Qty INTEGER,
 UnitPrice MONEY)
```

This code returns the following rowset:

ProductID	Qty	UnitPrice
11	1	12.9900
17	2	4.9900
21	1	11.9900

This Transact-SQL code can be viewed in the ComplexOrder.sql script in the Demos\Chapter7 folder on the companion CD. The *rowpattern* parameter can limit the rows being returned by including an XPath expression that defines some selection criteria. For example, the following sample code could be used to return a rowset that contains all items of which the customer has ordered more than one unit:

```
SELECT * FROM
OPENXML(@iTree, 'Order/Items/Item[@Qty>1]', 1)
WITH
(ProductID INTEGER,
 Qty INTEGER,
 UnitPrice MONEY)
```

This code returns the following rowset:

ProductID	Qty	UnitPrice
17	2	4.9900

Using Flags to Retrieve Attributes and Elements

The *flags* parameter determines whether the *OpenXML* function searches for attributes or elements by default. As I said earlier, you use the value 1 to denote an attribute-centric search, 2 for an element-centric search, and you can combine the values into 3, in which case both attributes and elements are searched.

The following code sample returns the *ProductID*, *Qty*, and *UnitPrice* attributes, as well as the *Discount* subelement value, from the *Item* elements in our sample document:

```
SELECT * FROM
OPENXML(@iTree, 'Order/Items/Item', 3)
WITH
(ProductID INTEGER,
 Qty INTEGER,
 UnitPrice MONEY,
 Discount REAL)
```

This code produces the following rowset:

ProductID	Qty	UnitPrice	Discount
11	1	12.9900	0.0
17	2	4.9900	0.5
21	1	11.9900	0.0

You can view this Transact-SQL code in the ComplexOrderFlags.sql script in the Demos\Chapter7 folder on the companion CD.

> **Note** Combining element and attribute flag values might impact application performance because the function needs to search both the attribute nodes and the element nodes for each element specified by the *rowpattern* parameter. Using a column pattern in the WITH clause can be a more efficient way to combine elements and attributes. I'll talk about column patterns later in this chapter.

Defining the Rowset Schema

The columns in the rowset returned by the *OpenXML* function are determined by the WITH clause. So far we've seen sample code in which I declared the rowset schema explicitly by listing the columns and their data types in the WITH clause. When you use this approach, the column names must match the names of the attributes or elements being retrieved and the specified data type must be compatible with the values in the XML document.

Using Column Patterns

You can customize the rowset schema definition by specifying *column patterns*. A column pattern is an XPath expression that identifies a node in the document relative to the element defined by the *rowpattern* parameter. Using column patterns allows you to solve two common problems:

- The name of the attribute doesn't match the name you want to use for the column in the rowset.
- The required data isn't within the immediate scope defined by the *rowpattern* and *flags* parameters.

Let's look at each of these problems in turn. First suppose you want to return the *Qty* attribute of the *Item* element as a column named Quantity. You could use the following Transact-SQL code:

```
SELECT * FROM
OPENXML(@iTree, 'Order/Items/Item', 1)
WITH
(ProductID INTEGER,
 Quantity INTEGER '@Qty')
```

Note that the XPath expression identifying the *Qty* attribute is used to map to the Quantity column in the WITH clause. This code produces the following rowset:

ProductID	Quantity
11	1
17	2
21	1

The second problem addressed by column patterns is a little more complex. To understand the nature of this problem, consider the schema of the following Order Details table definition:

```
CREATE TABLE [Order Details]
(OrderID INTEGER,
```

(continued)

```
 ProductID INTEGER,
 Qty INTEGER,
 UnitPrice MONEY,
 Discount REAL)
```

To retrieve a rowset from our purchase order document that could be inserted into this table, we need to be able to generate an OrderID column. However, the order ID in the XML document is represented by the *OrderID* attribute of the *Order* element, which is two levels above the *Item* level used to retrieve the rest of the columns in this table.

To solve this problem, you can use a column pattern specifying an XPath expression that navigates back up the tree hierarchy, as shown in this sample code:

```
SELECT * FROM
OPENXML(@iTree, 'Order/Items/Item', 1)
WITH
(OrderID INTEGER '../../@OrderID',
 ProductID INTEGER,
 Qty INTEGER,
 UnitPrice MONEY,
 Discount REAL 'Discount')
```

Note that the XPath expression *../../@OrderID* defines the *OrderID* attribute of the element two levels above the current *Item* element. This code retrieves the value of the *OrderID* attribute of the *Order* element. Notice also that a column pattern identifies the *Discount* element one level below the current one. This code allows us to retrieve the *Discount* subelement without combining element and attribute flag values. The following rowset is returned by this code:

OrderID	ProductID	Qty	UnitPrice	Discount
1001	11	1	12.9900	0.0
1001	17	2	4.9900	0.5
1001	21	1	11.9900	0.0

This Transact-SQL code can be viewed in the ComplexOrderColPatterns.sql script in the Demos\Chapter7 folder on the companion CD. The ability to retrieve data from anywhere in the XML hierarchy is extremely useful when, for example, you're inserting a foreign key into a table because XML documents often nest data in such a way that the primary key of a parent element is not repeated as a foreign key in the child elements.

Using a Table Name to Define the Rowset Schema

Sometimes the data in an XML element matches the structure of an existing table. In this case, you can specify the name of the table instead of defining the columns explicitly. For example, suppose you created an Orders table using the following schema:

```
CREATE TABLE Orders
(OrderID INTEGER,
 CustomerID nCHAR(5),
 EmployeeID INTEGER,
 OrderDate DATETIME)
```

You could use the following Transact-SQL statement to retrieve data from the purchase order XML document:

```
SELECT * FROM
OPENXML(@iTree, 'Order', 1)
WITH Orders
```

This code would return the rowset shown here:

OrderID	CustomerID	EmployeeID	OrderDate
1001	ALFKI	2	2001-01-01 00:00:00.000

Using *OpenXML* to Insert Data

The most practical application of the *OpenXML* function is to insert data from an XML document into tables in the database. Which Transact-SQL statement you use to do this depends on whether the table you want to store the data in already exists.

Inserting Data into an Existing Table

To insert data into an existing table, you use the Transact-SQL INSERT statement this way:

```
INSERT Orders
SELECT * FROM
OPENXML(@iTree, 'Order', 1)
WITH Orders
```

This statement inserts the data from the XML purchase order document into a matching Orders table. Of course, the Northwind database's Orders table, like those in many production scenarios, contains columns that can't be mapped to the attributes or elements in the XML document. Here's a simplified definition of the Northwind Orders table:

```
CREATE TABLE Orders
(OrderID INTEGER IDENTITY (1, 1) NOT NULL ,
 CustomerID nCHAR (5) NULL ,
 EmployeeID INTEGER NULL ,
 OrderDate DATETIME NULL ,
 RequiredDate DATETIME NULL ,
 ShippedDate DATETIME NULL ,
 ShipVia INTEGER NULL ,
 Freight MONEY NULL ,
 ShipName nVARCHAR (40) NULL ,
 ShipAddress nVARCHAR (60) NULL ,
 ShipCity nVARCHAR (15) NULL ,
 ShipRegion nVARCHAR (15) NULL ,
 ShipPostalCode nVARCHAR (10) NULL ,
 ShipCountry nVARCHAR (15) NULL)
```

All columns in the Orders table (except the *OrderID* column) allow NULL values to be inserted. This means that even though the information isn't supplied in the XML document, we can still insert either a NULL or an explicit value for the missing columns. Another issue is that the *OrderID* column is an IDENTITY column, which means that by default SQL Server automatically generates a value for each new record. This action can be overridden by setting the *IDENTITY_INSERT* property for the table to *ON*.

To incorporate these requirements in our Transact-SQL statement, we need to make a few changes. First we need to set the *IDENTITY_INSERT* option *ON* for the Orders table. Then we need to change the INSERT and SELECT clauses in the preceding Transact-SQL statement so that they include all the columns required for the Orders table. The columns must be listed in the INSERT clause when SQL Server explicitly inserts an IDENTITY column value, and the actual values to be inserted for the missing columns must be specified in the SELECT clause. Next we need to change the WITH clause in the *OpenXML* function to explicitly specify the columns retrieved from the XML document. Finally we need to return the *IDENTITY_INSERT* option to the *OFF* setting. The following Transact-SQL statement shows how a new row composed of data from the XML document and values explicitly assigned in the SELECT clause can be inserted into the Orders table.

```
SET IDENTITY_INSERT Orders ON
INSERT Orders (OrderID, CustomerID, EmployeeID, OrderDate,
```

```
              RequiredDate, ShippedDate, ShipVia, Freight,
              ShipName, ShipAddress, ShipCity, ShipRegion,
              ShipPostalCode, ShipCountry)
SELECT OrderID, CustomerID, EmployeeID, OrderDate,
       NULL, NULL, NULL, 0, NULL, NULL, NULL, NULL, NULL, NULL
FROM
OPENXML(@iTree, 'Order', 1)
WITH (OrderID INTEGER, EmployeeID INTEGER, OrderDate DATETIME,
      CustomerID nCHAR(5))
SET IDENTITY_INSERT Orders OFF
```

This code can be used to insert a new row in the Northwind Orders table. The *OrderID*, *CustomerID*, *EmployeeID*, and *OrderDate* values are retrieved from the XML document, and *NULL* is explicitly assigned for the rest of the columns apart from Freight, which is assigned a default value of 0.

Of course, the purchase order also contains data for the Order Details table, so the stored procedure to insert all of the data in the XML document would look something like this:

```
CREATE PROCEDURE InsertOrder @xmlOrder VARCHAR(2000)
AS
DECLARE @iTree INTEGER
EXEC sp_xml_preparedocument @iTree OUTPUT, @xmlOrder

SET IDENTITY_INSERT Orders ON
INSERT Orders (OrderID, CustomerID, EmployeeID, OrderDate,
              RequiredDate, ShippedDate, ShipVia, Freight,
              ShipName, ShipAddress, ShipCity, ShipRegion,
              ShipPostalCode, ShipCountry)
SELECT OrderID, CustomerID, EmployeeID, OrderDate,
       NULL, NULL, NULL, 0, NULL, NULL, NULL, NULL, NULL, NULL
FROM
OPENXML(@iTree, 'Order', 1)
WITH (OrderID INTEGER, EmployeeID INTEGER, OrderDate DATETIME,
      CustomerID nCHAR(5))
SET IDENTITY_INSERT Orders OFF

INSERT [Order Details]
SELECT * FROM
OPENXML(@iTree, 'Order/Items/Item', 1)
WITH (OrderID INTEGER '../../@OrderID', ProductID INTEGER,
      Qty INTEGER, UnitPrice MONEY, Discount REAL 'Discount')

EXEC sp_xml_removedocument @iTree
```

You can view code similar to this in the InsertOrder.sql script in the Demos\Chapter7 folder on the companion CD. This procedure receives the XML purchase order and creates an internal tree representation of the purchase order document. The procedure then inserts the data from the *Order* element into the Orders table and the data from the *Item* element into the Order Details table. Finally it reclaims the memory used by the node tree.

> **Note** Because the procedure inserts data into two tables, you should use a transaction to ensure data integrity isn't broken in the event of an error. You could do this by adding BEGIN TRAN and COMMIT TRAN statements to the stored procedure, using the *BeginTrans* and *CommitTrans* methods of an ADO *Connection* object; or you could ensure integrity by calling the stored procedure from a transactional COM+ or MTS component.

Creating a New Table

You might occasionally want to use the data in an XML document to create and populate a new table. This strategy might be a suitable approach were you revising a product catalog, say, for which the XML catalog document contained an updated version of the entire catalog. The most efficient way to update the database might be to simply drop the existing catalog table and re-create it with the new data.

To insert data into a new table, you use the SELECT...INTO syntax, as shown in the following example:

```
SELECT * INTO Products
FROM OPENXML(@iTree, 'Product', 1)
WITH (ProductID INTEGER,
      ProductName VARCHAR(20),
      UnitPrice MONEY)
```

This code creates a new table named *Products*, which uses the schema defined in the WITH clause, and populates it with the data from the XML document referenced by *@iTree*.

> **Note** In previous versions of SQL Server, the SELECT...INTO syntax could be used with permanent tables only when the *SELECT INTO/BULKCOPY* option was set to *ON*. In SQL Server 2000, this requirement is eliminated.

If the Products table already exists, the preceding Transact-SQL statement will fail, so any stored procedure using this approach would need to use the DROP TABLE statement to delete the existing table first. Of course, if an existing table is dropped, any constraints, such as primary keys or foreign keys, and any indexes will be dropped with it. Re-creating the necessary constraints and indexes after the table has been re-created and populated is so much work that you might not want to take this approach. A more suitable tactic might be to use a TRUNCATE TABLE statement to delete the existing records and then use an INSERT statement to insert the new data.

Using *OpenXML* to Retrieve XML Metadata

In addition to being useful for inserting XML data into tables, the *OpenXML* function can be used to retrieve metadata from an XML document. This functionality allows you to write code that queries the actual XML structure of the document, and you could use it to build your own XML-processing application.

A number of metaproperties are defined in the Microsoft xml-metaprop namespace. These metaproperties can be retrieved by specifying the metaproperty name in a column pattern. For example, you could retrieve the unique node ID, the name, and the name of the parent node for each *Item* XML node in a document by executing the following query:

```
SELECT * FROM
OpenXML(@iTree, 'Order/Items/Item', 1)
WITH
(NodeID INTEGER '@mp:id',
 NodeName VARCHAR(20) '@mp:localname',
 ParentNode VARCHAR(20) '@mp:parentlocalname')
```

This code would return the following rowset:

NodeID	NodeName	ParentNode
6	Item	Items
10	Item	Items
14	Item	Items

This Transact-SQL code can be viewed in the metadata.sql script in the Demos\Chapter7 folder on the companion CD. The metaproperties can be used to examine the structure of an XML document and process it accordingly. On the next page is the full list of metaproperties defined in the xml-metaprop namespace.

Metaproperty	Description
@mp:id	Unique identifier for the specified node.
@mp:localname	The name of the element.
@mp:namespaceuri	The namespace for the specified node. The value of this property is NULL if no namespace is defined.
@mp:prefix	The prefix used for the specified node.
@mp:prev	The ID of the previous sibling node.
@mp:xmltext	The textual representation of the node and its attributes and subelements.
@mp:parentid	The ID of the parent node.
@mp:parentlocalname	The name of the parent node.
@mp:parentnamespaceuri	The namespace of the parent node.
@mp:parentprefix	The prefix of the parent node.

Inserting Overflow Data

One of the most useful metaproperties is *xmltext*. This property returns the actual XML text from any part of the document. You can use the *xmltext* property to retrieve the whole XML document by specifying the root (/) as the row pattern, which of course means that you could insert the entire XML document into a single column of a table. However, it's more likely that you'd want to insert some data from the document into individual columns and perhaps insert the remaining unconsumed XML into an overflow column.

For example, suppose we wanted to store the order header information (*OrderID*, *CustomerID*, *EmployeeID*, and *OrderDate*) in the corresponding columns of the Orders table, and store the XML data representing the relevant items in an overflow column named *OrderDetailsXML*. You can use the *OpenXML* function to retrieve the necessary data from the *Order* element, and you can use the *xmltext* metaproperty to retrieve the remaining XML data. However, by default the *xmltext* metaproperty retrieves the entire XML text for the element defined in the *rowpattern* parameter (in this case, *Order*), even if some of its attributes and subelements have already been selected. To retrieve only the unconsumed XML, you must add the value 8 to the *flags* parameter. This action instructs SQL Server to copy only the elements and attributes that haven't already been explicitly selected to the overflow column.

In the case of the purchase order document, the following Transact-SQL statement could be used to retrieve the order header fields and the unconsumed XML data about order details:

```
SELECT * FROM
OpenXML(@iTree, 'Order', 9)
WITH
(OrderID INTEGER,
 CustomerID nCHAR(6),
 EmployeeID INTEGER,
 OrderDate DATETIME,
 OrderDetailsXML VARCHAR(2000) '@mp:xmltext')
```

Note that the *flags* parameter has been assigned the value *9*. This assignment instructs SQL Server to search for attributes (1) and to retrieve unconsumed data in an overflow column (8). Here's the resulting rowset from this query when used against the purchase order document I described earlier:

OrderID	CustomerID	EmployeeID	OrderDate	OrderDetailsXML
1001	ALFKI	2	01/01/2001	<Order><Items> <Item ProductID="11" Qty="1" UnitPrice="12.99"> <Discount>0</Discount> </Item> <Item ProductID="17" Qty="2" UnitPrice="4.99"> <Discount>0.5</Discount> </Item> <Item ProductID="21" Qty="1" UnitPrice="11.99"> <Discount>0</Discount> </Item> </Items></Order>

This Transact-SQL code can be viewed in the overflow.sql script in the Demos\Chapter7 folder on the companion CD. As you can see, the *OrderDetailsXML* column contains an XML representation of the entire order document apart from the nodes that were retrieved in the other columns.

Creating an Edge Table

You can retrieve additional metadata by generating an *edge table* from an XML document. An edge table gets its name from the fact that every edge (or node) in the XML document produces a row in the rowset. To retrieve an edge table, simply omit the *flags* parameter and the WITH clause in the *OpenXML* function, as shown here:

```
SELECT * FROM

OPENXML(@iTree, 'Order')
```

This code retrieves a rowset with the following columns:

Column	Description
Id	Unique identifier for the node
Parentid	Unique identifier of the parent node
Nodetype	XML DOM node type
Localname	Name of the node
Prefix	Node prefix
Namespaceuri	XML namespace for the node
Datatype	The XML datatype of the node
Prev	Unique identifier of the previous sibling node
Text	Attribute value or element content

This Transact-SQL code can be viewed in the EdgeTable.sql script in the Demos\Chapter7 folder on the companion CD. Notice that an edge table includes the *datatype* and *text* properties for each node. These properties aren't available by specifying metaproperty column patterns.

An edge table can be useful for calculating summary information about the document. For example, a simple way to find out how many different items have been ordered is to count the *Item* elements this way:

```
SELECT COUNT(*) ItemCount FROM
OpenXML(@iTree, 'Order')
WHERE localname='Item'
```

This query returns the number of nodes with the name *Item* in the document.

Summary

The main point of this chapter was to demonstrate how to use the *OpenXML* function to insert data from an XML document into tables in a database. This is the primary purpose of this function, and it can be a crucial aspect of an integration solution in which XML documents are received and need to be logged in a database.

A secondary use of the *OpenXML* function is to retrieve metadata from an XML document, which can be useful if you intend to write your own XML processing logic. This is certainly not a trivial task, however, and you can find many off-the-shelf tools and utilities to do this kind of work for you.

In the next chapter, we'll examine two alternative approaches to inserting XML data: updategrams and the XML bulk load component.

8

Additional XML Tools

In previous chapters, you saw how the XML-related functionality provided with Microsoft SQL Server 2000 can be used to great effect. However, that's only part of the story. The XML support in SQL Server 2000 can be enhanced by downloading and installing XML For SQL Server 2000 Web Release 1 from the MSDN Web site (*http://msdn.microsoft.com/downloads*). This update includes additional tools for building XML-based SQL Server applications. In particular, it includes *updategrams*, an XML-based way to modify data in a database, and the *XML bulk load component*, a programmable object for inserting large volumes of XML data into a database.

In this chapter, I'll explain how to download and install the XML For SQL Server 2000 Web Release and how to create applications using updategrams and the XML bulk load component.

Installing the XML For SQL Server 2000 Web Release

You can download the XML For SQL Server 2000 Web Release from the Downloads section of the MSDN Web site. The download consists of a single file named XML For SQL.exe. When you run this program on a computer with SQL Server 2000 installed, the extra XML-related tools will be added to the installation.

Once you've installed the update, you can open the documentation for the XML For SQL Server 2000 Web Release from the Microsoft SQL Server XML Tools program group. This documentation tells you about the XML-related enhancements to SQL Server, including updategrams and the XML bulk load component.

XML For SQL Server 2000 Web Release 1 at a Glance

So what exactly do you get for your trouble? The XML For SQL Server 2000 Web Release includes a number of improvements to the XML-related functionality in SQL Server 2000.

- **Updategrams** Support for updategrams means that you can use XML template-like documents to insert, update, and delete data in a SQL Server database. The Settings tab of the Virtual Directory Properties dialog box in the Configure SQL XML Support In IIS tool is updated to allow updategrams to be posted to a SQLISAPI virtual directory.
- **The bulk load component** The bulk load component is a scriptable COM component with which you can import large volumes of XML data into a database more efficiently than you can using the *OpenXML* function.
- **SQL data type support for schemas** In a standard SQL Server 2000 installation, annotated schemas support the *sql:datatype* annotation for binary data such as *image* or *text*. The XML For SQL Server 2000 Web Release adds support for all SQL Server built-in data types, including *varchar*, *money*, *integer*, and so on. This improved data type support is especially useful when you're bulk-loading data into a SQL Server database using the bulk load component.
- **Template enhancements** The *nullvalue* attribute is added to the XML-SQL namespace used in templates. This inclusion allows you to specify a parameter value that represents NULL in the header of a template. For example, you could include the annotation *sql:nullvalue="none"* in the header of a template and pass NULL to any of the parameters by specifying *none*. The *is-xml* attribute is also added to the namespace, allowing you to indicate that a string parameter containing XML characters (such as <) is to be treated as text rather than XML; you accomplish this task by including the annotation *sql:is-xml="0"* in a *param* element.

In the rest of this chapter, I'll describe how you can use the two main features of the XML For SQL Server 2000 Web Release (updategrams and the bulk load component) to build an XML-based application.

Modifying Data with Updategrams

I explained in previous chapters how you can use templates to retrieve data over ADO or HTTP connections. However, retrieving data solves only half the problem. We also need a way to modify data by updating records, deleting them, or adding new ones. For example, the Northwind Traders Web site might allow users to not only view the products available, but also place orders by adding records to the Orders and Order Details tables. Or Northwind Traders could use an intranet-based application to update employee records. Updategrams give developers an XML-based approach to data modification, in much the same way that templates allow you an XML-based way to retrieve data. An updategram is an XML document containing a before and after image of the data you want to modify, which you can submit to SQL Server much as you submit a template.

Anatomy of an Updategram

An updategram is based on the xml-updategram namespace and contains one or more *sync* elements. Each *sync* element represents a transactional unit of database modifications. *Sync* elements contain at least one pair of *before* and *after* elements representing an individual insert, update, or delete operation. For example, the following updategram could be used to change the HomePhone field in the Employees table for employee number 1:

```
<?xml version="1.0"?>
<employeeupdate xmlns:updg="urn:schemas-microsoft-com:xml-updategram">
    <updg:sync>
        <updg:before>
            <Employees EmployeeID="1"/>
        </updg:before>
        <updg:after>
            <Employees HomePhone="555-112233"/>
        </updg:after>
    </updg:sync>
</employeeupdate>
```

This updategram can be viewed in the UpdateEmployee.xml file in the Demos\Chapter8\Updategrams folder on the companion CD. You can execute it by opening the Update Employee shortcut in the Demos\Chapter8 folder. If you include more than one *sync* element in an updategram, each *sync* element is treated as a transaction. In other words, if an error causes an update to fail, all the other updates in that *sync* element will also fail. The updates in other *sync* elements, however, will be unaffected.

> **Note** Each element in the *before* element must identify only a single record for modification. In other words, you can't specify a *before* element that results in multiple records being updated. For this reason, the elements in the *before* element usually include either the primary key value of the row to be modified or multiple columns that represent a unique combination.

Mapping Data in an Updategram

You can map the XML data in an updategram to SQL Server tables and columns in two ways: you can use default mapping or a mapping schema.

Using the Default Mapping

The easiest approach to mapping XML data in an updategram is to use the default (or *intrinsic*) mapping, which assumes that the top-level tag in a *before* or *after* element is named after the table it represents, and that the columns in that table are represented by attributes or subelements. For example, the EmployeeID column in the Employees table could be mapped using either of the following XML elements:

```
<Employees EmployeeID="1"/>
```

or

```
<Employees>
    <EmployeeID>1</EmployeeID>
</Employees>
```

When more than one column is specified, you can use a mixture of attribute-centric and element-centric mappings, as shown in this sample code:

```
<Employees EmployeeID="1">
    <HomePhone>555-112233</HomePhone>
</Employees>
```

If a table name contains an illegal character (such as a space) for an XML element name, you must use the four-digit hexadecimal UCS-2 value for that character to encode it. For example, the following XML could be used to represent the OrderID column in the Order Details table:

```
<Order_x0020_Details OrderID="1000"/>
```

Using a Mapping Schema

An alternative approach to mapping data in an updategram to tables and columns in the database is to specify a mapping schema. I described how to use mapping schemas to map XML elements and attributes to data in the database in Chapter 6. To specify a mapping schema in an updategram, you use the *mapping-schema* annotation in a *sync* element, as shown in this example:

```
<?xml version="1.0"?>
<employeeupdate xmlns:updg="urn:schemas-microsoft-com:xml-updategram">
    <updg:sync updg:mapping-schema="EmployeeSchema.xml">
        <updg:before>
            <Employee EmpID="1"/>
        </updg:before>
        <updg:after>
            <Employee Phone="555-112233"/>
        </updg:after>
    </updg:sync>
</employeeupdate>
```

You can find this updategram in the UpdateEmployeesSchema.xml file in the Demos\Chapter8\Updategrams folder on the companion CD. The mapping schema referenced (in this case *EmployeeSchema.xml*) should contain the information necessary to map the elements in the updategram to data in the database. For example, the updategram could be mapped to the Employees table using the following schema:

```
<?xml version="1.0"?>
<Schema xmlns="urn:schemas-microsoft-com:xml-data"
    xmlns:sql="urn:schemas-microsoft-com:xml-sql">
    <ElementType name="Employee" sql:relation="Employees">
        <AttributeType name="EmpID"/>
        <AttributeType name="Phone"/>

        <attribute type="EmpID" sql:field="EmployeeID"/>
        <attribute type="Phone" sql:field="HomePhone"/>
    </ElementType>
</Schema>
```

This schema is also available in the EmployeeSchema.xml file in the Demos\Chapter8\Updategrams folder on the companion CD. You can execute the updategram that uses this schema by opening the Update Employees (Schema) shortcut in the Demos\Chapter8 folder. This schema maps the Employee element to the Employees table and the *EmpID* and *Phone* attributes to the EmployeeID and HomePhone columns, respectively.

Handling NULLs in an Updategram

Databases often use NULL to indicate that the value of a field is unknown. You can use the *nullvalue* attribute to retrieve or set a NULL value in an updategram. The *nullvalue* attribute is used in the *sync* element to assign a placeholder string used to represent NULL. You can then use this placeholder in the updategram to identify a column containing a NULL value or to set a column value to NULL. For example, the following updategram sets an employee's HomePhone field to NULL:

```
<?xml version="1.0"?>
<employeeupdate xmlns:updg="urn:schemas-microsoft-com:xml-updategram">
    <updg:sync updg:nullvalue="NoPhone">
        <updg:before>
            <Employees EmployeeID="1"/>
        </updg:before>
        <updg:after>
            <Employees HomePhone="NoPhone"/>
        </updg:after>
    </updg:sync>
</employeeupdate>
```

This updategram is also available in the UpdateEmployeesNull.xml file in the Demos\Chapter8\Updategrams folder on the companion CD. You can execute it by opening the Update Employees (NULL) shortcut in the Demos\Chapter8 folder.

Using Parameters in an Updategram

Because an updategram is essentially a specialized template, you'd expect to be able to pass parameters to an updategram in much the same way that you pass them to a template. But in fact, you need to observe a slight difference in the syntax when you're passing parameters to an updategram, which you may spot in this example:

```
<?xml version="1.0"?>
<employeeupdate xmlns:updg="urn:schemas-microsoft-com:xml-updategram">
    <updg:header>
        <updg:param name="EmployeeID"/>
        <updg:param name="HomePhone"/>
    </updg:header>
    <updg:sync>
        <updg:before>
            <Employees EmployeeID="$EmployeeID"/>
        </updg:before>
```

```
        <updg:after>
            <Employees HomePhone="$HomePhone"/>
        </updg:after>
    </updg:sync>
</employeeupdate>
```

The only difference between using parameters in an updategram and using parameters in a template (in case you didn't spot it) is that parameter placeholders in an updategram are prefixed by a dollar (*$*) symbol instead of the at (*@*) symbol used in templates. You can use parameters in an updategram either to identify the rows to be modified (by specifying the parameter in the *before* element) or to assign a new value to a column (by specifying the parameter in the *after* element).

Passing NULL as a Parameter

You can pass NULL as a parameter to an updategram by specifying the *nullvalue* attribute in the *header* element. The *nullvalue* attribute is used to assign a placeholder value for NULL, just as when that attribute is specified in the *sync* element. To pass NULL to the updategram, simply pass the placeholder string; the updategram will interpret it as NULL.

One potential gotcha here is that when using the *nullvalue* attribute in the *header* element, you should not specify a namespace qualifier (such as *updg:*) as you do when using the *nullvalue* attribute in the *sync* element.

The following example shows an updategram that uses two parameters. If you pass a value of *NoPhone* to the updategram, NULL is inserted into the HomePhone column of the specified employee.

```
<?xml version="1.0"?>
<employeeupdate xmlns:updg="urn:schemas-microsoft-com:xml-updategram">
    <updg:header nullvalue="NoPhone">
        <updg:param name="EmployeeID"/>
        <updg:param name="HomePhone"/>
    </updg:header>
    <updg:sync>
        <updg:before>
            <Employees EmployeeID="$EmployeeID"/>
        </updg:before>
        <updg:after>
            <Employees HomePhone="$HomePhone"/>
        </updg:after>
    </updg:sync>
</employeeupdate>
```

You can also find this updategram in the UpdateEmployeesParam.xml file in the Demos\Chapter8\Updategrams folder on the companion CD. You can execute it by opening the Update Employees (Parameter) shortcut in the Demos\Chapter8 folder.

Updating Multiple Rows

I told you earlier in this chapter that each element in the *before* element can identify only a single row. This restriction means that to update multiple rows, you must include an element for each row you want to modify.

Using the *id* Attribute

In addition to listing the *before* and *after* elements, you must provide SQL Server with a means of matching the *before* elements to their corresponding *after* elements. You can do this in one of two ways: by referencing a mapping schema in which the *key-fields* annotation is used to identify the primary key of the table being updated (and include the primary key in the *before* element), or by specifying the *id* attribute in the updategram. I explained *key-fields* annotation in Chapter 6, so I'll focus here on the *id* attribute.

You use the *id* attribute to specify a unique string value to match a *before* element with its corresponding *after* element. For example, the following updategram modifies two records. We use the *id* attribute to match the required modification in the *after* element with the row identified in the *before* element.

```
<?xml version="1.0"?>
<employeeupdate xmlns:updg="urn:schemas-microsoft-com:xml-updategram">
    <updg:sync>
        <updg:before>
            <Employees updg:id="U1" EmployeeID="1"/>
            <Employees updg:id="U2" EmployeeID="2"/>
        </updg:before>
        <updg:after>
            <Employees updg:id="U2" HomePhone="555-332211"/>
            <Employees updg:id="U1" HomePhone="555-112233"/>
        </updg:after>
    </updg:sync>
</employeeupdate>
```

This updategram can be viewed in the UpdateEmployeesMultiRow.xml file in the Demos\Chapter8\Updategrams folder on the companion CD. You can execute it by opening the Update Employees (Multiple Rows) shortcut in the Demos\Chapter8 folder. Because you use the *id* attribute to match the *before* and *after* elements, the order of appearance of the elements in the code is unimportant. The updategram sets the HomePhone field for employee 1 to *555-112233* while setting the same field for employee 2 to *555-332211*.

Using Multiple *before* and *after* Elements

You can also avoid ambiguity by using multiple *before* and *after* elements in an updategram. If you specify only one element in each *before* and *after* element pair, you can avoid having to specify an *id* attribute. For example, you could use the following updategram to change the HomePhone field for employees 1 and 2:

```
<?xml version="1.0"?>
<employeeupdate xmlns:updg="urn:schemas-microsoft-com:xml-updategram">
    <updg:sync>
        <updg:before>
            <Employees EmployeeID="1"/>
        </updg:before>
        <updg:after>
            <Employees HomePhone="555-112233"/>
        </updg:after>
        <updg:before>
            <Employees EmployeeID="2"/>
        </updg:before>
        <updg:after>
            <Employees HomePhone="555-332211"/>
        </updg:after>
    </updg:sync>
</employeeupdate>
```

You can view this updategram in the UpdateEmployeesMultiRow2.xml file in the Demos\Chapter8\Updategrams folder on the companion CD.

Updategram Results

When a client application executes an updategram, the result is returned as an XML document. In most cases, the document is simply the empty root element that was specified in the updategram. For example, the expected result of the employeeupdate updategram shown earlier would be this code:

```
<?xml version="1.0"?>
<employeeupdate xmlns:updg="urn:schemas-microsoft-com:xml-updategram">
</employeeupdate>
```

Updategram Error Messages

If any errors occur during the execution of the updategram, they're returned as an MSSQLError processing instruction, as shown here:

```
<?xml version="1.0"?>
<employeeupdate xmlns:updg="urn:schemas-microsoft-com:xml-updategram">
    <?MSSQLError HResult="0x80004005"
        Source="Microsoft XML Extensions to SQL Server"
        Description="All updategram nodes with siblings must have ids,
            either user-specified ones or mapping schema-based key
            field id"?>
</employeeupdate >
```

Applying a Style Sheet

You can apply an XSL style sheet to the updategram results the same way that you would for a template. A style sheet can be applied on the server by specifying the *xsl* attribute (defined in the XML-SQL namespace) in the root element of the updategram, as shown here:

```
<?xml version="1.0"?>
<employeeupdate xmlns:updg="urn:schemas-microsoft-com:xml-updategram"
    xmlns:sql="urn:schemas-microsoft-com:xml-sql"
    sql:xsl="Results.xsl">
    <updg:sync>
        <updg:before>
            <Employees EmployeeID="1"/>
        </updg:before>
        <updg:after>
            <Employees Lastname="Malcolm"/>
        </updg:after>
    </updg:sync>
</employeeupdate>
```

This updategram is also available in the UpdateEmployeeName.xml file in the Demos\Chapter8\Updategrams folder on the companion CD. You can execute it by opening the Update Employee (XSL) shortcut in the Demos\Chapter8 folder. This capability allows you to use updategrams in Web sites, while providing a suitable HTML result page when data has been modified or when an error has occurred.

Inserting Rows with an Updategram

You can use an updategram to insert data into the database. For example, you could build an e-commerce site that uses templates to allow customers to view the product data and updategrams to add customer orders to the Orders and Order Details tables. When you're using an updategram to insert data, you need to specify an empty *before* element, with the data to be inserted in the corresponding *after* element. For example, the following updategram could be used to add a row to the Order Details table. (Because the Northwind database contains a referential constraint between Orders and Order Details, this example assumes that an order with an OrderID of 10248 has already been inserted into the Orders table.)

```
<?xml version="1.0"?>
<neworder xmlns:updg="urn:schemas-microsoft-com:xml-updategram">
    <updg:sync>
        <updg:before>
        </updg:before>
        <updg:after>
        <Order_x0020_Details OrderID="10248" ProductID="13"
            UnitPrice="$10.99" Quantity="1" Discount="0"/>
        </updg:after>
    </updg:sync>
</neworder>
```

You can view this updategram in the InsertOrderDetail.xml file in the Demos\Chapter8\Updategrams folder on the companion CD. You can execute it by opening the Insert Order Details shortcut in the Demos\Chapter8 folder.

> **Note** Currency values, such as the UnitPrice column in the Order Details table, must either be mapped in a schema using the *dt:type* attribute with a value of *fixed.14.4*, or prefixed with a dollar ($) symbol, as shown in the preceding example. Because parameter values in an updategram are also prefixed with a dollar symbol, the only way to pass a currency parameter is to map the data using a mapping schema.

Inserting Multiple Rows

To insert multiple rows into the same table, you can simply specify multiple XML elements in the *after* element. For example, the following updategram inserts two rows into the Order Details table. (Again, the example assumes that an order with an order ID of 10248 has previously been inserted in the Orders table.)

```
<?xml version="1.0"?>
<neworder xmlns:updg="urn:schemas-microsoft-com:xml-updategram">
    <updg:sync>
        <updg:before>
        </updg:before>
        <updg:after>
            <Order_x0020_Details OrderID="10248" ProductID="14"
```

(continued)

```
                UnitPrice="$10.99" Quantity="1"
                Discount="0"/>
            <Order_x0020_Details OrderID="10248" ProductID="15"
                UnitPrice="$11.99" Quantity="2"
                Discount="0"/>
        </updg:after>
    </updg:sync>
</neworder>
```

This updategram is also available in the InsertMultipleOrderDetail.xml file in the Demos\Chapter8\Updategrams folder on the companion CD.

Using an IDENTITY Column Value

IDENTITY columns are automatically assigned a value by SQL Server. However, sometimes you need to know what value SQL Server has assigned in a primary key table (such as Orders) so that you can insert the same value for related rows in a foreign key table (such as Order Details). You can obtain an IDENTITY value using the *at-identity* attribute. This attribute allows you to use the same updategram to insert data into a primary key table that has an IDENTITY column and a foreign key table that references the primary key. For example, the following updategram would insert data into the Orders and Order Details tables:

```
<?xml version="1.0"?>
<neworder xmlns:updg="urn:schemas-microsoft-com:xml-updategram">
    <updg:sync>
        <updg:before>
        </updg:before>
        <updg:after>
            <Orders updg:at-identity="newID" CustomerID="ALFKI"
                EmployeeID="3" OrderDate="01/01/2001"/>
            <Order_x0020_Details OrderID="newID" ProductID="1"
                UnitPrice="$10.99" Quantity="1"
                Discount="0"/>
            <Order_x0020_Details OrderID="newID" ProductID="2"
                UnitPrice="$12.99" Quantity="2"
                Discount="0"/>
        </updg:after>
    </updg:sync>
</neworder>
```

Notice that the *at-identity* attribute is specified in the element representing the Orders table (which contains the IDENTITY column). A placeholder value is assigned, in this case *newID*, which can then be used elsewhere in the updategram to represent the IDENTITY value inserted into the Orders table. The *newID* placeholder is assigned to the *OrderID* attribute in the Order Details table for both the added Order Details records.

Returning the IDENTITY Value to the Client

Of course, if this were a real e-commerce application, you'd want to return the IDENTITY value to the browser so that the customer would know the OrderID assigned to his order. To retrieve the IDENTITY value, you can add a *returnid* attribute to the *after* element and specify the placeholder name for the IDENTITY column as its value. This process is shown in the following updategram:

```
<?xml version="1.0"?>
<neworder xmlns:updg="urn:schemas-microsoft-com:xml-updategram">
    <updg:sync>
        <updg:before>
        </updg:before>
        <updg:after updg:returnid="newID">
            <Orders updg:at-identity="newID" CustomerID="ALFKI"
                EmployeeID="3" OrderDate="01/01/2001"/>
            <Order_x0020_Details OrderID="newID" ProductID="1"
                UnitPrice="$10.99" Quantity="1"
                Discount="0"/>
            <Order_x0020_Details OrderID="newID" ProductID="2"
                UnitPrice="$12.99" Quantity="2"
                Discount="0"/>
        </updg:after>
    </updg:sync>
</neworder>
```

This updategram can be viewed in the InsertOrder.xml file in the Demos\Chapter8\Updategrams folder on the companion CD. When you execute this updategram, the value represented by the *newID* placeholder is returned as an element in the resulting XML document. For example, suppose the value 11088 was generated as an IDENTITY value. The following XML document would be returned:

```
<?xml  version="1.0"?>
<neworder xmlns:updg="urn:schemas-microsoft-com:xml-updategram">
    <returnid>
        <newID>11088</newID>
    </returnid>
</neworder>
```

Of course, in a Web environment, a style sheet could be applied to the updategram results and the order ID would be displayed in a suitable format.

Generating a Globally Unique Identifier (GUID)

Many applications use Globally Unique Identifiers (or GUIDs) as unique values to identify a business entity (such as a customer or product). GUIDs are unique 16-byte values such as *6F9619FF-8B86-D011-B42D-00C04FC964FF*. SQL Server supports the *uniqueidentifier* data type, which allows GUIDs to be stored in a SQL Server database column.

In an ordinary INSERT statement, you can use the *NEWID()* function to generate a GUID. However, in an updategram, you must use the *guid* attribute to generate a GUID for use anywhere within a *sync* block. As with the *at-identity* attribute, the *guid* attribute specifies a placeholder value representing the new GUID. For example, you could use the following updategram to insert rows into a SpecialOrder table and a SpecialOrderDetail table, in which a GUID is used to identify an order. (Note that these tables don't actually exist in the Northwind database.)

```
<NewSpecialOrder
    xmlns:updg="urn:schemas-microsoft-com:xml-updategram">
    <updg:sync>
        <updg:before>
        </updg:before>
        <updg:after>
            <SpecialOrder updg:guid="NewGUID">
                <OrderID>NewGUID</OrderID>
                <OrderDate>01/01/2001</OrderDate>
            </SpecialOrder>
            <SpecialOrderDetail>
                <OrderID>NewGUID</OrderID>
                <ProductID>1</ProductID>
                <Quantity>2</Quantity>
            </SpecialOrderDetail>
        </updg:after>
    </updg:sync>
</NewSpecialOrder>
```

Deleting Data with an Updategram

To delete rows from a table with an updategram, you essentially do the opposite of an INSERT operation. The row (or rows) to be deleted must be identified in the *before* element, with no corresponding elements in the *after* element. The principal difference in process to remember is that each element in the *before* element must uniquely identify a single row in the database; in an updategram, there's no equivalent of a wildcard delete operation (in which multiple records can be deleted based on a single criterion).

For example, the following updategram could be used to delete an employee record from the database:

```
<?xml version="1.0"?>
<DeleteEmployee xmlns:updg="urn:schemas-microsoft-com:xml-updategram">
    <updg:sync>
        <updg:before>
```

```
            <Employees EmployeeID="1"/>
        </updg:before>
        <updg:after>
        </updg:after>
    </updg:sync>
</DeleteEmployee>
```

To delete multiple rows, specify multiple elements in the *before* element, as the following code shows:

```
<?xml version="1.0"?>
<DeleteEmployee xmlns:updg="urn:schemas-microsoft-com:xml-updategram">
    <updg:sync>
        <updg:before>
            <Employees EmployeeID="1"/>
            <Employees EmployeeID="2"/>
        </updg:before>
        <updg:after>
        </updg:after>
    </updg:sync>
</DeleteEmployee>
```

> **Note** Updategrams don't support *cascading deletes* (the capacity to delete related records in other tables) unless the ON DELETE CASCADE option was specified when the table containing the data was created. For more information about the SQL Server 2000 support for cascading referential integrity, refer to SQL Server Books Online.

Updategrams and Concurrency

When a database is accessed by many users, you can encounter concurrency issues (such as excessive locking) as multiple users attempt to access the same data. Many database applications adopt different strategies to deal with locking—the most common approaches being *optimistic locking* and *pessimistic locking*. Optimistic locking takes its name from the fact that the application doesn't lock any data until an update takes place. (In other words, you're optimistic that no other user will change the data in the time between your access of the data and your update of the data.) This strategy results in much shorter lock times and better throughput but means that any data you retrieve can be updated (or even deleted) by another user while you're still working with it. Pessimistic locking takes the opposite approach; the application locks all data as soon as someone accesses it. (In other words, you're pessimistically assuming that some other user will attempt to change the data before you're finished with it.) This strategy prevents many concurrency errors but increases the amount of time data is locked, and therefore can degrade performance. Updategrams are based on an optimistic concurrency model, which means that other users can access the data affected by your updategram while it's in progress. However, you can control the updategram's behavior when this happens by using one of three levels of protection—low concurrency protection, intermediate concurrency protection, or high concurrency protection.

Low Concurrency Protection

You can use the lowest level of protection by simply specifying the primary key (or some unique combination identifying a single row) in the *before* element. For example, consider the following updategram:

```
<?xml version="1.0"?>
<UpdateShipper xmlns:updg="urn:schemas-microsoft-com:xml-updategram">
    <updg:sync>
        <updg:before>
            <Shippers ShipperID="1"/>
        </updg:before>
        <updg:after>
            <Shippers Phone="(503) 555-1122"/>
        </updg:after>
    </updg:sync>
</UpdateShipper>
```

When this updategram is executed, SQL Server retrieves the row identified in the *before* element and then updates the Phone column for that record. The equivalent Transact-SQL statement for the *after* element in this updategram would be the following:

```
UPDATE Shippers
SET Phone='(503) 555-1122'
WHERE ShipperID=1
```

The update happens regardless of any other activity in the database, even if another user changes the same field in the same record between the retrieval and the update. Effectively, this is what's known as a *blind update* because you update the record even though you can't see changes made by other users. This level of protection provides great performance but could lead to some unexpected results.

Intermediate Concurrency Protection

You can apply the next level of protection by specifying the column you're changing in the *before* element. This level ensures that the update takes place only if at the time of the update the field being updated still has the same value specified in the *before* element. For example, you could use the following updategram to update the shipper's phone number:

```
<?xml version="1.0"?>
<UpdateShipper xmlns:updg="urn:schemas-microsoft-com:xml-updategram">
    <updg:sync>
        <updg:before>
            <Shippers ShipperID="1" Phone="(503) 555-9831"/>
        </updg:before>
        <updg:after>
            <Shippers Phone="(503) 555-1122"/>
        </updg:after>
    </updg:sync>
</UpdateShipper>
```

In this case, the shipper record is updated only if the Phone field value remains (503) 555-9831 throughout the entire updategram operation. The equivalent Transact-SQL statement for the *after* element is the following:

```
UPDATE Shippers
SET Phone='(503) 555-1122'
WHERE ShipperID=1
AND Phone='(503) 555-9831'
```

If another user updates the Phone field for this record between the execution of the *before* element and the execution of the *after* element, the updategram returns an error message. Of course, any concurrent updates to the other field in the record (CompanyName) have no effect on your update operation and will be ignored, and the end result will be a merge of all the concurrent update operations.

High Concurrency Protection

The highest level of protection allows the update to take place only if the record hasn't been modified at all between the *before* and *after* element executions. You can achieve this level in one of two ways: you can specify all the fields in the *before* element, or you can make use of any timestamp columns in the table being updated. Of these two approaches, specifying all the fields is the most realistic because using a timestamp requires that you copy the current timestamp value from the row into the updategram before executing it.

The following updategram specifies all the fields in the Shippers table in the *before* element:

```
<?xml version="1.0"?>
<UpdateShipper xmlns:updg="urn:schemas-microsoft-com:xml-updategram">
    <updg:sync>
        <updg:before>
```

(continued)

```
            <Shippers ShipperID="1"
                CompanyName="Speedy Express"
                Phone="(503) 555-9831"/>
        </updg:before>
        <updg:after>
            <Shippers HomePhone="(503) 555-1122"/>
        </updg:after>
    </updg:sync>
</UpdateShipper>
```

In this case, an update of any of the columns by another user between the *before* and *after* elements causes this updategram to return an error message. The equivalent Transact-SQL statement for the *after* element is the following:

```
UPDATE Shippers
SET Phone='(503) 555-1122'
WHERE ShipperID=1
AND CompanyName='Speedy Express'
AND Phone='(503) 555-9831'
```

Combining INSERT, UPDATE, and DELETE Operations in an Updategram

So far, we've used updategrams to insert, update, or delete data, each operation by itself, which is probably the most realistic scenario. However, a business process might occasionally involve a combination of two, or all three, of these actions. You can use a single updategram to perform a combination of INSERT, UPDATE, and DELETE operations by using the *id* attribute to identify each individual data-modification operation.

For example, you could use the following updategram to update a customer record and add an order for that customer to the database:

```
<CustOrder xmlns:updg="urn:schemas-microsoft-com:xml-updategram">
    <updg:sync>
        <updg:before>
            <Customers updg:id="UpdtCust" CustomerID="ALFKI"/>
        </updg:before>
        <updg:after>
            <Customers updg:id="UpdtCust" ContactName="Charles"/>
            <Orders updg:id="InstOrd" updg:at-identity="NewID"
                CustomerID="ALFKI" OrderDate="01/01/2001"/>
            <Order_x0020_Details updg:id="InstOrdDet" OrderID="NewID"
                ProductID="11"
                UnitPrice="$1.00"
                Quantity="1"
                Discount="0.00"/>
        </updg:after>
    </updg:sync>
</CustOrder>
```

You can view this updategram in the UpdateAndInsert.xml file in the Demos\Chapter8\Updategrams folder on the companion CD. You can execute it by opening the Update And Insert shortcut in the Demos\Chapter8 folder. Notice that a different *id* attribute is used for each operation in the updategram. The *UpdtCust* string matches the *before* and *after* elements of the UPDATE operation (which changes the customer's ContactName field), and the *InstOrd* and *InstOrdDet id* attributes identify the INSERT operations (which insert a record into the Orders and OrderDetails tables, respectively).

The XML Bulk Load Component

As you've just seen, updategrams can be used to insert data in a SQL Server database. You might recall that you can also use the *OpenXML* function to add data to a table. Although both of these approaches are ideal for business processes that involve adding one, or a few, records, neither of them is ideally suited to importing a large volume of XML data.

To assist you in bulk load operations, the XML For SQL Server 2000 Web Release includes the XML bulk load component. This COM component can be used from any COM-aware programming language (such as Microsoft VBScript) to import XML data into SQL Server.

How the Bulk Load Component Works

To use the XML bulk load component, you define a mapping schema that matches the XML data you want to import with the tables and columns you want to load it into. The component then reads the XML data as a stream, inserting each row into the database as the corresponding XML element is read.

For example, consider the following annotated schema:

```
<?xml version="1.0" ?>
<Schema xmlns="urn:schemas-microsoft-com:xml-data"
    xmlns:dt="urn:schemas-microsoft-com:datatypes"
    xmlns:sql="urn:schemas-microsoft-com:xml-sql" >

    <ElementType name="Catalog" sql:is-constant="1">
        <element type="Category"/>
    </ElementType>

    <ElementType name="Category" sql:relation="Categories">
        <AttributeType name="CategoryID"/>
        <AttributeType name="CategoryName"/>
        <AttributeType name="Description"/>
```

(continued)

```
        <attribute type="CategoryID" sql:field="CategoryID"/>
        <attribute type="CategoryName" sql:field="CategoryName"/>
        <attribute type="Description" sql:field="Description"/>
        <element type="Product">
            <sql:relationship  key-relation="Categories"
                key="CategoryID"
                foreign-key="CategoryID"
                foreign-relation="Products"/>
        </element>
    </ElementType>

    <ElementType name="Product" sql:relation="Products">
        <AttributeType name="ProductID"/>
        <AttributeType name="ProductName"/>
        <AttributeType name="SupplierID"/>
        <AttributeType name="QuantityPerUnit"/>
        <AttributeType name="UnitPrice"/>

        <attribute type="ProductID" sql:field="ProductID"/>
        <attribute type="ProductName" sql:field="ProductName"/>
        <attribute type="SupplierID" sql:field="SupplierID"/>
        <attribute type="QuantityPerUnit"
            sql:field="QuantityPerUnit"/>
        <attribute type="UnitPrice" sql:field="UnitPrice"/>
    </ElementType>

</Schema>
```

This schema maps each *Category* element in an XML document to a row in the Categories table, and each *Product* element to a row in the Products table. This schema could be used to import the following XML data into the Northwind database:

```
<?xml version="1.0"?>
<Catalog>
    <Category CategoryID="99"
        CategoryName="Scottish Foods"
        Description="Traditional food from Scotland">
        <Product ProductID="101"
            ProductName="Porridge"
            SupplierID="1"
            QuantityPerUnit="10 boxes x 20 bags"
            UnitPrice="16"/>
        <Product ProductID="102"
            ProductName="Haggis"
            SupplierID="1"
            QuantityPerUnit="12 Boxes"
            UnitPrice="19"/>
```

```
    </Category>
    <Category CategoryID="100"
        CategoryName="Scottish Drinks"
        Description="Traditional drinks from Scotland">
        <Product ProductID="103"
            ProductName="Single Malt Whisky"
            SupplierID="1"
            QuantityPerUnit="12 - 550 ml bottles"
            UnitPrice="100"/>
    </Category>
</Catalog>
```

When the bulk load component reads the XML data file, it uses the schema to determine the *scope* of each row to be inserted. In the case of the preceding catalog data, the bulk load component would read the first *<Category>* tag and begin constructing a new row for the Categories table. When the closing tag (*</Category>*) is read, the row will be written to the database.

Another interesting aspect of the way the bulk load component maps XML data to rows in the database is the way in which it handles nested relationships. In the catalog example, the schema declares that each *Product* subelement of a *Category* element maps to a row in the Products table. You define the relationship between the two tables by using the relationship annotation to join the tables on the CategoryID field. When the bulk load component reads a *<Product>* tag, it begins constructing a new row for the Products table. Notice, however, that the CategoryID field for the Products table isn't included as an attribute of the *Product* element. In cases like this, the bulk load component uses the relationship annotation to retrieve the appropriate value from the parent element (in this case, *Category*) and inserts that value into the new row. For this tactic to work, the key field for the parent element must be declared in the schema before the subelement representing the related table because the bulk load component reads the data as a stream, and if the key field hasn't been read by the time the closing tag for the subelement is read, the insert can't take place.

If the subelement contains an explicit key field value, however, use the value in the subelement instead of the key field in the parent. The CategoryID value could be repeated in the *Product* subelement, for example, in which case the order of the *CategoryID* attribute declaration and the *Product* subelement in the schema wouldn't matter.

Bulk Loading XML Data

If you want to bulk load XML data, you can use a *SQLXMLBulkLoad* object. You create an instance of this object programmatically by using the ProgID *SQLXMLBulkLoad.SQLXMLBulkLoad*. You then need to connect the component to the database either by setting the *ConnectionString* property of the *SQLXMLBulkLoad* object to a valid OLE-DB connection string or by setting the *ConnectionCommand* property of this object to an existing ADO *Command* object. Once connected, you can use the bulk load component to import XML data into the database by calling the *Execute* method of this object, which requires the path to the schema file and the XML data to be imported.

For example, the following code is the minimum required to import the data in the *C:\CatalogData.xml* file into the Northwind database using the *C:\CatalogSchema.xml* schema:

```
Set objBulkLoad = CreateObject("SQLXMLBulkLoad.SQLXMLBulkLoad")
objBulkLoad.ConnectionString = _
    "provider=SQLOLEDB;data source=DBServer1;database=Northwind;" & _
    "Integrated Security=SSPI;"
objBulkLoad.Execute c:\CatalogSchema.xml, c:\CatalogData.xml
Set objBulkLoad = Nothing
```

The bulk load component also allows you to specify a stream rather than a file as the XML data to be imported, which makes it easy to retrieve data as an XML stream from one database and import it into another.

Bulk Loading from XML Fragments

You can import data from an XML fragment (an XML document with no root element) by specifying the *XMLFragment* property, as shown here:

```
Set objBulkLoad = CreateObject("SQLXMLBulkLoad.SQLXMLBulkLoad")
objBulkLoad.ConnectionString = _
    "provider=SQLOLEDB;data source=DBServer1;database=Northwind;" & _
    "Integrated Security=SSPI;"
objBulkLoad.XMLFragment = True
objBulkLoad.Execute c:\CatalogSchema.xml, c:\CatalogFragment.xml
Set objBulkLoad = Nothing
```

Maintaining Referential Integrity

When you import data into a database, it's important to maintain referential integrity by ensuring that no duplicate rows exist and that relationship constraints between tables are enforced. The bulk load component gives you a number of options to ensure that data can be imported without compromising the integrity of the database.

Enforcing Constraints

Constraints are rules that data in the database must obey. You can use constraints to ensure that values in a particular column meet a specified criterion or to enforce relationships between tables. You can use the *CheckConstraints* property of the *SQLXMLBulkLoad* object to specify whether the bulk load component should check constraints. If this component imports a large volume of data, checking constraints for each row inserted can impair performance. For this reason, the bulk load component doesn't check constraints by default when bulk loading XML data.

To force the bulk load component to check constraints, you can set the *CheckConstraints* property to True, as shown in this code sample:

```
Set objBulkLoad = CreateObject("SQLXMLBulkLoad.SQLXMLBulkLoad")
objBulkLoad.ConnectionString = _
    "provider=SQLOLEDB;data source=DBServer1;database=Northwind;" & _
    "Integrated Security=SSPI;"
objBulkLoad.CheckConstraints = True
objBulkLoad.Execute c:\CatalogSchema.xml, c:\CatalogData.xml
Set objBulkLoad = Nothing
```

If you attempt to insert a row that breaks a constraint when the *CheckConstraints* property is set to True, the bulk load component will return an error.

Ignoring Duplicate Keys

The foundation of any good database design is that there should be no duplicate key values in a table. By default, the bulk load component issues an error message if you attempt to insert a duplicate key, and the bulk load process halts. In some circumstances, however, you don't want your application to behave this way. For example, suppose that after performing the previous bulk load of Scottish produce, you need to update the catalog by inserting the new products in the following XML document:

```
<?xml version="1.0"?>
<Catalog>
    <Category CategoryID="99"
        CategoryName="Scottish Foods"
        Description="Traditional food from Scotland">
        <Product ProductID="104"
            ProductName="Smoked Salmon"
            SupplierID="1"
            QuantityPerUnit="5 Crates"
            UnitPrice="16"/>
        <Product ProductID="105"
            ProductName="Fresh Lobster"
            SupplierID="1"
            QuantityPerUnit="12 Boxes"
            UnitPrice="19"/>
    </Category>
    <Category CategoryID="100"
        CategoryName="Scottish Drinks"
```

(continued)

```
        Description="Traditional drinks from Scotland">
        <Product ProductID="106"
            ProductName="Blended Whisky"
            SupplierID="1"
            QuantityPerUnit="12 - 550 ml bottles"
            UnitPrice="100"/>
    </Category>
</Catalog>
```

This document contains three new products (smoked salmon, fresh lobster, and blended whisky), but the categories (*Scottish Foods* and *Scottish Drinks*) already exist in the database. If we attempt to load this data, the operation will fail at the first hurdle because the database already has a category with a *CategoryID* of 99.

The solution to this problem is to set the *IgnoreDuplicateKeys* property of the *SQLXMLBulkLoad* object to True, as shown in this code:

```
Set objBulkLoad = CreateObject("SQLXMLBulkLoad.SQLXMLBulkLoad")
objBulkLoad.ConnectionString = _
    "provider=SQLOLEDB;data source=DBServer1;database=Northwind;" & _
    "Integrated Security=SSPI;"
objBulkLoad.IgnoreDuplicateKeys = True
objBulkLoad.Execute c:\CatalogSchema.xml, c:\CatalogData.xml
Set objBulkLoad = Nothing
```

When you set the *IgnoreDuplicateKeys* property to True, any inserts that would cause a duplicate key value will fail, but the bulk load process doesn't stop, which allows you to import the remaining data.

Inserting IDENTITY Column Values

As I explained earlier, IDENTITY columns are often used to automatically generate a unique key for each row in a table. In the Northwind database, the ProductID column in the Products table and the CategoryID column in the Categories table are both IDENTITY columns.

By default, if an XML document contains a value for an IDENTITY column, the value in the XML document will be used instead of an automatic value generated by SQL Server. You can change this behavior by setting the *KeepIdentity* property of the *SQLXMLBulkLoad* object to False, in which case the bulk load operation will ignore the value in the XML document and SQL Server will generate a new IDENTITY value for each row. The following code shows how to set the *KeepIdentity* property to False:

```
Set objBulkLoad = CreateObject("SQLXMLBulkLoad.SQLXMLBulkLoad")
objBulkLoad.ConnectionString = _
    "provider=SQLOLEDB;data source=DBServer1;database=Northwind;" & _
    "Integrated Security=SSPI;"
objBulkLoad.KeepIdentity = False
```

```
objBulkLoad.Execute c:\CatalogSchema.xml, c:\CatalogData.xml
Set objBulkLoad = Nothing
```

Be careful when you use the *KeepIdentity* property because it's an all-or-nothing choice that can sometimes lead to unexpected results. For example, you might want to insert some new catalog data and assign an IDENTITY value to each new product using the following code:

```
Set objBulkLoad = CreateObject("SQLXMLBulkLoad.SQLXMLBulkLoad")
objBulkLoad.ConnectionString = _
    "provider=SQLOLEDB;data source=DBServer1;database=Northwind;" & _
    "Integrated Security=SSPI;"
objBulkLoad.CheckConstraints = True
objBulkLoad.IgnoreDuplicateKeys = True
objBulkLoad.KeepIdentity = False
objBulkLoad.Execute c:\CatalogSchema.xml, c:\CatalogData.xml
Set objBulkLoad = Nothing
```

This code will create a new IDENTITY value for the products, but it will also create a new row for each *Category* element in the Categories table, with an IDENTITY column for each row. This means there are now two rows in the Categories table for Scottish Foods and for Scottish Drinks.

Inserting NULLs

Maybe you have a table that includes some columns that are not mapped in the schema. By default, the bulk load component inserts the column's default value for any column not mapped. If the unmapped column doesn't have a default value, the bulk load component inserts a NULL in that column. And if the unmapped column doesn't allow NULLs, you'll get an error message.

You can force the bulk load component to insert a NULL value for unmapped columns even when a default value is defined. To do this, simply set the *KeepNulls* property of the *SQLXMLBulkLoad* object to True, as shown in this code:

```
Set objBulkLoad = CreateObject("SQLXMLBulkLoad.SQLXMLBulkLoad")
objBulkLoad.ConnectionString = _
    "provider=SQLOLEDB;data source=DBServer1;database=Northwind;" & _
    "Integrated Security=SSPI;"
objBulkLoad.KeepNulls = True
objBulkLoad.Execute c:\CatalogSchema.xml, c:\CatalogData.xml
Set objBulkLoad = Nothing
```

Forcing a Table Lock

When bulk loading XML data, the bulk load component locks the table receiving the data for each individual insert. You can force the bulk load component to lock a table for the entire duration of the bulk load operation by setting the *ForceTableLock* property of the *SQLXMLBulkLoad* object to True, as shown at the top of the next page.

```
Set objBulkLoad = CreateObject("SQLXMLBulkLoad.SQLXMLBulkLoad")
objBulkLoad.ConnectionString = _
    "provider=SQLOLEDB;data source=DBServer1;database=Northwind;" & _
    "Integrated Security=SSPI;"
objBulkLoad.ForceTableLock = True
objBulkLoad.Execute c:\CatalogSchema.xml, c:\CatalogData.xml
Set objBulkLoad = Nothing
```

Using Transactions

You can force a bulk load operation to be transactional (in which case the whole import either succeeds or fails) by setting the *Transaction* property of the *SQLXMLBulkLoad* object to True. This setting makes the overall bulk load process slower by caching all inserts in a temporary file until the entire XML document has been read, but using this setting can be a very important way to maintain the integrity of your database in the case of a bulk load error.

> **Note** You must not set the *Transaction* property to True when you're bulk loading binary data such as images.

You can control the location of the temporary file that the bulk load component creates for a transacted bulk load by setting the *TempFilePath* property of the *SQLXMLBulkLoad* object. If you're importing data to a SQL Server database on the local computer, this setting can take the form of an ordinary file path, such as *c:\tempdata*. However, in most circumstances, you won't actually be sitting at the SQL Server machine when you run the bulk load process, so you should use a Universal Naming Convention (UNC) network path. UNC paths take the form *\\ServerName\ShareName*. To use a share named *Data* on a server called *DBServer1*, for example, you would set the *TempFilePath* property to *\\DBServer1\Data*.

The following code shows how a transaction can be used in a bulk load operation:

```
Set objBulkLoad = CreateObject("SQLXMLBulkLoad.SQLXMLBulkLoad")
objBulkLoad.ConnectionString = _
    "provider=SQLOLEDB;data source=DBServer1;database=Northwind;" & _
    "Integrated Security=SSPI;"
objBulkLoad.Transaction = True
objBulkLoad.TempFilePath = "\\DBServer1\Data"
objBulkLoad.Execute c:\CatalogSchema.xml, c:\CatalogData.xml
Set objBulkLoad = Nothing
```

In the preceding sample code, the bulk load component operates in its own transaction context. In the case of an error, the bulk load component issues a ROLLBACK command to abort the transaction. When you're using the *ConnectionCommand* property to piggy back on an existing OLE-DB connection, the transaction is controlled by the client application, which must explicitly commit or abort the transaction. The following code shows how to use the ADO *Connection* object's *RollbackTrans* and *CommitTrans* methods to control a transaction:

```
On Error Resume Next
Err.Clear
Set objCmd = CreateObject("ADODB.Command")
objCmd.ActiveConnection= _
    "provider=SQLOLEDB;data source=DBServer1;database=Northwind;" & _
    "Integrated Security=SSPI;"
Set objBulkLoad = CreateObject("SQLXMLBulkLoad.SQLXMLBulkLoad")
objBulkLoad.Transaction = True
objBulkLoad.ConnectionCommand = objCmd
objBulkLoad.Transaction = True
objBulkLoad.Execute c:\CatalogSchema.xml, c:\CatalogData.xml
If Err.Number = 0 Then
    objCmd.ActiveConnection.CommitTrans
    Set objBulkLoad = Nothing
Else
    objCmd.ActiveConnection.RollbackTrans
End If
```

Note The *Transaction* property *must* be set to True when you're using the *ConnectionCommand* property to connect to the database.

Logging Errors

You can log error messages from the bulk load component to a file by specifying the *ErrorLogFile* property of the *SQLXMLBulkLoad* object, as shown here:

```
Set objBulkLoad = CreateObject("SQLXMLBulkLoad.SQLXMLBulkLoad")
objBulkLoad.ConnectionString = _
    "provider=SQLOLEDB;data source=DBServer1;database=Northwind;" & _
    "Integrated Security=SSPI;"
objBulkLoad.ErrorLogFile = "c:\BulkLoadErrors.xml"
objBulkLoad.Execute c:\CatalogSchema.xml, c:\CatalogData.xml
Set objBulkLoad = Nothing
```

If an error occurs during the bulk load operation, the error message returned will be written to the file specified as an XML document that resembles the following example:

```
<?xml version="1.0"?>
<Error>
    <Record>
        <HResult>0x80040E2F</HResult>
        <SQLState>01000</SQLState>
        <NativeError></NativeError>
        <ErrorState>1</ErrorState>
        <Severity>0</Severity>
        <Source>Microsoft OLE DB Provider for SQL Server</Source>
        <Description>
            <![CDATA[The statement has been terminated.]]>
        </Description>
    </Record>
    <Record>
        <HResult>0x80040E2F</HResult>
        <SQLState>23000</SQLState>
        <NativeError></NativeError>
        <ErrorState>1</ErrorState>
        <Severity>14</Severity>
        <Source>Microsoft OLE DB Provider for SQL Server</Source>
        <Description>
            <![CDATA[Violation of PRIMARY KEY constraint
                'PK_TestCategories'. Cannot insert duplicate key in
                object 'TestCategories'.]]>
        </Description>
    </Record>
</Error>
```

The file contains a *Record* element for each error that occurred, with the most recent error at the beginning of the document. These elements can be useful for tracing problems during insert operations. The ImportCatalogData.vbs script in the Demos\Chapter8 folder on the companion CD can be used to import data into the Categories and Products tables in the Northwind database.

Generating the Database Schema

Sometimes you might want to perform a bulk load that creates the tables for the new data as part of the import process. You can achieve this by setting the *SchemaGen* property of the *SQLXMLBulkLoad* object to True, as shown here:

```
Set objBulkLoad = CreateObject("SQLXMLBulkLoad.SQLXMLBulkLoad")
objBulkLoad.ConnectionString = _
    "provider=SQLOLEDB;data source=DBServer1;database=Northwind;" & _
```

```
    "Integrated Security=SSPI;"
objBulkLoad.SchemaGen = True
objBulkLoad.Execute c:\GenCatalogSchema.xml, c:\CatalogData.xml
Set objBulkLoad = Nothing
```

Executing this script causes the tables mapped in the schema to be created if they don't already exist. (If they do already exist, the data is simply inserted into the existing tables.) The table definitions are based on the information in the mapping schema, in which the table and column names, together with the data types, can be declared. For example, you could use the following mapping schema to create a new *SpecialProducts* table:

```
<?xml version="1.0" ?>
<Schema xmlns="urn:schemas-microsoft-com:xml-data"
    xmlns:dt="urn:schemas-microsoft-com:datatypes"
    xmlns:sql="urn:schemas-microsoft-com:xml-sql">

    <ElementType name="Catalog" sql:is-constant="1">
        <element type="Category"/>
    </ElementType>

    <ElementType name="Category" sql:relation="NewCategories">
        <AttributeType name="CategoryID" sql:datatype="int"/>
        <AttributeType name="CategoryName"/>
        <AttributeType name="Description"/>

        <attribute type="CategoryID" sql:field="CategoryID"/>
        <attribute type="CategoryName" sql:field="CategoryName"/>
        <attribute type="Description" sql:field="Description"/>
        <element type="Product">
            <sql:relationship key-relation="NewCategories"
                key="CategoryID"
                foreign-key="CategoryID"
                foreign-relation="SpecialProducts"/>
        </element>
    </ElementType>

    <ElementType name="Product" sql:relation="SpecialProducts">
        <AttributeType name="ProductID" sql:datatype="int"/>
        <AttributeType name="ProductName" sql:datatype="nvarchar(40)"/>
        <AttributeType name="SupplierID" sql:datatype="int"/>
        <AttributeType name="QuantityPerUnit"
            sql:datatype="nvarchar(40)"/>
        <AttributeType name="UnitPrice" sql:datatype="money"/>

        <attribute type="ProductID" sql:field="ProductID"/>
        <attribute type="ProductName" sql:field="ProductName"/>
        <attribute type="SupplierID" sql:field="SupplierID"/>
```

(continued)

```
        <attribute type="QuantityPerUnit" sql:field="QuantityPerUnit"/>
        <attribute type="UnitPrice" sql:field="UnitPrice"/>
    </ElementType>

</Schema>
```

When you use this schema to import data with the *SchemaGen* property set to True, a new table will be created, based on the following Transact-SQL statement:

```
CREATE TABLE SpecialProducts
(
    CategoryID int NULL ,
    ProductID int NULL ,
    ProductName nvarchar (40),
    SupplierID int NULL ,
    QuantityPerUnit nvarchar (40),
    UnitPrice money NULL
)
```

By default, the data in the specified XML data source will be imported into the new tables. You can choose to override this behavior by setting the *BulkLoad* property of the *SQLXMLBulkLoad* object to False, as shown here:

```
Set objBulkLoad = CreateObject("SQLXMLBulkLoad.SQLXMLBulkLoad")
objBulkLoad.ConnectionString = _
    "provider=SQLOLEDB;data source=DBServer1;database=Northwind;" & _
    "Integrated Security=SSPI;"
objBulkLoad.SchemaGen = True
objBulkLoad.BulkLoad = False
objBulkLoad.Execute c:\GenCatalogSchema.xml
Set objBulkLoad = Nothing
```

Notice that when the *BulkLoad* property is set to False, you can omit the data source parameter to the *Execute* method. This code simply creates the tables defined in the schema if the tables don't already exist; no data will be imported.

Specifying a Primary Key

The tables created using the *SchemaGen* property use the information in the mapping schema to define the columns. In particular, the *sql:datatype* annotation is used to define the column data types. You can also get the bulk load component to define a primary key column by including an *id* attribute in the schema and setting the *SGUseID* property of the *SQLXMLBulkLoad* object to True. For example, you could change the *Product* element declaration in the catalog schema to the following:

```
<ElementType name="Product" sql:relation="SpecialProducts">
    <AttributeType name="ProductID" sql:datatype="int" dt:type="id"/>
```

```
    <AttributeType name="ProductName" sql:datatype="nvarchar(40)"/>
    <AttributeType name="SupplierID" sql:datatype="int"/>
    <AttributeType name="QuantityPerUnit" sql:dataype="nvarchar(40)"/>
    <AttributeType name="UnitPrice" sql:datatype="money"/>

    <attribute type="ProductID" sql:field="ProductID"/>
    <attribute type="ProductName" sql:field="ProductName"/>
    <attribute type="SupplierID" sql:field="SupplierID"/>
    <attribute type="QuantityPerUnit" sql:field="QuantityPerUnit"/>
    <attribute type="UnitPrice" sql:field="UnitPrice"/>
</ElementType>
```

Then you could perform the bulk load with the *SchemaGen* and *SGUseID* properties set appropriately, as you see here:

```
Set objBulkLoad = CreateObject("SQLXMLBulkLoad.SQLXMLBulkLoad")
objBulkLoad.ConnectionString = _
    "provider=SQLOLEDB;data source=DBServer1;database=Northwind;" & _
    "Integrated Security=SSPI;"
objBulkLoad.SchemaGen = True
objBulkLoad.SGUseID = True
objBulkLoad.Execute c:\GenCatalogSchema.xml, c:\CatalogData.xml
Set objBulkLoad = Nothing
```

The combination of the *id* attribute in the schema and the *SGUseID* property in the code would cause the following table to be created:

```
CREATE TABLE SpecialProducts
(
    CategoryID int NULL ,
    ProductID int NOT NULL ,
    ProductName nvarchar (40) NULL,
    SupplierID int NULL ,
    QuantityPerUnit nvarchar (40) NULL ,
    UnitPrice money NULL ,
    PRIMARY KEY  CLUSTERED (ProductID)
)
```

Dropping Existing Tables

Sometimes you'll want to completely refresh the data in the database by dropping the existing tables, re-creating them, and importing the new data. For example, you might want to perform a bulk load of a catalog that not only includes new products, but also includes updated prices for existing products. The easiest way to update the entire catalog is to delete the existing records and replace them with the new data.

You can instruct the bulk load component to drop the tables mapped in the mapping schema by setting the *SGDropTables* property of the *SQLXMLBulkLoad* object to True, as shown in this code:

```
Set objBulkLoad = CreateObject("SQLXMLBulkLoad.SQLXMLBulkLoad")
objBulkLoad.ConnectionString = _
    "provider=SQLOLEDB;data source=DBServer1;database=Northwind;" & _
    "Integrated Security=SSPI;"
objBulkLoad.SchemaGen = True
objBulkLoad.SGDropTables = True
objBulkLoad.Execute c:\GenCatalogSchema.xml, c:\CatalogData.xml
Set objBulkLoad = Nothing
```

Executing the preceding code drops the tables referenced in the schema and then re-creates them and imports the data from the *CatalogData.xml* file. So you should set the *SchemaGen* property to True when using the *SGDropTables* property. The ImportGenSchema.vbs script in the Demos\Chapter8 folder on the companion CD can be used to create new tables in the Northwind database.

Summary

In this chapter, you've seen how the addition of the XML For SQL Server 2000 Web Release can provide some useful XML-related functionality. In particular, you can use updategrams to insert, update, or delete data in the same way that you can use templates to retrieve data. You've also seen how the XML bulk load component can be used to import large volumes of XML data into a SQL Server database.

In the next chapter, I'll discuss a sample e-commerce application that uses the SQL Server XML support throughout. I'll also introduce another key Microsoft product that can help you integrate applications and trading partners: BizTalk Server 2000.

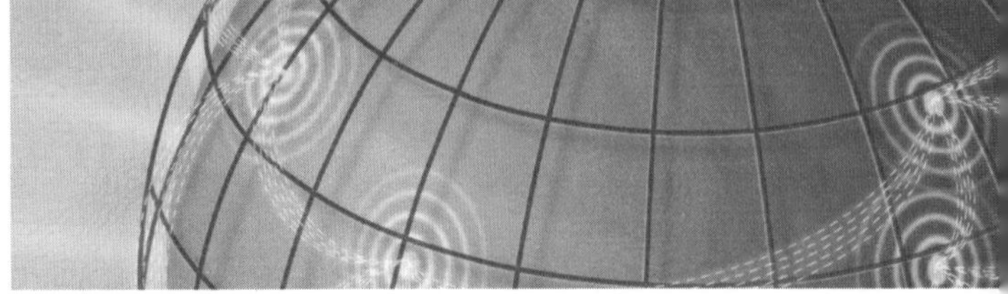

9

Building an E-Commerce Solution with SQL Server and XML

If you've read the previous chapters in this book, you should by now have a good understanding of the XML-related functionality in SQL Server 2000. I hope you can think of some ways to use this functionality to build XML-based integrated solutions. I'll use this final chapter to examine a sample e-commerce application that uses SQL Server's XML support throughout. This chapter allows you to see the technologies we've looked at in earlier chapters working within the context of a real (well, real-ish) application. I also want to introduce another important server application that can be used with SQL Server and XML to build integrated solutions—Microsoft BizTalk Server.

The Sample E-Commerce Scenario

Various aspects of this chapter's sample e-commerce application include business to consumer as well as business to business functionality. I'll describe how SQL Server's support for XML has been used to implement functionality within the application and also how BizTalk Server 2000 has been used to enhance the B2B aspects of the solution.

The sample application isn't intended to represent a fully functional application that can be deployed in a production environment. In particular, the sample is limited to single-machine installations and makes no use of compiled software components or SSL encryption. Nevertheless, by means of this application I can show you how to solve common e-commerce problems using SQL Server and XML.

The application is available in the Sample Application folder on the companion CD and can be installed by extracting the source files to your hard disk and running Setup.bat. Refer to the Introduction for the system requirements for installing and running the sample application.

When installed, the application creates a number of shortcuts on your desktop. Closer inspection reveals that the installation script has created three SQL Server databases (RetailSite, SupplierSite, and DeliveryCo); four folders in your WWWRoot directory (RetailSite, SupplierSite, OrderPicking, and DeliveryCo); and three SQLISAPI applications (SupplierSiteXML, OrderPickingXML, and DeliveryCo).

Overview of the E-Commerce Scenario

The scenario on which the sample application is based involves the exchange of data among three trading partners: an online retailer, a supplier, and a package delivery company. Customers can order goods through the online retailer's Web site using a browser. The orders are then forwarded to the supplier, where warehouse employees use an intranet-based order picking application to prepare the goods for delivery. When the various items in an order have been prepared, a delivery request is sent to the package delivery company, which arranges to pick the goods up from the supplier and deliver them to the customer. Each time the supplier receives an order, an invoice is generated and sent to the retailer that placed the order. Additionally, the supplier publishes its product catalog in an extranet, allowing retailers to download it and update their own databases. You can see this scenario represented graphically in Figure 9-1.

As I said before, this scenario gives us a number of commonly faced e-commerce challenges and provides a relatively realistic context in which to evaluate the use of SQL Server and XML to meet those challenges.

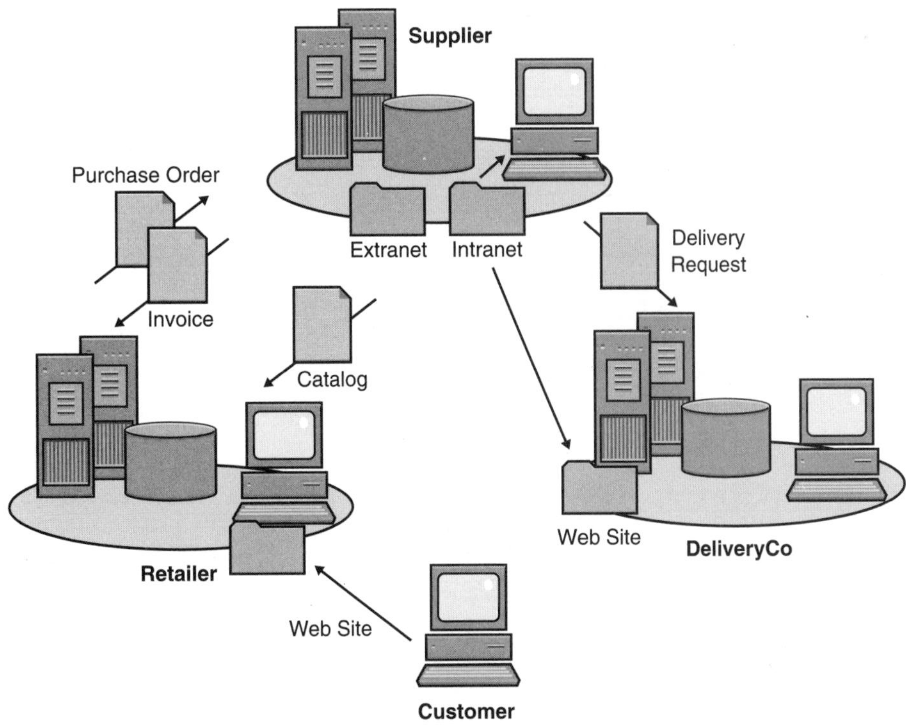

Figure 9-1 The sample e-commerce scenario

Challenges in the E-Commerce Scenario

The challenges in the sample e-commerce scenario include many of the common issues relating to the building of an effective e-commerce solution. Most of these issues involve solving one of two problems: getting data out of a database and sending it to its destination, or receiving data and inserting it into a database. As we've seen throughout this book, SQL Server provides a number of ways to extract data in XML format from a database and insert XML data into a database. We'll see many of these techniques used in the sample application, and we'll examine various ways to transmit the data from source to destination.

Here are the specific areas of functionality that I'll cover in this chapter:

- The online retail Web site
- Order processing at the supplier
- Arranging package deliveries
- Updating the catalog
- Invoicing the retailer

As we examine each of these aspects of the solution, I'll explain the rationale behind the design and assess possible extensions or alternative solutions. Remember that this application is for illustrative purposes only: you could choose from countless other ways to implement the solution.

The Online Retail Web Site

The first part of an e-commerce solution that most people think of is a Web site at which customers can view products and make purchases online. In our application, this part of the solution is implemented as an ASP-based Web site in the WWWRoot\RetailSite folder. The pages at this site submit requests for XML data using ADO to the SQL Server RetailSite database, as illustrated in Figure 9-2.

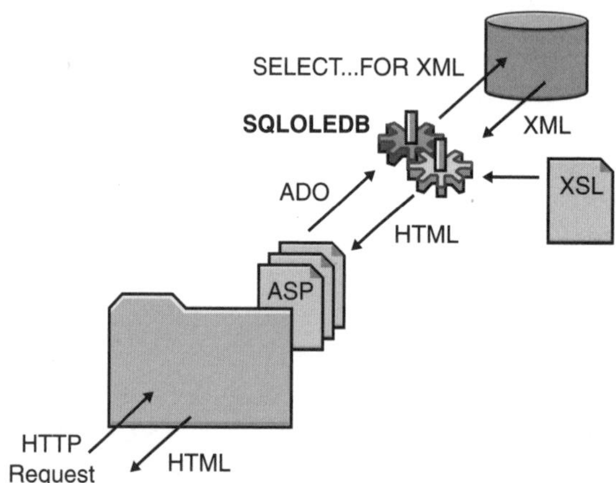

Figure 9-2 Architecture of the RetailSite Web site

I decided to implement the retail site as an ASP-based application because the site requires custom user authentication and state management functionality, and these could be easily handled using server-side scripts on the Active Server Pages in the site. I might have realized some performance gains by implementing the site as a SQLISAPI application, using templates to publish data and updategrams to allow customer and order data to be entered. That strategy, however, would have made it more difficult to include the kind of custom business logic that scripting (or calls to custom components) allows.

Displaying Product Categories

When users first navigate our retail site, they're presented with a frame-based home page. A list of product categories is displayed in the left pane, allowing the user to browse products by category. The list of categories is retrieved as XML by the code on the Menu.asp page, and transformed to HTML by means of a style sheet. Here's the code that retrieves the data and applies the style sheet:

```
Dim strQry
Dim conDB
Dim cmdCategories
Dim strmQuery
Dim strmResult

'Root element and namespace for the XML query
Const XML_HEADER = _
    "<categorylist xmlns:sql='urn:schemas-microsoft-com:xml-sql'>"
Const XML_FOOTER = "</categorylist>"

'Define query string.
strQry = XML_HEADER
strQry = strQry & "<sql:query>"
strQry = strQry & "EXEC getCategories"
strQry = strQry & "</sql:query>"
strQry = strQry & XML_FOOTER

'Connect to database and configure Command object.
Set conDB = CreateObject("ADODB.Connection")
conDB.ConnectionString = strCon
conDB.Open
Set cmdCategories = CreateObject("ADODB.Command")
Set cmdCategories.ActiveConnection = conDB
```

(continued)

```
'Create Query stream for inbound XML query.
Set strmQuery = CreateObject("ADODB.Stream")
strmQuery.Open
strmQuery.WriteText strQry, adWriteChar
strmQuery.Position = 0
Set cmdCategories.CommandStream = strmQuery

'Specify the style sheet to be used.
cmdCategories.Properties("XSL") = Server.MapPath("AppFiles\Menu.xsl")

'Create result stream for the retrieved document.
Set strmResult = CreateObject("ADODB.Stream")
strmResult.Open
cmdCategories.Properties("Output Stream") = strmResult

'Execute query.
cmdCategories.Execute , , adExecuteStream

Response.Write strmResult.ReadText
Set strmResult = Nothing
Set strmQuery = Nothing
Set cmdCategories = Nothing
Set conDB = Nothing
```

I defined the connection string and various constants used in this page in an include file named ADOData.asp so that I could reuse them throughout the site. The code calls the *getCategories* stored procedure, defined as follows:

```
CREATE PROC getCategories
AS
SELECT CategoryID, CategoryName FROM Categories
FOR XML AUTO, ELEMENTS
```

Using a stored procedure, rather than embedding the query in the template on the ASP, yields a performance boost on subsequent executions of the procedure because the compiled execution plan will be cached on the SQL Server. So I took this approach in the retail site solution for most occasions that data must be retrieved from the database. The *getCategories* procedure retrieves the list of categories in the following XML format:

```
<categorylist xmlns:sql="urn:schemas-microsoft-com:xml-sql">
    <Categories>
        <CategoryID>1</CategoryID>
        <CategoryName>Computers</CategoryName>
    </Categories>
```

```
    <Categories>
        <CategoryID>2</CategoryID>
        <CategoryName>Monitors</CategoryName>
    </Categories>
    <Categories>
        <CategoryID>3</CategoryID>
        <CategoryName>Printers</CategoryName>
    </Categories>
    <Categories>
        <CategoryID>4</CategoryID>
        <CategoryName>Cables Etc.</CategoryName>
    </Categories>
    <Categories>
        <CategoryID>5</CategoryID>
        <CategoryName>Software</CategoryName>
    </Categories>
</categorylist>
```

The Menu.xml style sheet, which is applied to this XML data, is reproduced here:

```
<?xml version="1.0"?>
<xsl:stylesheet xmlns:xsl="http://www.w3.org/1999/XSL/Transform"
    version="1.0">
    <xsl:template match="/">
        <HTML>
            <HEAD>
                <Title>
                    Category List
                </Title>
            </HEAD>
            <BODY bgcolor='Gainsboro'>
                <FONT face= 'Arial'>
                <P><A target='Products' href="Main.asp">Home</A></P>
                <P><A target='Products' href="Login.htm">Login</A>
                /<A target='Products' href="Logout.asp">Logout</A></P>
                <P><A target='Products' href="Basket.asp">Basket</A></P>
                <TABLE border="0">
                    <TR><TD><B>Product Categories</B></TD></TR>
                    <xsl:for-each select="categorylist/Categories">
                    <TR>
                        <TD>
                            <A TARGET="Products">
                                <xsl:attribute name="HREF">
                                    Browse.asp?categoryID=
                                    <xsl:value-of select="CategoryID"/>
```

(continued)

```
                                        </xsl:attribute>
                                        <xsl:value-of select="CategoryName"/>
                                    </A>
                                </TD>
                            </TR>
                            </xsl:for-each>
                        </TABLE>
                        </FONT>
                    </BODY>
                </HTML>
            </xsl:template>
        </xsl:stylesheet>
```

As you can see, this style sheet constructs the entire menu pane and creates links to Browse.asp that include the category ID of the category clicked by the user as a parameter. You can see the menu pane produced by this code in Figure 9-3.

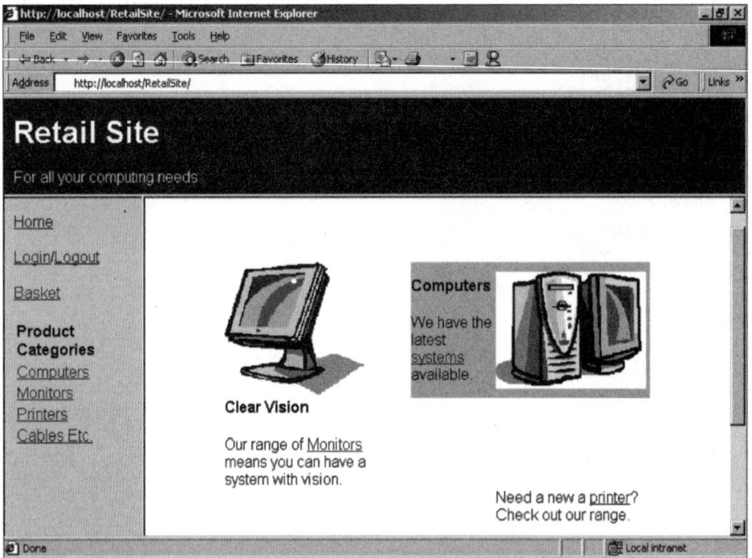

Figure 9-3 The main RetailSite page, including Menu.asp in the left pane

Displaying the Products in a Specified Category

When a user clicks a category, Browse.asp is executed and the results are displayed in the main pane. The code in Browse.asp is shown here:

```
Response.Write RenderCatalog(Request.QueryString("CategoryID"))

Function RenderCatalog(intCategory)
'Function to retrieve products in a specified catalog

Dim ConDB
Dim cmdProducts
Dim strmResult

'Connect to database.
Set conDB = CreateObject("ADODB.Connection")
conDB.Open strCon
Set cmdProducts = CreateObject("ADODB.Command")
Set cmdProducts.ActiveConnection = conDB

'Use the CatalogSchema.xml annotated schema.
cmdProducts.Dialect = "{ec2a4293-e898-11d2-b1b7-00c04f680c56}"
cmdProducts.Properties("mapping schema") = _
    Server.MapPath("AppFiles\CatalogSchema.xml")
'XPath for category
cmdProducts.CommandText = "Catalog/Category/Product[../@CategoryID=" & _
    intCategory & "]"

'Specify output stream for results.
Set strmResult = CreateObject("ADODB.Stream")
strmResult.Open
cmdProducts.Properties("Output Stream") = strmResult

'Specify the root element for the returned document.
cmdProducts.Properties("XML Root") = "CatalogData"

'Specify the XSL to be used.
cmdProducts.Properties("XSL") = Server.MapPath("AppFiles\Products.xsl")

cmdProducts.Execute , , adExecuteStream
RenderCatalog = strmResult.ReadText

Set strmResult = Nothing
Set cmdProducts = Nothing
Set conDB = Nothing
End Function
```

The products in the specified category are retrieved by using the selected category ID in an XPath expression against an annotated schema. The schema is used to define a product catalog document that can be downloaded from the supplier and reused here to retrieve the product list. Reusing a schema in this way means that should any minor changes be made to the definition of a product catalog, the impact of those changes on the application can be minimized.

Here's the CatalogSchema.xml schema:

```
<?xml version="1.0"?>
<Schema xmlns="urn:schemas-microsoft-com:xml-data"
    xmlns:sql="urn:schemas-microsoft-com:xml-sql">

    <ElementType name="Catalog" sql:is-constant="1">
        <element type="Category"/>
    </ElementType>

    <ElementType name="Category" sql:relation="Categories">
        <AttributeType name="CategoryID"/>
        <AttributeType name="CategoryName"/>
        <attribute type="CategoryID" sql:field="CategoryID"/>
        <attribute type="CategoryName" sql:field="CategoryName"/>
        <element type="Product">
            <sql:relationship key-relation="Categories"
                key="CategoryID"
                foreign-key="CategoryID"
                foreign-relation="Products"/>
        </element>
    </ElementType>

    <ElementType name="Product" sql:relation="Products">
        <AttributeType name="ProductID"/>
        <AttributeType name="ProductName"/>
        <AttributeType name="UnitPrice"/>
        <AttributeType name="Tax"/>
        <attribute type="ProductID" sql:field="ProductID"/>
        <attribute type="ProductName" sql:field="ProductName"/>
        <attribute type="UnitPrice" sql:field="UnitPrice"/>
        <attribute type="Tax" sql:field="Tax"/>
    </ElementType>

</Schema>
```

This schema maps data in an XML catalog document to the Categories and Products tables in the RetailSite database. The XPath used in Browse.asp retrieves the *Product* elements that have a parent *Category* element with a *CategoryID* attribute value the same as the one passed to the page in the URL.

The following XML shows the result of passing a CategoryID value of 1 to Browse.asp:

```
<?xml version="1.0" encoding="utf-8" ?>
<CatalogData>
    <Product ProductID="1" ProductName="Desktop System"
        UnitPrice="1000" Tax="250"/>
    <Product ProductID="2" ProductName="Server System"
        UnitPrice="1500" Tax="375"/>
```

```
    <Product ProductID="3" ProductName="Laptop System"
        UnitPrice="1300" Tax="325"/>
</CatalogData>
```

This XML is rendered as HTML using the Products.xsl style sheet:

```
<?xml version="1.0"?>
<xsl:stylesheet xmlns:xsl="http://www.w3.org/1999/XSL/Transform"
    version="1.0">
    <xsl:template match="/">
    <Title>
        ProductList
    </Title>
    <Body>
        <FONT face= "Arial" color="navy">
            <TABLE border="0" cellspacing="5">
                <TR>
                    <TD><B>Product ID</B></TD>
                    <TD><B>Product Name</B></TD>
                    <TD><B>Price</B></TD>
                    <TD><B>Tax</B></TD>
                </TR>
                <xsl:for-each select="CatalogData/Product">
                    <TR>
                        <TD>
                            <xsl:value-of select="@ProductID"/>
                        </TD>
                        <TD>
                            <A TARGET="Products">
                                <xsl:attribute name="HREF">
                                    Product.asp?ProductID=<xsl:value-of
                                    select="@ProductID"/>
                                </xsl:attribute>
                                <xsl:value-of select="@ProductName"/>
                            </A>
                        </TD>
                        <TD>
                            <xsl:value-of select="@UnitPrice"/>
                        </TD>
                        <TD>
                            <xsl:value-of select="@Tax"/>
                        </TD>
                    </TR>
                </xsl:for-each>
            </TABLE>
        </FONT>
    </Body>
    </xsl:template>
</xsl:stylesheet>
```

The list of products is displayed in the main pane of the site, as shown in Figure 9-4.

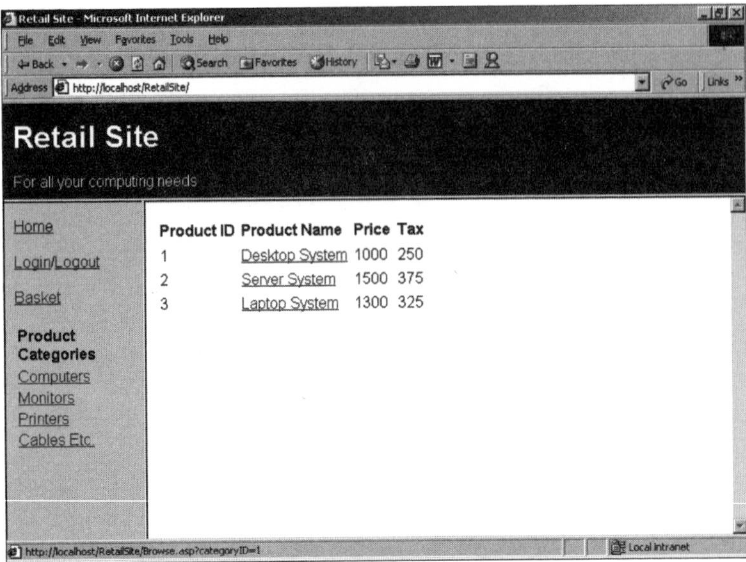

Figure 9-4 The product list produced by Browse.asp

Displaying Product Details

When the user clicks a product in Browse.asp, the product ID is passed to Product.asp and the following code is used to retrieve the product details:

```
Dim objXML
'Call RenderProduct function, passing the requested product ID.
Response.Write RenderProduct(Request.QueryString("ProductID"))

Function RenderProduct(intProductID)
'Method to retrieve product details in HTML format
Dim cmdProduct
Dim strmQuery
Dim strmResult
Dim strQry
Dim conDB

'Root element and namespace for XML query
Const XML_HEADER = _
    "<productdetails xmlns:sql='urn:schemas-microsoft-com:xml-sql'>"
Const XML_FOOTER = "</productdetails>"
```

```
'Define query string.
strQry = XML_HEADER
strQry = strQry & "<sql:query>"
strQry = strQry & "EXEC getProductDetails " & intProductID
strQry = strQry & "</sql:query>"
strQry = strQry & XML_FOOTER

'Connect to database and configure Command object.
Set conDB = CreateObject("ADODB.Connection")
conDB.ConnectionString = strCon
conDB.Open
Set cmdProduct = CreateObject("ADODB.Command")
Set cmdProduct.ActiveConnection = conDB

'Create Query stream.
Set strmQuery = CreateObject("ADODB.Stream")
strmQuery.Open
strmQuery.WriteText strQry, adWriteChar
strmQuery.Position = 0
Set cmdProduct.CommandStream = strmQuery

'Specify the style sheet to be used.
cmdProduct.Properties("XSL") = _
    Server.MapPath("AppFiles\ProductDetails.xsl")

'Create result stream.
Set strmResult = CreateObject("ADODB.Stream")
strmResult.Open
cmdProduct.Properties("Output Stream") = strmResult

'Execute query.
cmdProduct.Execute , , adExecuteStream

RenderProduct = strmResult.ReadText
Set strmResult = Nothing
Set strmQuery = Nothing
Set cmdProduct = Nothing
Set conDB = Nothing
End Function
```

This code is very similar to the code in Menu.asp. It calls the *getProductDetails* stored procedure, passing the product ID as a parameter, to retrieve the product data. The definition of the *getProductDetails* stored procedure is shown here:

```
CREATE PROC getProductDetails @ProductID integer
AS
SELECT * FROM products WHERE ProductID = @ProductID
FOR XML AUTO, ELEMENTS
```

This query returns the following XML when a *ProductID* parameter of 1 is passed:

```
<productdetails xmlns:sql="urn:schemas-microsoft-com:xml-sql">
    <products>
        <ProductID>1</ProductID>
        <ProductName>Desktop System</ProductName>
        <CategoryID>1</CategoryID>
        <UnitPrice>1000</UnitPrice>
        <Tax>250</Tax>
    </products>
</productdetails>
```

This data is rendered as HTML using the ProductDetails.xsl style sheet, which you can see here:

```
<?xml version="1.0"?>
<xsl:stylesheet xmlns:xsl="http://www.w3.org/1999/XSL/Transform"
    version="1.0">
    <xsl:template match="/">
        <HTML>
            <BODY>
                <FONT face='Arial'>
                    <FORM id='FORM1' name='FORM1' action='AddItem.asp'
                        method='post'>
                    <P>
                        <STRONG>ProductID:</STRONG>
                        <INPUT readOnly='true' name='txtProductID'>
                            <xsl:attribute name='value'>
                                <xsl:value-of select=
                                    "productdetails/products/ProductID"/>
                            </xsl:attribute>
                        </INPUT>
                    </P>
                    <P>
                        <STRONG>Product Name:</STRONG>
                        <INPUT readOnly='true' size='57'
                            name= 'txtProductName'>
                            <xsl:attribute name='value'>
                                <xsl:value-of select=
                                    "productdetails/products/ProductName"/>
                            </xsl:attribute>
                        </INPUT>
                    </P>
                    <P>
                        <STRONG>Price:</STRONG>
                        <INPUT readOnly='true' name='txtUnitPrice'>
                            <xsl:attribute name='value'>
```

```
                    <xsl:value-of select=
                        "productdetails/products/UnitPrice"/>
                </xsl:attribute>
            </INPUT>
        </P>
        <P>
            <STRONG>Tax:</STRONG>
            <INPUT readOnly='true' size='55' name='txtTax'>
                <xsl:attribute name='value'>
                    <xsl:value-of select=
                        "productdetails/products/Tax"/>
                </xsl:attribute>
            </INPUT>
        </P>
        <P></P>
        <P>
            Add <INPUT size='7' value='1' name='txtQuantity'/>
            to shopping basket
            <INPUT type='submit' value='Submit'
                name='submit1'/>
        </P>
        </FORM>
      </FONT>
    </BODY>
  </HTML>
 </xsl:template>
</xsl:stylesheet>
```

This style sheet causes the product details to be displayed in read-only fields in a form and creates an additional field that allows the customer to specify the quantity he'd like to add to his shopping basket. When the user clicks the Submit button on the form, the data in the fields is posted to AddItem.asp.

Customer Authentication

Before users can add any items to their shopping baskets, they must log in and be authenticated by the site. Each user is identified by means of a Globally Unique Identifier (GUID) and must provide a user name and password to log in. User data is stored in the Users table in the RetailSite database and the application accesses that data by using the *addUser* and *getUserID* stored procedures.

To register, a new user must fill in the form on the Register.htm page. The application then posts the details to Register.asp, which calls the *addUser* stored procedure to add the user data to the Users table. The *addUser* stored procedure is defined at the top of the next page.

```
CREATE PROC addUser  @UserName varchar(30),
                     @Password varchar(20),
                     @UserID varchar(36) OUTPUT
AS
SET @UserID = NewID()
INSERT Users
VALUES
(@UserID, @UserName, @Password)
GO
```

This procedure generates a new GUID to identify the user, which is passed back to the calling application when the details have been entered into the Users table so that the user can be immediately logged in.

On subsequent visits, the user must log in using the Login.htm form, which posts data to the Login.asp script. Login.asp calls the *getUserID* stored procedure to authenticate the user and retrieve her user ID. The *getUserID* stored procedure is shown here:

```
CREATE PROC getUserID  @Username varchar(30),
                       @Password varchar(20),
                       @UserID varchar(36) OUTPUT
AS
SELECT @UserID = UserID
FROM Users
WHERE username = @UserName AND userpassword = @Password
```

If this procedure returns a row, the user has been authenticated. If no row is returned, the login has failed.

> **Note** In a production site, both Register.asp and Login.asp should be accessed over an encrypted connection by means of the HTTPS protocol.

Maintaining Authentication State

Once a user has been authenticated, the application must maintain her authenticated status for the rest of the session. Information that must be maintained between user requests is called *state*, and there are a number of problems associated with managing it in an e-commerce solution. Although the ASP object model provides a *Session* object in which data can be persisted, you should generally avoid maintaining state here because of performance issues and server-affinity problems that occur when you use a Web farm to load balance user requests.

The strategy that most e-commerce sites adopt is to send a key value to the client that can be resubmitted with each subsequent request and used to track the user throughout the session. In our RetailSite solution, the customer's ID is sent to the browser as a cookie and checked on subsequent requests. Here's the code in Login.asp that writes the cookie:

```
Dim strUserName 'As String
Dim strPassword 'As String
Dim strUserID 'As String
Dim objSecurity

'Clear existing cookies.
Response.Cookies("userauthid") = ""

'Retrieve supplied user name and password.
'(In reality we'd use an HTTPS connection for this.)
strUserName = Request.Form("txtUserName")
strPassword = Request.Form("txtPassword")

strUserID = GetUserID(strUserName, strPassword)

If strUserID= "invalid" Then
    'Incorrect details have been supplied; redirect back to logon page.
    Response.Write "<H2>Invalid Logon</H2>"
    Response.Write "Please try again."
    Server.Transfer "Login.htm"
Else
    'Write UserID to cookie so we know the user has been authenticated.
    Response.Cookies("userauthid")= strUserID
    Server.Execute "Main.asp"
End If

Function GetUserID(strUserName, strPassword)
'Function to authenticate a user and return his user ID

Dim cmd
Dim conDB
Dim strUserID
'Initialize strUserID variable.
strUserID = "invalid"

'Check valid data has been supplied, then call the getUserID
'stored procedure.
If ValidData(strUserName, strPassword) Then
    Set cmd = CreateObject("ADODB.Command")
```

(continued)

```
        With cmd
            .ActiveConnection = strCon
            .CommandText = "getUserID"
            .CommandType = adCmdStoredProc
            .Parameters(1).Value = strUserName
            .Parameters(2).Value = strPassword
            .Execute
        End With
        'Check for returned user ID.
        If Not IsNull(cmd.Parameters(3).Value) Then
            strUserID = cmd.Parameters(3).Value
        End If
    End If
    GetUserID = strUserID
    Set cmd = Nothing
    End Function
```

This code clears the authentication cookie (in case the user had already logged in using different credentials), and then calls the *getUserID* stored procedure. If the user hasn't provided a valid username and password combination, she's redirected back to the Login.htm page. If authentication is successful, the user's ID is assigned to the cookie.

Managing the Shopping Basket

Once a user has been authenticated, she can use a shopping basket to manage the goods she wants to purchase. The shopping basket is implemented as a table named Basket, in which a customer's ID is used to track the items placed in the basket by that particular customer. The items aren't removed from the basket until the customer explicitly deletes them or checks out; therefore, items added to the basket will remain in the basket between sessions.

Adding Items to the Shopping Basket

When a customer views the product details for a product she wants to buy, she can click the Submit button on Product.asp, which posts the product data and quantity required to the AddItem.asp page. Here's the code in AddItem.asp:

```
Dim strUserID
Dim lngProductID
Dim intQuantity
Dim curUnitPrice
Dim curTax
```

```
'Check for authentication cookie.
strUserID = Request.Cookies("userauthid")
If strUserID = "" Then
    Response.Write "You must log in before making any purchases."
    Server.transfer "Login.htm"
End If

'Get item data from form.
lngProductID = Request.Form("txtProductID")
intQuantity = Request.Form("txtQuantity")
curUnitPrice = Request.Form("txtUnitPrice")
curTax = Request.Form("txtTax")

AddItemToBasket strUserID, lngProductID, intQuantity, curUnitPrice, curTax
Response.Write intQuantity & _
    " units have been added to your <A href='Basket.asp'>" & _
    "Shopping Basket</A>."

Sub AddItemToBasket(strCustomer, lngProductID, intQuantity,
                    curUnitPrice, curTax)
'Procedure to add an item to the shopping basket
Dim cmd

'If one or more items is ordered, use the addItem stored procedure.
If intQuantity > 0 Then
Set cmd = CreateObject("ADODB.Command")
    With cmd
        .ActiveConnection = strCon
        .CommandText = "addItem"
        .CommandType = adCmdStoredProc
        .Parameters(1).Value = strCustomer
        .Parameters(2).Value = lngProductID
        .Parameters(3).Value = intQuantity
        .Parameters(4).Value = curUnitPrice
        .Parameters(5).Value = curTax
        .Execute
    End With
End If
Set cmd = Nothing
End Sub
```

First of all, this page checks for an authentication cookie. If the user hasn't been authenticated, she's redirected to the Login.htm page. Next a local procedure is used to make sure that if the quantity requested is greater than zero, a stored procedure will be used to add the item to the Basket table. Finally the application displays a confirmation message, with a link to Basket.asp.

The stored procedure used to add items to the Basket table is defined as follows:

```
CREATE PROC addItem  @Customer varchar(40),
@ProductID int,
@Quantity int,
@UnitPrice money,
@Tax money
AS
INSERT Basket
VALUES
(@Customer, @ProductID, @Quantity, @UnitPrice, @Tax)
```

This procedure simply inserts a row containing the specified values into the Basket table.

Viewing the Shopping Basket

Customers can view the contents of their shopping baskets by navigating to Basket.asp (by following either the link created by AddItem.asp or the Basket link in the menu pane of the retail site). To provide more meaningful information, Basket.asp retrieves data from a view that combines data from the Basket and Products tables. This view is named BasketView and is defined as follows:

```
CREATE VIEW BasketView
AS
SELECT   P.ProductID, P.ProductName,
B.UnitPrice, B.Tax,
B.Quantity, B.Customer
FROM Products P
JOIN Basket B
ON P.ProductID = B.ProductID
```

The code in Basket.asp retrieves data from this view in XML format as shown in the following code:

```
Dim strUser
Dim objShopping

'Check for authentication cookie.
strUser = Request.Cookies("userauthid")
If struser = "" Then
    server.transfer "Login.htm"
End If

Response.Write ViewBasket(strUser)

Function ViewBasket(strCustomer)
'Method to view the contents of the shopping basket as HTML
Dim cmdBasket
```

```
Dim strmQuery
Dim strmResult
Dim strQry
Dim conDB

'Root element and namespace for XML query
Const XML_HEADER = _
    "<basketcontents xmlns:sql='urn:schemas-microsoft-com:xml-sql'>"
Const XML_FOOTER = "</basketcontents>"


'Define query string.
strQry = XML_HEADER
strQry = strQry & "<sql:query>"
strQry = strQry & "EXEC getBasket '" & strCustomer & "'"
strQry = strQry & "</sql:query>"
strQry = strQry & XML_FOOTER

'Connect to database and configure Command object.
Set conDB = CreateObject("ADODB.Connection")
conDB.ConnectionString = strCon
conDB.Open
Set cmdBasket = CreateObject("ADODB.Command")
Set cmdBasket.ActiveConnection = conDB

'Create Query stream for the inbound XML query.
Set strmQuery = CreateObject("ADODB.Stream")
strmQuery.Open
strmQuery.WriteText strQry, adWriteChar
strmQuery.Position = 0
Set cmdBasket.CommandStream = strmQuery

'Specify the style sheet to be used to transform the results to HTML.
cmdBasket.Properties("XSL") = Server.MapPath("AppFiles\Basket.xsl")

'Create result stream for the query results.
Set strmResult = CreateObject("ADODB.Stream")
strmResult.Open
cmdBasket.Properties("Output Stream") = strmResult

'Execute query.
cmdBasket.Execute , , adExecuteStream

ViewBasket = strmResult.ReadText
Set strmResult = Nothing
Set strmQuery = Nothing
Set cmdOrders = Nothing
Set conDB = Nothing

End Function
```

The *getBasket* stored procedure called by this code is defined as follows:

```
CREATE PROC getBasket @customer varchar(40)
AS
SELECT * FROM BasketView
WHERE Customer = @customer
FOR XML AUTO, ELEMENTS
```

This stored procedure returns the items in the Basket table belonging to the specified customer. The XML returned by this procedure is similar to the following example:

```
<basketcontents xmlns:sql="urn:schemas-microsoft-com:xml-sql">
    <BasketView>
        <ProductID>1</ProductID>
        <ProductName>Desktop System</ProductName>
        <UnitPrice>1000</UnitPrice>
        <Tax>250</Tax>
        <Quantity>1</Quantity>
        <Customer>AA5733A9-712A-4389-9DA4-4F6408F39F74</Customer>
    </BasketView>
    <BasketView>
        <ProductID>5</ProductID>
        <ProductName>Flat Panel Screen</ProductName>
        <UnitPrice>1000</UnitPrice>
        <Tax>250</Tax>
        <Quantity>1</Quantity>
        <Customer>AA5733A9-712A-4389-9DA4-4F6408F39F74</Customer>
    </BasketView>
</basketcontents>
```

This XML is rendered using the Basket.xsl style sheet, which is reproduced here:

```
<?xml version="1.0"?>
<xsl:stylesheet xmlns:xsl="http://www.w3.org/1999/XSL/Transform"
    version="1.0">
    <xsl:template match="/">
        <Title>Basket</Title>
        <Body>
            <FONT face= "Arial" color="navy">
                <P><B>Contents of Your Shopping Basket</B></P>
                <TABLE border="0" cellspacing="5">
                    <TR>
                        <TD><B>Product ID</B></TD>
                        <TD><B>Product Name</B></TD>
                        <TD><B>Price</B></TD>
                        <TD><B>Tax</B></TD>
                        <TD><B>Quantity</B></TD>
                    </TR>
```

```
                    <xsl:for-each select="basketcontents/BasketView">
                        <TR>
                            <TD>
                                <xsl:value-of select="ProductID"/>
                            </TD>
                            <TD>
                                <xsl:value-of select="ProductName"/>
                            </TD>
                            <TD>
                                <xsl:value-of select="UnitPrice"/>
                            </TD>
                            <TD>
                                <xsl:value-of select="Tax"/>
                            </TD>
                            <TD>
                                <xsl:value-of select="Quantity"/>
                            </TD>
                            <TD>
                                <FONT size='-2'>
                                    <A TARGET="Products">
                                        <xsl:attribute name="HREF">
                                            RemoveItem.asp?ProductID=
                                            <xsl:value-of select=
                                                "ProductID"/>
                                        </xsl:attribute>
                                        Remove
                                    </A>
                                </FONT>
                            </TD>
                        </TR>
                    </xsl:for-each>
                </TABLE>
                <FORM name='Form1' action='Payment.asp'>
                    <INPUT type='submit' value='Checkout' name='submit1'/>
                </FORM>
                <A Target="Products" HREF="MyOrders.asp">
                    Invoices From Past Orders
                </A>
            </FONT>
        </Body>
    </xsl:template>
</xsl:stylesheet>
```

This style sheet renders the basket information in a table and provides a link allowing individual items to be removed. It also includes a form that the user can use to check out as well as a link that allows the user to view previous invoices. The HTML produced by Basket.asp is shown in Figure 9-5.

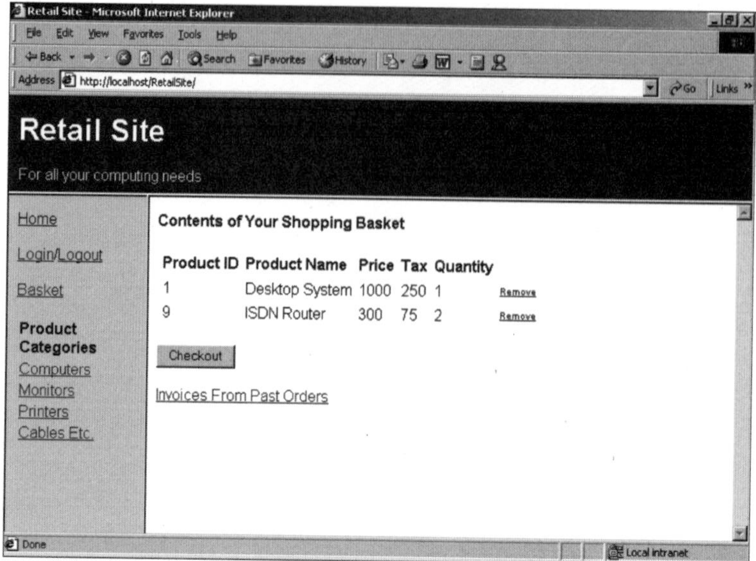

Figure 9-5 The Shopping Basket

Removing Items from the Shopping Basket

Customers can click a link on Basket.asp to remove an individual item from the basket. The Remove link passes the ProductID as a parameter to RemoveItem.asp, and the code in RemoveItem.asp calls a stored procedure to delete the record from the Basket table, as shown here:

```
Dim objShopping
Dim strUserID
Dim lngProductID

'Check authentication cookie.
strUserID = Request.Cookies("userauthid")
If strUserID = "" Then
    Server.Transfer "Login.htm"
End If

'Retrieve requested product ID.
lngProductID = Request.QueryString("ProductID")

'Call RemoveItemFromBasket function.

RemoveItemFromBasket strUserID, lngProductID
Server.transfer "Basket.asp"

Public Sub RemoveItemFromBasket(strCustomer, lngProductID)
'Function to remove an item from the shopping basket
Dim cmd
```

```
'Call the removeItem stored procedure.
Set cmd = CreateObject("ADODB.Command")
With cmd
    .ActiveConnection = strCon
    .CommandText = "removeItem"
    .CommandType = adCmdStoredProc
    .Parameters(1).Value = strCustomer
    .Parameters(2).Value = lngProductID
    .Execute
End With
Set cmd = Nothing
End Sub
```

This code passes the customer's ID and the ID of the product to be removed to the *removeItem* stored procedure, which is defined as follows:

```
CREATE PROC removeItem @Customer varchar(40), @ProductID int
AS
DELETE Basket
WHERE Customer = @Customer
AND ProductID = @ProductID
```

The *removeItem* stored procedure simply deletes the record in the Basket table that relates to the specified product and customer. The code in RemoveItem.asp then transfers the user back to the Basket.asp page.

Checking Out

When a user is ready to complete his purchase, he clicks the Submit button in the form on Basket.asp to start the check-out process. The customary first stage of this process is to allow the customer to enter delivery and payment information; our application uses Payment.asp for this purpose. This page displays a form in which the customer enters his credit card number and the card's expiration date, the name of the credit card holder, and the address to which the goods should be delivered. This information is then passed to Checkout.asp where the actual check-out process occurs. (In this sample application, we use only the delivery address data—the credit card data is discarded.)

The code in Checkout.asp performs three main tasks. First it calls a stored procedure to enter the order details into the Orders and OrderDetails tables and remove those items from the basket. Next it uses an annotated schema to retrieve the order information as an XML purchase order. And finally it posts the purchase order to the supplier site. Here's the code for Checkout.asp:

```
Dim strUserID
Dim strAddress
Dim strOrderNo
```

(continued)

```
'Check for authentication cookie.
strUserID = Request.Cookies("userauthid")
If strUserID = "" Then
    Server.Transfer "Login.htm"
End If

'Get the delivery address.
strAddress = Request.Form("txtAddress")

'Call Checkout function passing the user's ID and address.
strOrderNo = CheckOut(strUserID, strAddress)

Response.Write "Your order has been placed successfully.<BR>"

'The order number is returned by the Checkout function.
Response.Write "The order number is " & strOrderNo
Response.Write "<BR>Take a note of this number. " & _
    "You will need to quote it in the event of any enquiries."

Function CheckOut(strCustomer, strAddress)
'Function to check out.
'This function clears the basket and logs the order data.
'Then the order is retrieved as XML and sent to the supplier using HTTP.

Dim cmd
Dim conDB
Dim OrderNo

'Use Checkout stored procedure to clear basket and log order in the
'database.
Set conDB = CreateObject("ADODB.Connection")
conDB.Open strCon
Set cmd = CreateObject("ADODB.Command")
With cmd
    Set .ActiveConnection = conDB
        .CommandText = "checkOut"
        .CommandType = adCmdStoredProc
        .Parameters(1).Value = strCustomer
        .Parameters(2).Value = strAddress
        .Execute
End With
If Not IsNull(cmd.Parameters(3).Value) Then
    OrderNo = cmd.Parameters(3).Value
Else
    OrderNo = "Invalid Order"
End If
```

```
If OrderNo <> "Invalid Order" Then
'Retrieve Order detail as XML using the OrderSchema.xml annotated schema.
Dim cmdOrder
Dim strmResult

Set cmdOrder = CreateObject("ADODB.Command")
Set cmdOrder.ActiveConnection = conDB

'XPath Dialect
cmdOrder.Dialect = "{ec2a4293-e898-11d2-b1b7-00c04f680c56}"
cmdOrder.Properties("mapping schema") = _
    Server.MapPath("AppFiles\OrderSchema.xml")
'XPath for the order data
cmdOrder.CommandText = "Order[@OrderNo='" & OrderNo & "']"

Set strmResult = CreateObject("ADODB.Stream")
strmResult.Open

cmdOrder.Properties("Output Stream") = strmResult
'Root element
cmdOrder.Properties("XML Root") = "PurchaseOrder"
cmdOrder.Execute , , adExecuteStream

Dim strXML
strXML = strmResult.ReadText

'Post the XML Order over HTTP to the supplier.
Dim objHTTP
Set objHTTP = CreateObject("Microsoft.XMLHTTP")
objHTTP.Open "POST", _
    "HTTP://localhost/SupplierSite/PlaceOrder.asp?txtOrder=" & _
    strXML, False
objHTTP.send
Set strmResult = Nothing
Set cmdOrder = Nothing
Set conDB = Nothing
End If
CheckOut = OrderNo
Set cmd = Nothing
End Function
```

The *checkOut* stored procedure is used to insert the order data into the Orders and OrderDetails tables, and remove the items from the Basket table. This stored procedure is defined as follows:

```
CREATE PROC checkOut @Customer varchar(40),
                     @Address varchar(255), @OrderNo integer OUTPUT
AS
BEGIN TRAN
```

(continued)

```
-- Get the next order number.
SELECT @OrderNo = MAX(OrderNo) + 1 FROM Orders

--Insert the order header.
INSERT Orders
VALUES
(@OrderNo,GetDate(), 'RetailerSite','SupplierSite',
 @Customer, @Address, 'placed')

--Insert order details and order number into a temporary table.
SELECT @OrderNo OrderNo, ProductID, Quantity, UnitPrice, Tax
INTO #OrderDetails
FROM Basket

--Insert the contents of the temporary table into the Order Details table.
INSERT OrderDetails
SELECT OrderNo, ProductID, Quantity, UnitPrice, Tax FROM #OrderDetails

--Remove all items from the basket for this user.
DELETE Basket
WHERE Customer = @Customer

--Clean up.
DROP TABLE #OrderDetails
COMMIT TRAN
```

This stored procedure encapsulates the process in a transaction. The next available order number is retrieved from the Orders table, and the order data is inserted. Then all records belonging to the current customer are removed from the Basket table and the order number is returned to the caller.

Once the order data has been entered into the database, a purchase order document must be sent to the supplier in an XML format the trading partners have agreed to use. The format is defined in the OrderSchema.xml XDR schema, which has been annotated to make it easy to extract the data from the database. The OrderSchema.xml schema is shown here:

```
<?xml version="1.0" ?>
<Schema xmlns="urn:schemas-microsoft-com:xml-data"
    xmlns:dt="urn:schemas-microsoft-com:datatypes"
    xmlns:sql="urn:schemas-microsoft-com:xml-sql">

    <ElementType name="ProductID"/>
    <ElementType name="Quantity"/>
    <ElementType name="UnitPrice"/>
    <ElementType name="Tax"/>
```

```
    <ElementType name="OrderDetail" model="closed"
        sql:relation="OrderDetails">
        <element type="ProductID" sql:field="ProductID" minOccurs="1"
            maxOccurs="1"/>
        <element type="Quantity" sql:field="Quantity" minOccurs="1"
            maxOccurs="1"/>
        <element type="UnitPrice" sql:field="UnitPrice" minOccurs="1"
            maxOccurs="1"/>
        <element type="Tax" sql:field="Tax" minOccurs="1" maxOccurs="1"/>
    </ElementType>

    <AttributeType name="OrderNo"/>
    <ElementType name="RetailerID"/>
    <ElementType name="SupplierID"/>
    <ElementType name="Customer"/>
    <ElementType name="DeliveryAddress"/>
    <ElementType name="OrderDate"/>
    <ElementType name="OrderStatus"/>

    <ElementType name="Order" model="closed" sql:relation="Orders">
        <attribute type="OrderNo" sql:field="OrderNo" required="yes"/>
        <element type="OrderDate" sql:field="OrderDate" minOccurs="1"
            maxOccurs="1"/>
        <element type="RetailerID" sql:field = "RetailerID" minOccurs="1"
            maxOccurs="1"/>
        <element type="SupplierID" sql:field = "SupplierID" minOccurs="1"
            maxOccurs="1"/>
        <element type="Customer" sql:field="Customer" minOccurs="1"
            maxOccurs="1"/>
        <element type="DeliveryAddress" sql:field="DeliveryAddress"
            minOccurs="1" maxOccurs="1"/>
        <element type="OrderStatus" sql:field="OrderStatus" minOccurs="1"
            maxOccurs="1"/>
        <element type="OrderDetail" minOccurs = "1" maxOccurs="*">
            <sql:relationship key-relation="Orders"
                key="OrderNo"
                foreign-key="OrderNo"
                foreign-relation="OrderDetails"/>
        </element>
    </ElementType>

    <ElementType name="PurchaseOrder" model="closed" sql:is-constant="1">
        <element type="Order" minOccurs="1" maxOccurs="1"/>
    </ElementType>

</Schema>
```

This schema defines a *PurchaseOrder* element that contains a single *Order* element. The *Order* element in turn contains one or more *OrderDetail* elements. The following example shows the structure of a purchase order document defined by this schema:

```
<?xml version="1.0" encoding="utf-8" ?>
<PurchaseOrder>
    <Order OrderNo="1000">
        <OrderDate>2001-03-13T14:37:59.453</OrderDate>
        <RetailerID>RetailerSite</RetailerID>
        <SupplierID>SupplierSite</SupplierID>
        <Customer>0A00497C-DFC6-4F1C-AAED-959943A63A86</Customer>
        <DeliveryAddress>1 Any Street, Anytown</DeliveryAddress>
        <OrderStatus>placed</OrderStatus>
        <OrderDetail><ProductID>1</ProductID>
            <Quantity>1</Quantity>
            <UnitPrice>1000</UnitPrice>
            <Tax>250</Tax>
        </OrderDetail>
        <OrderDetail>
            <ProductID>9</ProductID>
            <Quantity>1</Quantity>
            <UnitPrice>300</UnitPrice>
            <Tax>75</Tax>
        </OrderDetail>
    </Order>
</PurchaseOrder>
```

The application then sends this document to the supplier site by using the Microsoft *XMLHTTP* object. This object comes with the Microsoft XML parser and can be used to make HTTP POST and GET requests over the Internet. In this case, the document is posted asynchronously to the PlaceOrder.asp page in the supplier's extranet site. In the sample application, the data is sent anonymously and unencrypted. In a production environment, however, you would probably need to specify a username and password in the call to the *Open* method and use an HTTPS URL to open a secure session.

Order Processing at the Supplier

So what happens to an order once it is received by the supplier? The order data first needs to be inserted into a database. Then the individual items for the order need to be gathered in the warehouse and prepared for shipment. Finally, the details of the order need to be sent to a package delivery company so that the goods can be delivered to the customer.

Inserting the Order in the Supplier Database

As you might recall, when a customer places an order at the online retail site, the application sends the order information as an XML document to the PlaceOrder.asp page in the SupplierSite extranet. The PlaceOrder.asp page receives the order and passes it to a stored procedure, as you can see from the following code:

```
Dim strXML
Dim cmd
Dim con
Const adCmdStoredProc = 4

strXML = Request.QueryString("txtOrder")
Set con = CreateObject("ADODB.Connection")
con.Open "PROVIDER=SQLOLEDB; INTEGRATED SECURITY=SSPI;" & _
    "DATA SOURCE=(local);INITIAL CATALOG=SupplierSite;"

Set cmd = CreateObject("ADODB.Command")
strXML = Replace(strXML, "encoding=""utf-8""", "")
With cmd
    Set .ActiveConnection = con
    .CommandText = "importOrder"
    .CommandType = adCmdStoredProc
    .Parameters(1).Value = strXML
    .Execute
End With

Set cmd = Nothing
Set con = Nothing
```

> **Note** PlaceOrder.asp also includes code that sends an invoice back to the retailer through BizTalk Server. I'll discuss this aspect of the SupplierSite application in the "BizTalk Server Messaging" section later in this chapter.

The unnecessary encoding information is removed from the document and then the XML purchase order is passed to the *importOrder* stored procedure in the SupplierSite database, which is defined as follows:

```
CREATE PROC ImportOrder @xml ntext
AS
BEGIN TRAN
DECLARE @idoc int
EXEC sp_xml_preparedocument @idoc OUTPUT, @xml
```

(continued)

```
-- Extract order header details from XML purchase order and insert into
-- Orders table.
INSERT Orders
    SELECT * FROM OpenXML(@idoc, 'PurchaseOrder/Order', 3)
    WITH (OrderNo integer,
          OrderDate datetime,
          RetailerID varchar(30),
          SupplierID varchar(30),
          Customer varchar(40),
          DeliveryAddress varchar(255),
          OrderStatus varchar(40))
-- Extract order details from XML and insert into OrderDetails table.
INSERT OrderDetails
    SELECT * FROM OpenXML(@idoc, 'PurchaseOrder/Order/OrderDetail', 2)
    WITH (OrderNo integer '../@OrderNo',
          ProductID int,
          Quantity int,
          UnitPrice money,
          Tax money)

EXEC sp_xml_removedocument @idoc
COMMIT TRAN
```

This stored procedure parses the XML document and creates an internal tree representation using the *sp_xml_preparedocument* system stored procedure and then uses two INSERT statements containing the *OpenXML* function to insert the data into the Orders and OrderDetails tables.

Preparing Goods for Shipment with the Order Picking Application

Now that the order information is in the SupplierSite database, warehouse employees can use the Order Picking intranet application to prepare the items for shipment. The Order Picking application is implemented as an intranet site in a virtual directory named OrderPicking that retrieves data from a SQLISAPI virtual directory named OrderPickingXML. The need for two virtual directories arises because we want to use an HTML page with frames as the default page in the site, but conventional HTML pages can't be hosted in a SQLISAPI virtual directory. Both virtual directories reference the same physical folder.

Default.htm, which is the home page in the OrderPicking virtual directory, defines three horizontal frames. The top frame contains Header.htm, a static heading for the site. The middle frame retrieves data from the Orders.xml template in the OrderPickingXML virtual directory, and the bottom frame retrieves data from the OrderDetails.xml template in the OrderPickingXML virtual directory. Users arrive at this page by using the URL *http://localhost/OrderPicking*. Here's the HTML code for Default.htm:

```
<HTML>
    <HEAD>
        <TITLE>Supplier Intranet</TITLE>
    </HEAD>
    <FRAMESET rows="100,*" framespacing="0" border="0">
        <FRAME name='header' target='header' scrolling='0'
            src='Header.htm'/>
        <FRAMESET rows="50%,*">
            <FRAME name="Orders" target="OrderDetails" scrolling="auto"
            src="http://localhost/OrderPickingXML/Templates/Orders.xml"/>
            <FRAME name="OrderDetails" scrolling="auto" src=
            "http://localhost/OrderPickingXML/Templates/OrderDetails.xml"/>
        </FRAMESET>
        <NOFRAMES>
            <BODY>
                <P>This page uses frames, but your browser doesn't
                    support them.</P>
            </BODY>
        </NOFRAMES>
    </FRAMESET>
</HTML>
```

The Orders.xml template is defined in the *Templates* virtual name in the OrderPickingXML virtual directory. It retrieves the list of current orders using a FOR XML query, as shown here:

```
<?xml-stylesheet type="text/xsl" href="Orders.xsl"?>
<Orders xmlns:sql="urn:schemas-microsoft-com:xml-sql">
    <sql:query>
        SELECT OrderNo, Customer, OrderDate
        FROM Orders CustomerOrder
        FOR XML AUTO, ELEMENTS
    </sql:query>
</Orders>
```

The XML retrieved by this template looks like this:

```
<?xml-stylesheet type="text/xsl" href="Orders.xsl"?>
<Orders xmlns:sql="urn:schemas-microsoft-com:xml-sql">
    <CustomerOrder>
        <OrderNo>1000</OrderNo>
        <Customer>C0842D3B-A712-47E5-9045-7A91DC07A6F7</Customer>
        <OrderDate>2001-03-13T14:37:58.503</OrderDate>
    </CustomerOrder>
    <CustomerOrder>
        <OrderNo>1001</OrderNo>
        <Customer>2F72FEB7-7436-4BA2-B5C5-03EB4275FD5A</Customer>
        <OrderDate>2001-03-13T14:38:36.317</OrderDate>
    </CustomerOrder>
```

(continued)

```
    <CustomerOrder>
        <OrderNo>1002</OrderNo>
        <Customer>2F72FEB7-7436-4BA2-B5C5-03EB4275FD5A</Customer>
        <OrderDate>2001-03-13T17:04:22.460</OrderDate>
    </CustomerOrder>
</Orders>
```

This template contains a processing instruction so that the Orders.xsl style sheet will be applied to the XML results by the browser. We can safely rely on the browser to apply the style sheet because the application will only ever be used in an intranet environment in which the use of an XML-aware browser such as Internet Explorer can be mandated. The Orders.xsl style sheet is shown below:

```
<?xml version="1.0"?>
<xsl:stylesheet xmlns:xsl="http://www.w3.org/1999/XSL/Transform"_
    version="1.0">
    <xsl:template match="/">
        <Title>
            Customer-Order Browsing
        </Title>
        <BODY bgproperties="fixed" bgcolor="white">
            <P><FONT face="Arial" size="4">
                Choose an order to see details...
                </FONT></P>
            <TABLE border="0" width="100%" bordercolor="#009900">
                <TR STYLE="font-size:12pt;
                    font-family:Verdana; font-weight:bold;
                    text-decoration:underline">
                    <TD>Order Number</TD>
                    <TD>Customer No</TD>
                    <TD>Order Date</TD>
                </TR>
                <xsl:for-each select="Orders/CustomerOrder">
                    <TR>
                        <TD>
                            <A TARGET="OrderDetails">
                                <xsl:attribute name="HREF">
                                    OrderDetails.xml?OrderNo=
                                    <xsl:value-of select="OrderNo"/>
                                </xsl:attribute>
                                <xsl:value-of select="OrderNo"/>
                            </A>
                        </TD>
                        <TD>
                            <xsl:value-of select="Customer"/>
                        </TD>
                        <TD>
                            <xsl:value-of select="OrderDate"/>
                        </TD>
                    </TR>
```

```
            </xsl:for-each>
        </TABLE>
    </BODY>
</xsl:template>
</xsl:stylesheet>
```

This style sheet creates an HTML document containing a list of orders. Each order number is a link that causes the details for that order to be displayed in the bottom pane of the site by executing the OrderDetails.xml template, which passes the *OrderNo* field as a parameter.

The OrderDetails.xml template retrieves the details for a particular order as shown here:

```
<?xml-stylesheet type="text/xsl" href="OrderDetails.xsl"?>
<OrderDetails xmlns:sql="urn:schemas-microsoft-com:xml-sql">
    <sql:header>
        <sql:param name="OrderNo">1000</sql:param>
    </sql:header>
    <sql:query>
        SELECT OrderNo, LineItem.ProductID, Quantity, ProductName
        FROM OrderDetails LineItem
        JOIN Products on LineItem.ProductID = Products.ProductID
        WHERE LineItem.OrderNo = @OrderNo for XML AUTO, ELEMENTS
    </sql:query>
</OrderDetails>
```

The XML results produced by this template look like this:

```
<?xml-stylesheet type="text/xsl" href="OrderDetails.xsl"?>
<OrderDetails xmlns:sql="urn:schemas-microsoft-com:xml-sql">
    <LineItem>
        <OrderNo>1000</OrderNo>
        <ProductID>1</ProductID>
        <Quantity>1</Quantity>
        <Products>
            <ProductName>Desktop System</ProductName>
        </Products>
    </LineItem>
    <LineItem>
        <OrderNo>1000</OrderNo>
        <ProductID>9</ProductID>
        <Quantity>1</Quantity>
        <Products>
            <ProductName>ISDN Router</ProductName>
        </Products>
    </LineItem>
</OrderDetails>
```

Again, the template includes a processing instruction to apply a style sheet. This time the style sheet is OrderDetails.xsl, which you can see here:

```
<?xml version="1.0"?>
<xsl:stylesheet xmlns:xsl="http://www.w3.org/1999/XSL/Transform"
    version="1.0">
    <xsl:template match="/">
        <HTML>
            <HEAD>
                <TITLE>Order Details</TITLE>
   <!-- DHTML Scripting -->
   <SCRIPT language='vbscript'>
   Sub Window_onload
       frmDispatch.cmdSubmit.disabled = True
   End Sub

   Sub validate
   Dim bValid
   Dim ifields
   Dim iField
   bValid = True
   Set ifields = document.getElementsByTagName("input")
   For each iField in ifields
       If iField.Type = "checkbox" and iField.checked = False Then
           bValid = False
       End If
   Next
   If bValid = True Then
       frmDispatch.cmdSubmit.disabled = False
   Else
       frmDispatch.cmdSubmit.disabled = True
   End If
   End Sub
   </SCRIPT>
            </HEAD>
            <BODY bgproperties="fixed" bgcolor="white">
                <H3>Pick List</H3>
                <TABLE border="0" bordercolor="#009900" width='100%'>
                    <TR STYLE="font-size:12pt; font-family:Verdana;
                           font-weight:bold; text-decoration:underline">
                        <TD>Product Code</TD>
                        <TD>Product Name</TD>
                        <TD>Units</TD>
                        <TD>Picked?</TD>
                    </TR>
```

```
                    <xsl:for-each select="OrderDetails/LineItem">
                    <TR>
                        <TD>
                            <xsl:value-of select="ProductID"/>
                        </TD>
                        <TD>
                            <xsl:value-of select="Products/ProductName"/>
                        </TD>
                        <TD>
                            <xsl:value-of select="Quantity"/>
                        </TD>
                        <TD>
                            <INPUT type='checkbox' value='off'
                                onclick='validate'/>
                        </TD>
                    </TR>
                    </xsl:for-each>
                </TABLE>
                <P/>
                <FORM name='frmDispatch' id='frmDispatch' method='post'
                    action='http://localhost/OrderPicking/Dispatch.asp'>
                    <INPUT type='hidden' name='txtOrderNo'>
                        <xsl:attribute name='value'>
                            <xsl:value-of select=
                                "OrderDetails/LineItem/OrderNo"/>
                        </xsl:attribute>
                    </INPUT>
                    <INPUT id='cmdSubmit' type='submit'
                        value='Ready for Dispatch'/>
                </FORM>
            </BODY>
        </HTML>
    </xsl:template>
</xsl:stylesheet>
```

This style sheet includes some client-side DHTML script, which enables or disables a Submit button named *Ready For Dispatch* depending on whether all the items have been checked. The application uses a form to post the order information to the Dispatch.asp page in the OrderPicking virtual directory when the order has been assembled for shipping.

Figure 9-6 shows the Order Picking application user interface.

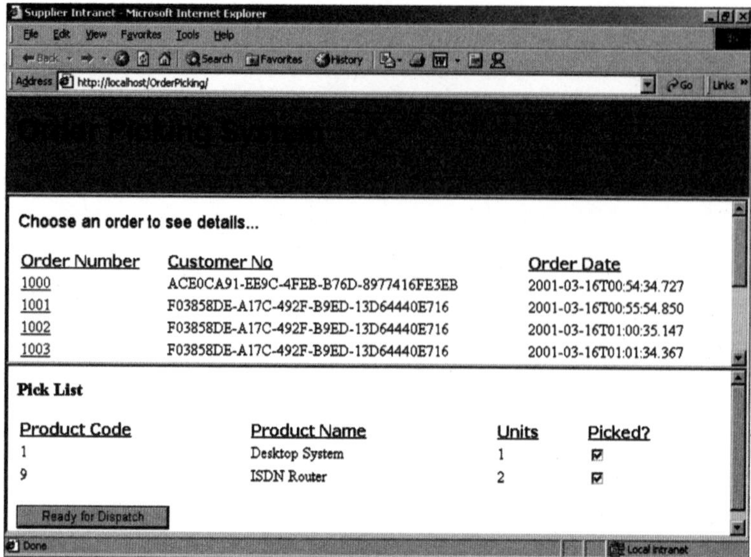

Figure 9-6 The Order Picking application

Sending the Order Details to the Delivery Company

Once an order has been prepared for shipment, the details of that order are sent to the delivery company by the code in Dispatch.asp. Dispatch.asp retrieves the order data from the database as an XML document and uses a style sheet to create an updategram that will be posted to the delivery company's Web site.

Dispatch.asp contains the following code:

```
Const XML_HEADER = "<deliverynote " & _
    "xmlns:sql='urn:schemas-microsoft-com:xml-sql'>"
Const XML_FOOTER = "</deliverynote>"
Const adExecuteStream = 1024
Const adWriteChar = 0
Dim strOrderNo

strOrderNo = Request.Form("txtOrderNo")

Dim strQuery
strQuery = XML_HEADER
strQuery = strQuery & "<sql:query>"
strQuery = strQuery & "SELECT OrderNo reference, " & _
    DeliveryAddress delivery_address "
strQuery = strQuery & "FROM Orders package WHERE OrderNo = " & _
    strOrderno & " FOR XML AUTO, ELEMENTS"
strQuery = strQuery & "</sql:query>"
strQuery = strQuery & XML_FOOTER
```

```
'Execute query using ADO.
Dim cmdPackage
Dim strmResult
Dim strmQuery
Set cmdPackage = CreateObject("ADODB.Command")
cmdPackage.ActiveConnection = "provider=SQLOLEDB;data source=(local)" & _
    ";initial catalog=SupplierSite;integrated security=sspi;"

Set strmQuery = CreateObject("ADODB.Stream")
strmQuery.Open
strmQuery.WriteText strQuery, adWriteChar
strmQuery.Position = 0
Set cmdPackage.CommandStream = strmQuery

Set strmResult = CreateObject("ADODB.Stream")
strmResult.Open
cmdPackage.Properties("Output Stream") = strmResult
cmdPackage.Properties("XSL") = Server.MapPath("Dispatch.xsl")

cmdPackage.Execute , , adExecuteStream

Dim strXML
strXML = strmResult.ReadText

Response.Write strXML
```

This script includes a query template that retrieves the order data from the SupplierSite database. The order data is retrieved in the following XML format:

```
<deliverynote xmlns:sql="urn:schemas-microsoft-com:xml-sql">
    <package>
        <reference>1000</reference>
        <delivery_address>1 Any Street, Anytown</delivery_address>
    </package>
</deliverynote>
```

The application uses the Dispatch.xsl style sheet to format this XML data. Here's the Dispatch.xsl style sheet:

```
<?xml version="1.0"?>
<xsl:stylesheet xmlns:xsl="http://www.w3.org/1999/XSL/Transform"
    version="1.0">
    <xsl:template match="/">
        <HTML>
            <HEAD>
                <TITLE>Dispatch Order</TITLE>
            </HEAD>
            <BODY bgproperties="fixed" bgcolor="white">
                <H3>Arrange Delivery</H3>
```

(continued)

```
                <P>Click Submit to send this delivery request to the
                    shipping company</P>
                <BR/>
                <B>Order No:</B>
                <xsl:value-of select="deliverynote/package/reference"/>
                <BR/>
                <B>Address:</B>
                <xsl:value-of select=
                    "deliverynote/package/delivery_address"/>
                <BR/>

                <FORM name='frmDelivery' id='frmDelivery' method='post'
                    action='http://localhost/DeliveryCo'>
                    <INPUT type='hidden' name='xsl' value='Delivery.xsl'/>
                    <INPUT type='hidden' name='template'>
                        <xsl:attribute name='value'>
                        &lt;deliveryrequest xmlns:updg=
                            "urn:schemas-microsoft-com:xml-updategram"&gt;;
                        &lt;updg:sync&gt;
                        &lt;updg:before&gt;
                        &lt;/updg:before&gt;
                        &lt;updg:after&gt;
                        &lt;deliveries customer='1'
                        reference='<xsl:value-of
                            select="deliverynote/package/reference"/>'
                        delivery_address='<xsl:value-of
                            select="deliverynote/package/delivery_address"/>'
                        package_type='1' shipping_method='2'/&gt;
                        &lt;/updg:after&gt;
                        &lt;/updg:sync&gt;
                        &lt;/deliveryrequest&gt;
                        </xsl:attribute>
                    </INPUT>
                    <INPUT type='submit' value="Send Delivery Request"/>
                </FORM>
            </BODY>
        </HTML>
    </xsl:template>
</xsl:stylesheet>
```

The style sheet generates an HTML page containing a form that posts an XML updategram to the DeliveryCo Web site. The updategram looks like this:

```
<deliveryrequest xmlns:updg="urn:schemas-microsoft-com:xml-updategram">
    <updg:sync>
        <updg:before>
        </updg:before>
        <updg:after>
```

```
            <deliveries customer='1'
                reference='1000'
                delivery_address='1 Any Street, Anytown'
                package_type='1' shipping_method='2'/>
        </updg:after>
    </updg:sync>
</deliveryrequest>
```

The posted updategram inserts a record in the Deliveries table in the DeliveryCo database.

Using an updategram to send delivery requests allows us to update the DeliveryCo database over HTTP. In a production environment, this task is likely to be performed over an HTTPS connection, and the supplier site would need to be authenticated at the DeliveryCo site in some way.

Viewing Delivery Information

The DeliveryCo Web site isn't fully implemented in the sample application. Its primary purpose is to allow you to easily confirm the insertion of orders into the Deliveries table.

As I mentioned, the site is implemented as a SQLISAPI virtual directory named DeliveryCo, which contains a single template named Deliveries.xml. This template retrieves delivery information from the Deliveries table, as shown here:

```
<?xml version="1.0"?>
<deliveries xmlns:sql="urn:schemas-microsoft-com:xml-sql"
    sql:xsl="Deliveries.xsl">
    <sql:query>
        SELECT reference, delivery_address
        FROM Deliveries delivery for XML AUTO, ELEMENTS
    </sql:query>
</deliveries>
```

The template includes a *sql:xsl* attribute, which causes the specified style sheet to be applied by the OLE-DB provider on the server before the IIS server sends the results to the browser. This strategy means that the browser receives HTML rather than XML, making this template more suitable for use on the Internet than those that require client-side style sheet processing. To ensure the HTML produced by the style sheet is displayed properly on the client, the URL you use to request the page must include a *contenttype* parameter, as shown in this example:

```
http://localhost/DeliveryCo/templates/deliveries.xml?contenttype=text/html
```

The output from the Deliveries.xml template is shown in Figure 9-7.

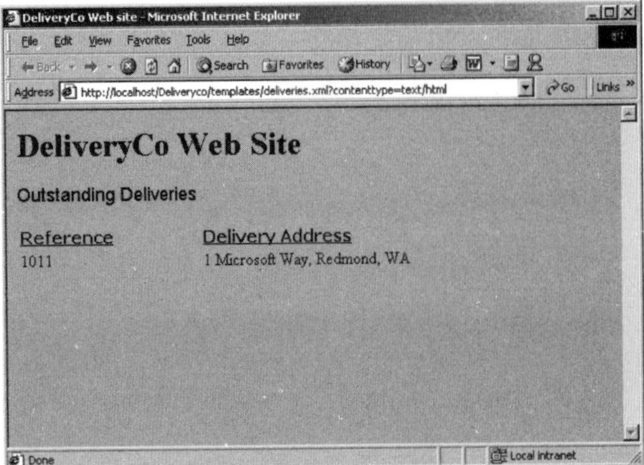

Figure 9-7 The DeliveryCo Web site

Updating the Catalog

Another aspect of the sample e-commerce scenario requires the retailer to update the catalog information for the site based on an XML catalog document downloaded from the supplier's extranet site. In the sample application, the retailer and supplier have agreed on the structure of a catalog document by defining an XDR schema. Both the retailer and the supplier have added annotations to the schema so that they can map the elements and attributes in a catalog document to data in their respective databases. The catalog schema is shown here:

```
<?xml version="1.0"?>
<Schema xmlns="urn:schemas-microsoft-com:xml-data"
    xmlns:sql="urn:schemas-microsoft-com:xml-sql">

    <ElementType name="Catalog" sql:is-constant="1">
        <element type="Category"/>
    </ElementType>

    <ElementType name="Category" sql:relation="Categories">
        <AttributeType name="CategoryID"/>
        <AttributeType name="CategoryName"/>

        <attribute type="CategoryID" sql:field="CategoryID"/>
        <attribute type="CategoryName" sql:field="CategoryName"/>
        <element type="Product">
            <sql:relationship  key-relation="Categories"
                key="CategoryID"
                foreign-key="CategoryID"
```

```
            foreign-relation="Products"/>
        </element>
    </ElementType>

    <ElementType name="Product" sql:relation="Products">
        <AttributeType name="ProductID"/>
        <AttributeType name="ProductName"/>
        <AttributeType name="UnitPrice"/>
        <AttributeType name="Tax"/>

        <attribute type="ProductID" sql:field="ProductID"/>
        <attribute type="ProductName" sql:field="ProductName"/>
        <attribute type="UnitPrice" sql:field="UnitPrice"/>
        <attribute type="Tax" sql:field="Tax"/>
    </ElementType>
</Schema>
```

Downloading the Catalog

The first step in updating the catalog is to download the latest data from the supplier. To make this possible, the supplier has published the annotated schema in a SQLISAPI virtual directory. This preparation allows retailers to access the catalog data over HTTP.

For the RetailSite solution, I use a Microsoft VBScript application to make an HTTP connection to the SupplierSiteXML virtual directory and to download the data from the schema. The downloaded data is then written into a local file. The script contains the following two procedures to download the catalog data and write it to a file:

```
Function DownloadCatalog()
    Dim objHTTP
    Dim strXML

    Set objHTTP = CreateObject("Microsoft.XMLHTTP")
    objHTTP.Open "GET", _
    "http://localhost/SupplierSiteXML/Schemas/CatalogSchema.xml/Catalog", _
        False
    objHTTP.Send
    strXML = objHTTP.responseText
    DownloadCatalog = strXML
    Set objHTTP = Nothing
End Function

Sub WriteFile(strData, strFileName)
    Dim FSO
    Dim TxtStrm
```

(continued)

```
    Set FSO = CreateObject("Scripting.FileSystemObject")
    Set TxtStrm = FSO.CreateTextFile(strFileName, True)
    TxtStrm.Write strData
    TxtStrm.Close
End Sub
```

The *DownloadCatalog* function uses the *XMLHTTP* object to download the data from the CatalogSchema.xml schema. Notice that no root element needs to be specified because the schema contains a constant *Catalog* element. The *WriteFile* procedure is simply a utility function to save a text file in a specified location. In the ImportCatalog.vbs script, the file is saved in the same directory as the script itself.

The XML catalog data downloaded from the supplier looks like this:

```
<Catalog>
    <Category CategoryID="1" CategoryName="Computers">
        <Product ProductID="1" ProductName="Desktop System"
            UnitPrice="1000" Tax="250"/>
        <Product ProductID="2" ProductName="Server System"
            UnitPrice="1500" Tax="375"/>
        <Product ProductID="3" ProductName="Laptop System"
            UnitPrice="1300" Tax="325"/>
    </Category>
    <Category CategoryID="2" CategoryName="Monitors">
        <Product ProductID="4" ProductName="17 inch Monitor"
            UnitPrice="500" Tax="125"/>
        <Product ProductID="5" ProductName="Flat Panel Screen"
            UnitPrice="1000" Tax="250"/>
    </Category>
    <Category CategoryID="3" CategoryName="Printers">
        <Product ProductID="6" ProductName="Color Ink Jet Printer"
            UnitPrice="300" Tax="75"/>
        <Product ProductID="7" ProductName="Laser Printer"
            UnitPrice="800" Tax="200"/>
    </Category>
    <Category CategoryID="4" CategoryName="Cables Etc.">
        <Product ProductID="8" ProductName="Workgroup Hub"
            UnitPrice="50" Tax="12.5"/>
        <Product ProductID="9" ProductName="ISDN Router"
            UnitPrice="300" Tax="75"/>
        <Product ProductID="10" ProductName="UTP Cable (100 M)"
            UnitPrice="35" Tax="8.75"/>
    </Category>
    <Category CategoryID="5" CategoryName="Software">
        <Product ProductID="11" ProductName="Word Processing Package"
            UnitPrice="100" Tax="25"/>
```

```
        <Product ProductID="12" ProductName="Spreadsheet"
            UnitPrice="120" Tax="30"/>
        <Product ProductID="13" ProductName="Database Management Software"
            UnitPrice="200" Tax="50"/>
        <Product ProductID="14" ProductName="Arcade Game Collection"
            UnitPrice="35" Tax="8.75"/>
        <Product ProductID="15" ProductName="Strategy Game Collection"
            UnitPrice="35" Tax="8.75"/>
    </Category>
</Catalog>
```

Importing the Catalog Data

The XML bulk load component does the actual work of importing the data. The bulk load component drops the existing tables, re-creates them, and imports the data from the newly created file. Here's the procedure used to import the data:

```
Sub LoadCatalog(strXMLFile, strSchemaFile, strErrLog)
    Dim objBL

    Set objBL = CreateObject("SQLXMLBulkLoad.SQLXMLBulkLoad")
    objBL.ConnectionString = "provider=SQLOLEDB.1;" & _
        "data source=localhost;" & _
        "database=RetailSite;" & _
        "Integrated Security=SSPI;"
    objBL.ErrorLogFile = strErrLog

    objBL.SchemaGen = True
    objBL.SGDropTables = True

    objBL.Execute strSchemaFile, strXMLFile
    Set objBL = Nothing
End Sub
```

Although this script works satisfactorily for a sample application, you should remember that dropping and re-creating a table means that any indexes you might have built to improve query performance will be lost. A production system would need to re-create the indexes and constraints after data had been imported by this method. Also, tables can't be dropped while users are accessing them, so you might want to adopt the strategy of using a script like ImportCatalog.vbs to refresh a staging database, and then replicate the contents of the tables to the production databases to avoid having to drop and re-create the production tables.

Invoicing the Retailer

The final aspect of the scenario that we need to discuss is the sending of invoices from the supplier to the retailer. I could have implemented this functionality in the application in a number of ways—I could have sent an updategram or used the *OpenXML* function to insert an XML invoice that I posted to an ASP. But those strategies don't address the fact that the invoice is generated from the order document, and some fields must be transformed. I could have solved this problem simply by applying an XSL style sheet, but yet another issue needed to be addressed: the supplier could receive orders from multiple retailers. So I needed to find some way to route the invoice to the correct retailer.

Introducing BizTalk Server 2000

Business document routing and transformation are two tasks that Microsoft BizTalk Server 2000 was designed to perform. BizTalk Server 2000 is a business process management and document exchange handling application that can be used in all kinds of integration solutions.

BizTalk Server provides two main services: *orchestration* and *messaging*. The orchestration functionality in BizTalk Server allows you to define business processes graphically (using a Microsoft Visio–based interface) and to generate compiled schedules to automate the key processes in your business. The messaging functionality provides support for the automated routing and translation of business documents between trading partners and internal systems. These documents can be in virtually any format including Electronic Data Interchange (EDI) standards such as X.12 or EDIFACT, SAP IDoc documents, and XML. A full discussion of BizTalk Server is beyond the scope of this book, but I want to examine some ways in which BizTalk Server messaging functionality can be used together with SQL Server's XML support to build integrated e-commerce solutions.

BizTalk Server Messaging

BizTalk Server messaging involves the creation of a number of conceptual objects. BizTalk Server provides several tools that you can use in this task.

Defining Business Documents

Your first task when building a messaging solution is to define the business documents you'll be exchanging. These can be XML, EDI or virtually any other kind of document; however, BizTalk Server always uses XML internally to represent the documents that flow through the messaging service. You can use the BizTalk Editor to create a new document definition from scratch, or you can import a definition from an existing document. When using XML, you can import an XDR schema, including annotated schemas that are used in SQL Server–based solutions. Figure 9-8 shows the BizTalk Editor.

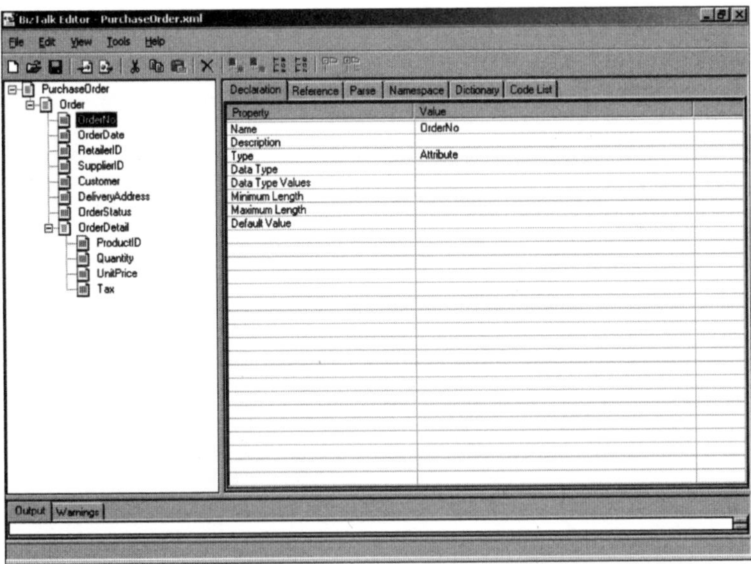

Figure 9-8 The BizTalk Editor

In the sample scenario, we used two documents in the messaging solution. The first is a purchase order defined by the following XML schema:

```
<?xml version="1.0"?>
<!-- Generated by using BizTalk Editor on Thu, Mar 08 2001 04:53:54 PM -->
<!-- Microsoft Corporation (c) 2000 (http://www.microsoft.com) -->
<Schema name="PurchaseOrder" b:BizTalkServerEditorTool_Version="1.0"
    b:root_reference="PurchaseOrder" b:standard="XML"
    xmlns="urn:schemas-microsoft-com:xml-data"
    xmlns:dt="urn:schemas-microsoft-com:datatypes"
    xmlns:b="urn:schemas-microsoft-com:BizTalkServer"
    xmlns:sql="urn:schemas-microsoft-com:xml-sql">
    <b:SelectionFields/>

    <ElementType name="UnitPrice">
        <b:FieldInfo/>
    </ElementType>
    <ElementType name="Tax">
        <b:FieldInfo/>
    </ElementType>
    <ElementType name="SupplierID">
        <b:FieldInfo/>
    </ElementType>
```

(continued)

```
<ElementType name="RetailerID">
    <b:FieldInfo/>
</ElementType>
<ElementType name="Quantity">
    <b:FieldInfo/>
</ElementType>
<ElementType name="PurchaseOrder" sql:is-constant="1">
    <b:RecordInfo/>
    <element type="Order" maxOccurs="1" minOccurs="1"/>
</ElementType>
<ElementType name="ProductID">
    <b:FieldInfo/>
</ElementType>
<ElementType name="OrderStatus">
    <b:FieldInfo/>
</ElementType>
<ElementType name="OrderDetail" sql:relation="OrderDetails">
    <b:RecordInfo/>
    <element type="ProductID" maxOccurs="1" minOccurs="1"
        sql:field="ProductID"/>
    <element type="Quantity" maxOccurs="1" minOccurs="1"
        sql:field="Quantity"/>
    <element type="UnitPrice" maxOccurs="1" minOccurs="1"
        sql:field="UnitPrice"/>
    <element type="Tax" maxOccurs="1" minOccurs="1" sql:field="Tax"/>
</ElementType>
<ElementType name="OrderDate">
    <b:FieldInfo/>
</ElementType>
<ElementType name="Order" sql:relation="Orders">
    <b:RecordInfo/>
    <AttributeType name="OrderNo">
        <b:FieldInfo/>
    </AttributeType>
    <attribute type="OrderNo" required="yes" sql:field="OrderNo"/>
    <element type="OrderDate" maxOccurs="1" minOccurs="1"
        sql:field="OrderDate"/>
    <element type="RetailerID" maxOccurs="1" minOccurs="1"
        sql:field="RetailerID"/>
    <element type="SupplierID" maxOccurs="1" minOccurs="1"
        sql:field="SupplierID"/>
    <element type="Customer" maxOccurs="1" minOccurs="1"
        sql:field="Customer"/>
    <element type="DeliveryAddress" maxOccurs="1" minOccurs="1"
        sql:field="DeliveryAddress"/>
    <element type="OrderStatus" maxOccurs="1" minOccurs="1"
        sql:field="OrderStatus"/>
    <element type="OrderDetail" maxOccurs="*" minOccurs="1">
```

```
            <sql:relationship key-relation="Orders"
                key="OrderNo"
                foreign-key="OrderNo"
                foreign-relation="OrderDetails">
            </sql:relationship>
        </element>
    </ElementType>
    <ElementType name="DeliveryAddress">
        <b:FieldInfo/>
    </ElementType>
    <ElementType name="Customer">
        <b:FieldInfo/>
    </ElementType>
</Schema>
```

The BizTalk Editor generates this schema from the OrderSchema.xml annotated schema used by the retailer and supplier to define a purchase order. An XML document based on this schema looks like this:

```
<PurchaseOrder>
    <Order OrderNo="1000">
        <OrderDate>2001-03-16T00:54:36.120</OrderDate>
        <RetailerID>RetailerSite</RetailerID>
        <SupplierID>SupplierSite</SupplierID>
        <Customer>053F4A23-05AC-4D4B-8898-FABF502E45B9</Customer>
        <DeliveryAddress>1 Any Street, Anytown</DeliveryAddress>
        <OrderStatus>placed</OrderStatus>
        <OrderDetail>
            <ProductID>1</ProductID>
            <Quantity>1</Quantity>
            <UnitPrice>1000</UnitPrice>
            <Tax>250</Tax>
        </OrderDetail>
        <OrderDetail>
            <ProductID>9</ProductID>
            <Quantity>1</Quantity>
            <UnitPrice>300</UnitPrice>
            <Tax>75</Tax>
        </OrderDetail>
    </Order>
</PurchaseOrder>
```

The second document defined in the sample scenario messaging solution is an invoice. The schema for the invoice document is shown here:

```
<?xml version="1.0"?>
<!-- Generated using BizTalk Editor on Mon, Oct 02 2000 09:36:47 AM -->
<!-- Microsoft Corporation (c) 2000 (http://www.microsoft.com) -->
```

(continued)

```
<Schema name="Invoice" b:BizTalkServerEditorTool_Version="1.0"
    b:root_reference="Invoice" b:standard="XML"
    xmlns="urn:schemas-microsoft-com:xml-data"
    xmlns:dt="urn:schemas-microsoft-com:datatypes"
    xmlns:b="urn:schemas-microsoft-com:BizTalkServer">
    <b:SelectionFields/>

    <ElementType name="Total">
        <b:FieldInfo/>
    </ElementType>
    <ElementType name="SupplierID">
        <b:FieldInfo/>
    </ElementType>
    <ElementType name="Sale">
        <b:RecordInfo/>
        <AttributeType name="OrderDate">
            <b:FieldInfo/>
        </AttributeType>
        <AttributeType name="InvoiceNo">
            <b:FieldInfo/>
        </AttributeType>
        <attribute type="InvoiceNo" required="yes"/>
        <attribute type="OrderDate" required="yes"/>
        <element type="CustomerID" maxOccurs="1" minOccurs="1"/>
        <element type="SupplierID" maxOccurs="1" minOccurs="1"/>
        <element type="CustomerRef" maxOccurs="1" minOccurs="1"/>
        <element type="LineItem" maxOccurs="*" minOccurs="1"/>
        <element type="Total" maxOccurs="1" minOccurs="1"/>
    </ElementType>
    <ElementType name="Quantity">
        <b:FieldInfo/>
    </ElementType>
    <ElementType name="ProductName">
        <b:FieldInfo/>
    </ElementType>
    <ElementType name="Price">
        <b:FieldInfo/>
    </ElementType>
    <ElementType name="LineItem">
        <b:RecordInfo/>
        <element type="ProductName" maxOccurs="1" minOccurs="1"/>
        <element type="Quantity" maxOccurs="1" minOccurs="1"/>
        <element type="Price" maxOccurs="1" minOccurs="1"/>
    </ElementType>
```

```
    <ElementType name="Invoice">
        <b:RecordInfo/>
        <element type="Sale" maxOccurs="1" minOccurs="1"/>
    </ElementType>
    <ElementType name="CustomerRef">
        <b:FieldInfo/>
    </ElementType>
    <ElementType name="CustomerID">
        <b:FieldInfo/>
    </ElementType>
</Schema>
```

A document based on this schema might contain the following data:

```
<Invoice>
    <Sale InvoiceNo="1000" OrderDate="01/01/2001">
        <CustomerID>RetailerSite</CustomerID>
        <SupplierID>SupplierSite</SupplierID>
        <CustomerRef>053F4A23-05AC-4D4B-8898-FABF502E45B9</CustomerRef>
        <LineItem>
            <ProductName>Desktop System</ProductName>
            <Quantity>1</Quantity>
            <Price>1250</Price>
        </LineItem>
        <LineItem>
            <ProductName>ISDN Router</ProductName>
            <Quantity>1</Quantity>
            <Price>375</Price>
        </LineItem>
        <Total>1825</Total>
    </Sale>
</Invoice>
```

This is the kind of invoice that a supplier sends to acknowledge an order from a retailer.

Both the purchase order and invoice document definitions are stored in the BizTalk Server repository, a local Web site accessed using the HTTP-DAV protocol.

Creating a Map Between the Order and Invoice Documents

Invoices are generated from orders, and the simplest way to create an invoice is to map fields in the order to fields in the invoice. BizTalk Server provides the BizTalk Mapper, a tool that can be used to define a mapping between two different document specifications. Figure 9-9 shows the BizTalk Mapper and the map created between the purchase order and invoice document definitions.

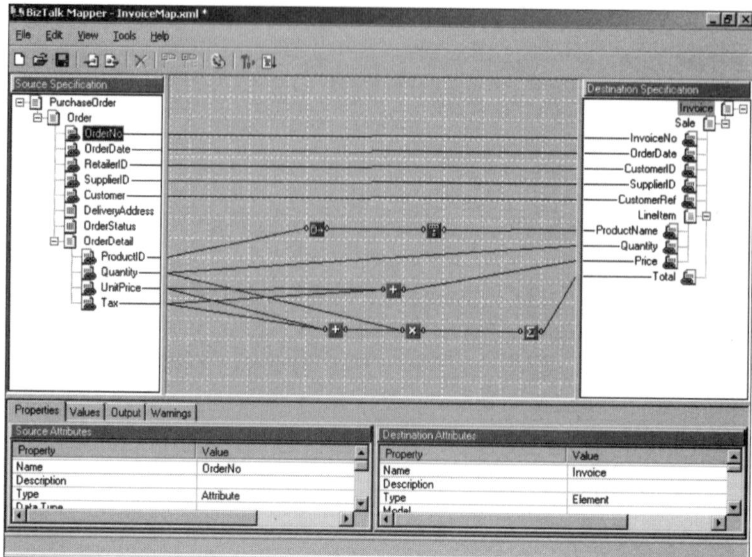

Figure 9-9 The BizTalk Mapper

In many cases, fields can simply be mapped directly from one document to another. For example, you can see in Figure 9-9 that the *OrderNo* field in the purchase order document is mapped directly to the *InvoiceNo* field in the invoice document. However, some mappings aren't so straightforward. The BizTalk Mapper provides some mapping functions (known as *functoids*) that you can use to define more complex mappings between fields.

The map created for the sample scenario uses a number of functoids to map fields in the purchase order document to fields in the invoice document. First of all, the BizTalk Mapper uses the Database Lookup functoid to retrieve the row in the Products table for each product ID in the order, and then uses the Value Extractor functoid to extract the corresponding product name and write it to the invoice. Second, the BizTalk Mapper uses the Addition functoid to add the price and tax for each item in the order and store the total unit price in the invoice. Finally, it uses the Addition functoid once again to add the price and tax fields, and the Multiplication functoid to multiply the total unit price by the quantity ordered. This produces the total price for each item, and the BizTalk Mapper then uses the Sum functoid to calculate the total value of the invoice.

When you create a map with the BizTalk Mapper, the map is stored in the BizTalk Server repository as an XSL style sheet that can be applied during document exchanges in which the source document must be transformed into a different destination document. Because you can transform a document in this way, you can build solutions to automate business processes, such as generating an invoice from an order or translating a specific type of document from one format to another so that organizations using different document definitions can be integrated. For example, you could use a FOR XML query to extract an XML invoice from a database and then submit that invoice to BizTalk Server, which could use a map to translate the invoice to an EDI format such as X.12 before sending it to its destination.

Configuring a Messaging Solution

Once you have defined the documents and maps that you'll use in your exchange, you can use the BizTalk Messaging Manager to define the messaging architecture for your integration solution. A messaging architecture can include the following entities:

- *Organization*: An organization represents a trading partner with which you'll exchange documents. Your own organization is represented as the *Home Organization*, and you can add as many other organizations as necessary. The Home Organization can include one or more applications, representing internal line-of-business (LOB) applications that need to exchange documents.
- *Document*: A document is, unsurprisingly, a document specification from the BizTalk Server repository that you will exchange with trading partners or among internal applications.
- *Channel*: A channel is used to define the processing that must take place during a particular document exchange. You can create a channel that defines the source and destination documents, and a map that should be applied as the document is routed to its destination.
- *Port*: A port defines how a document is transmitted to its destination. It can be used to route documents to a specific HTTP, FILE, or MSMQ address, or to pass the document to a component that will perform further processing.
- *Distribution List*: A distribution list is a group of ports that can be used to route a single document to multiple destinations. For example, a supplier could use a distribution list to send a catalog document to multiple retailers.
- *Envelope*: An envelope is used to encapsulate a document, perhaps by adding routing or manifest information.

Figure 9-10 shows the BizTalk Messaging Manager, which you can use to create and configure all of the preceding entities.

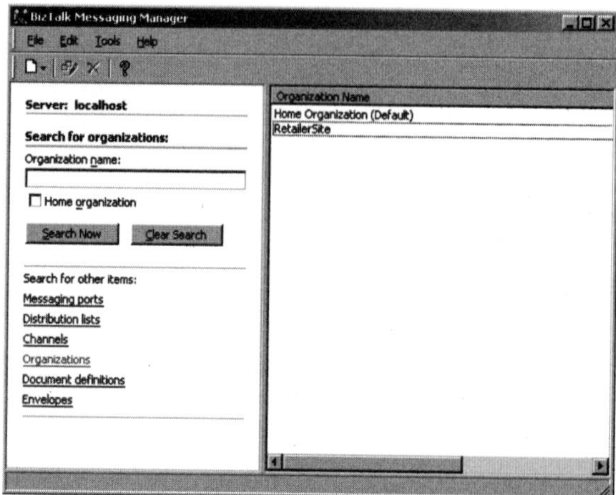

Figure 9-10 The BizTalk Messaging Manager

In the sample scenario, two organizations participate in the document exchange process: the Home Organization, representing the supplier, and RetailerSite, representing the retailer. The purchase order and invoice documents defined earlier are used as the source and destination documents respectively in a channel named *InvoiceChannel*. This channel applies the map I described earlier to the purchase order to generate an invoice. The resulting invoice document is then sent to a port named *InvoicePort*, where it is routed over HTTP to the RetailSite Web site.

Submitting a Document to BizTalk Server

So we've configured a messaging solution using BizTalk Server. The challenge now is to find a way to pass instances of the business documents we want to exchange into BizTalk Server so that they can be routed through the correct channel and sent to their destinations.

We can choose from two main techniques to submit documents to BizTalk Server: the *IInterchange* interface or a *receive* function.

IInterchange is a COM interface that COM-aware clients can use to submit a document programmatically. It provides *Submit* and *SubmitSync* methods so that you can choose to pass documents asynchronously or synchronously.

Receive functions are specified folders or messaging queues that BizTalk Server polls for new documents. Applications that can't use COM can deliver documents into a *receive* function so that BizTalk Server will pick them up for processing. You can create *receive* functions using the BizTalk Server Administration tool.

In the sample scenario, the purchase order document is submitted to BizTalk Server from an ASP script. Because COM components can be created in script, we use the *IInterchange* interface. Here's the code from PlaceOrder.asp that passes the document to BizTalk Server:

```
Dim oBTS, BIZTALK_OPENNESS_TYPE_NOTOPEN

BIZTALK_OPENNESS_TYPE_NOTOPEN = 1
Set oBTS = Server.CreateObject("BizTalk.Interchange")

'Submit document asynchronously, specifying the channel.
oBTS.Submit BIZTALK_OPENNESS_TYPE_NOTOPEN, strXML,,, ,,, "InvoiceChannel"
Set oBTS = Nothing
```

As you can see, we use the *Submit* method of the *IInterchange* interface to pass the purchase order document to BizTalk Server. This method can accept several parameters to identify the correct channel through which to route the document. In this case, I've taken the most simple option of simply specifying the channel name in the method call. However, you can choose from a number of approaches to routing a document in which either the source or the destination (or both) is defined in the channel and port as *open*, and the document is routed dynamically. You can specify the source and destination organizations in the call, allowing you to use the same code to route documents to different destinations, or you can use "self-routing" documents that include fields designated as source or destination identifiers so that BizTalk Server routes the document dynamically, based on data in the document itself.

Receiving a Document from BizTalk Server

Once a document is submitted to BizTalk Server, it passes through a channel and is routed to its destination through a port. The port can send the document to a specified URL over HTTP, a message queue, or a file system location, or the port can send the document in e-mail using SMTP. Furthermore, you can build an Application Integration Component (AIC) and send the document to your component for further custom processing.

In the sample scenario, the document is sent over HTTP to the Invoice.asp page in the RetailSite Web site. Here it's received and read into a DOM document object. The XML is then passed as a string to the *importInvoice* stored procedure in the RetailSite database. The code in Invoice.asp is shown here:

```
Dim objXML

'Load the incoming XML document.
Set objXML = server.CreateObject("Microsoft.XMLDom")
objXML.Load Request.BinaryRead(Request.TotalBytes)
```

(continued)

```
RecordInvoice objXML.xml

Sub RecordInvoice(strXML)
Dim cmd' As ADODB.Command

'Connect to the database.
Set conDB = CreateObject("ADODB.Connection")
conDB.ConnectionString = strCon
conDB.Open

'Call the importInvoice stored procedure, passing the XML invoice.
Set cmd = CreateObject("ADODB.Command")
With cmd
    Set .ActiveConnection = conDB
        .CommandText = "importInvoice"
        .CommandType = adCmdStoredProc
        .Parameters(1).Value = strXML
        .Execute
End With
End Sub
```

The *importInvoice* stored procedure uses the *OpenXML* function to insert the invoice data into the Invoices and LineItems tables as shown here:

```
CREATE PROC importInvoice @xml ntext
AS
DECLARE @idoc int
BEGIN
EXEC sp_xml_preparedocument @idoc OUTPUT, @xml
--Insert invoice header data from XML into Invoices table.
INSERT Invoices
    SELECT * FROM OpenXML(@idoc, 'Invoice/Sale', 3)
    WITH (InvoiceNo integer,
          OrderDate datetime,
          RetailerID varchar(30),
          SupplierID varchar(30),
          CustomerRef varchar(40),
          Total money
          )
--Insert line items from XML into LineItems table.
INSERT LineItems
    SELECT * FROM OpenXML(@idoc, 'Invoice/Sale/LineItem', 2)
    WITH (InvoiceNo integer '../@InvoiceNo',
          ProductName varchar(40),
          Quantity int,
          Price money
          )

EXEC sp_xml_removedocument @idoc
END
```

Summary

Throughout this book, I've tried to show how XML is the key to building integrated solutions and how SQL Server 2000's support for XML makes it easier to bridge the gap between the relational format we store data in and the XML format we want to use to exchange that data. In this final chapter, I've shown you a sample application that makes use of the XML-related functionality in SQL Server to integrate multiple organizations and build a flexible e-commerce solution. I've also introduced BizTalk Server and shown how you can use it to build a document messaging solution.

As I said at the beginning of this book, people conduct more and more business on the Internet. As they do so, we can see an increasing need for technologies that allow organizations to integrate with each other and that support the use of multiple devices to access business information. XML is such a technology, and support for XML is becoming a must-have feature for any development environment or server application that will be used to build integrated business solutions. In the past few years, we've seen Microsoft add XML functionality to nearly all of the products the company produces, from established products like SQL Server to brand-new products like BizTalk Server. The challenge now is for us to use these XML-enabled tools to build the business applications that will succeed in the Internet age.

Appendix

Introduction to XML

Although I wrote this book with experienced XML developers in mind, I know that readers from a primarily SQL-based background might need some additional information about XML and related technologies. If you fall into this category, read this appendix before you read the rest of the book. It isn't an exhaustive XML reference, but it does provide enough XML knowledge to help you understand some of the more complex XML-related functionality in SQL Server 2000.

What Is XML?

Way back in the mists of time (around 20 or so years ago), a language called the Standardized General Markup Language (SGML) was developed. SGML is a *metalanguage,* a language for defining markup languages, and although you might not be familiar with SGML itself, you certainly have heard of one of the languages based on it: Hypertext Markup Language (HTML).

HTML is the language of the Web. HTML uses markup tags to encode information so that the information can be parsed (usually by a browser) and displayed. A typical HTML document might contain code similar to this:

```
<P align="center">Welcome to the <STRONG>Northwind</STRONG> Web
    site</P>
```

This HTML code contains two markup tags, <P> and <STRONG>. The tags surround the data to which they apply, and a closing tag such as </STRONG> or </P> indicates the end of the data the tag applies to. The entire data within an opening and closing tag is referred to as an *element.* The <P> tag contains an *align* attribute to provide additional formatting information for the data in the *P* element. Because the tags in HTML are used to format data for presentation, an HTML parser needs to understand what kind of formatting the tags represent. An HTML parser would interpret the preceding example as the following instructions:

1. Start a new paragraph, and align the text to the center of the page (<P align="center">).
2. Display the text *Welcome to the.*

3. Display the text *Northwind* emphatically (<STRONG>Northwind </STRONG>).
4. Display the text *Web site.*
5. End the paragraph (</P>).

To process HTML code like the preceding example, an HTML parser must not only be able to find the HTML tags in a document, it must also know what those tags mean. When a browser renders an HTML document for display, it needs to be able to apply the various formats indicated by the markup tags.

Like HTML, Extensible Markup Language (XML) is also based on SGML, and it too uses markup tags to encode data. The main difference between HTML and XML is that while HTML tags provide formatting instructions that should be applied to the data, XML tags describe the structure of the data itself. For example, an XML order document might look like this:

```
<Order OrderNo="1234">
    <OrderDate>2001-01-01</OrderDate>
    <Customer>Graeme Malcolm</Customer>
    <Item>
        <ProductID>1</ProductID>
        <Quantity>2</Quantity>
    </Item>
    <Item>
        <ProductID>4</ProductID>
        <Quantity>1</Quantity>
    </Item>
</Order>
```

The XML order document contains no formatting information; it contains only data. This means that an XML parser doesn't need to understand the meaning of the tags in an XML document. It needs only to be able to find the tags and verify that the document is in fact an XML document. Because parsers aren't required to understand the tags, any tags can be used. This is why the X in XML stands for *extensible.* (I guess EML wasn't catchy enough!)

> **Note** Attribute values in XML can be enclosed in either double or single quotation marks. For example, you can represent an *Order* element with an *OrderNo* attribute of *1234* using either <Order OrderNo='1234'> or <Order OrderNo='1234'>. To an XML parser, these tags are the same.

XML Tags Up Close

Let's examine some XML tags and see how an XML document is composed. Each tag indicates the beginning of a new element in the document. Elements can have attributes and can contain values and other elements. For example, the *Order* element in the XML order example in the previous section has an *OrderNo* attribute with a value of *1234* and contains the following data:

- An *OrderDate* child element containing the value *2001-01-01*
- A *Customer* child element containing the value *Graeme Malcolm*
- Two *Item* child elements, each containing a *ProductID* child element and a *Quantity* child element

Of course you might need to include an element in your document that doesn't contain anything—for example, if you need to indicate an optional piece of data that hasn't been provided on this occasion. The most obvious way to represent an empty element is simply to place the closing tag immediately after the opening tag, as shown in the *MiddleInitial* element in the following XML customer data:

```
<Customer>
    <FirstName>Graeme</FirstName>
    <MiddleInitial></MiddleInitial>
    <LastName>Malcolm</LastName>
</Customer>
```

This approach to representing an empty element is acceptable, but it results in the unnecessary repetition of the element name. To cut down on the amount of text in your XML document, you can use the shorthand syntax for an empty element: a tag with a slash at the end, as shown in this revised customer data:

```
<Customer>
    <FirstName>Graeme</FirstName>
    <MiddleInitial/>
    <LastName>Malcolm</LastName>
</Customer>
```

Of course, empty elements can still have attributes, as shown in the second *PhoneNumber* element in the following example:

```
<Customer>
    <FirstName>Graeme</FirstName>
    <MiddleInitial/>
    <LastName>Malcolm</LastName>
    <PhoneNumber Location="Home">555 112233</PhoneNumber>
    <PhoneNumber Location="Work"/>
</Customer>
```

Representing Data in an XML Document

XML documents must be well formed and valid. Although these two terms are similar, they refer to two different aspects of verifying an XML document. The term *well formed* indicates that an XML document is suitable for interpretation by an XML parser. In other words, an XML document must follow all the rules for XML documents so that a parser can read it and identify all the elements, attributes, and values it contains. Note that a well-formed document isn't necessarily a useful document in a business process; being well formed merely ensures that the structure of the document is correct. To be suitable for processing in a business solution, the XML document must not only be well formed, but also valid. A document is *valid* if it contains all the data required in a document of that type or class. For example, an order document might be required to contain an *Order* element with an *OrderNo* attribute and an *OrderDate* child element. The parser validates XML documents by comparing the contents of the document to a specification defined for that class of document, which could be in a Document Type Definition (DTD) document or a schema. We'll discuss document validation later in this appendix; first let's look at what it takes to make a well-formed document.

Creating Well-Formed XML

To be well formed, an XML document must obey the following rules:

- There must be a single root element that contains all the other elements in the document.
- Each opening tag must be matched with a corresponding closing tag.
- XML tags are case sensitive, so opening tags must match exactly their corresponding closing tags.
- Each element inside the root element must be wholly nested within its parent element.

The first rule states that to be well formed, an XML document must have a single root element. The following example is *not* a well-formed document because there is no single top-level element:

```
<Product ProductID="1">Chai</Product>
<Product ProductID="2">Chang</Product>
```

An XML document with no root element is known as an XML *fragment.* To make this fragment into a well-formed XML document, we need to add a root element, as shown here:

```
<Catalog>
    <Product ProductID="1">Chai</Product>
    <Product ProductID="2">Chang</Product>
</Catalog>
```

The second rule states that each opening tag must have a corresponding closing tag. In other words, each tag that is opened must be closed. Empty elements indicated with the shorthand tag (<MiddleInitial/>, for example) are considered self-closing. All other tags must have a closing tag. For example, the following document is *not* well formed because it contains an <Item> tag with no matching </Item> tag:

```
<Order>
    <OrderDate>2001-01-01</OrderDate>
    <Customer>Graeme Malcolm</Customer>
    <Item>
        <ProductID>1</ProductID>
        <Quantity>2</Quantity>
    <Item>
        <ProductID>4</ProductID>
        <Quantity>1</Quantity>
    </Item>
</Order>
```

To make this well formed, a closing tag must be added for the first *Item* element, as shown here:

```
<Order>
    <OrderDate>2001-01-01</OrderDate>
    <Customer>Graeme Malcolm</Customer>
    <Item>
        <ProductID>1</ProductID>
        <Quantity>2</Quantity>
    </Item>
    <Item>
        <ProductID>4</ProductID>
        <Quantity>1</Quantity>
    </Item>
</Order>
```

The third rule is that XML tags are case sensitive, so a tag you use to close an element must match the case of the corresponding opening tag. Thus, in an XML document, <Product> isn't the same as <product>, so <Product> can't be closed using </product>. The example at the top of the next page is *not* well formed because a different case is used for the opening and closing tags of the *OrderDate* element.

```
<Order>
    <OrderDate>2001-01-01</Orderdate>
    <Customer>Graeme Malcolm</Customer>
</Order>
```

To be well formed, the case used for all tags must match, as shown in this example:

```
<Order>
    <OrderDate>2001-01-01</OrderDate>
    <Customer>Graeme Malcolm</Customer>
</Order>
```

The final rule states that each element must be contained within its parent. In other words, elements can't overlap. For example, the following document is *not* well formed because a *Category* element overlaps a *Product* element:

```
<Catalog>
    <Category CategoryName="Beverages">
        <Product ProductID="1">
            Chai
        </Category>
    </Product>
</Catalog>
```

To make this document well formed, the *Product* element needs to be closed before the *Category* element, as shown here:

```
<Catalog>
    <Category CategoryName="Beverages">
        <Product ProductID="1">
            Chai
        </Product>
    </Category>
</Catalog>
```

Processing Instructions and Comments

As well as containing data meant for use in a business process, XML documents can contain *processing instructions* to provide additional information to an XML parser and *comments* to provide additional information to a human reader.

Processing instructions are contained within <? and ?> tags. They're commonly used to indicate the version of the XML specification that a document adheres to or to instruct the parser to apply a style sheet. Although processing instructions aren't required to make a document well formed, it's generally good practice to include a processing instruction in the XML prologue before the root element of an XML document to indicate the XML version. The following example shows an XML document with a processing instruction in the prologue:

```
<?xml version="1.0"?>
<Order OrderNo="1234">
    <OrderDate>2001-01-01</OrderDate>
    <Customer>Graeme Malcolm</Customer>
    <Item>
        <ProductID>1</ProductID>
        <Quantity>2</Quantity>
    </Item>
    <Item>
        <ProductID>4</ProductID>
        <Quantity>1</Quantity>
    </Item>
</Order>
```

You can also include comments in an XML document by enclosing them in <!-- and --> tags, as shown in the following example:

```
<?xml version="1.0"?>
<!-- This is a purchase order. -->
<Order OrderNo="1234">
    <OrderDate>2001-01-01</OrderDate>
    <Customer>Graeme Malcolm</Customer>
    <!-- The items in the order are listed here. -->
    <Item>
        <ProductID>1</ProductID>
        <Quantity>2</Quantity>
    </Item>
    <Item>
        <ProductID>4</ProductID>
        <Quantity>1</Quantity>
    </Item>
</Order>
```

Namespaces

Another important concept in XML is the *namespace*. A namespace is a mechanism for allowing two different types of element with the same name in a single XML document. For example, the following order might be taken in a bookstore:

```
<?xml version="1.0"?>
<BookOrder OrderNo="1234">
    <OrderDate>2001-01-01</OrderDate>
    <Customer>
        <Title>Mr.</Title>
        <FirstName>Graeme</FirstName>
        <LastName>Malcolm</LastName>
    </Customer>
```

(continued)

```
    <Book>
        <Title>Treasure Island</Title>
        <Author>Robert Louis Stevenson</Author>
    </Book>
</BookOrder>
```

Close inspection of this document reveals a possible source of confusion. The document has two *Title* elements, but they represent two different things. The *Customer* element contains a *Title* element to identity the title of the customer (Mr., Mrs., Ms., Dr., and so on). The *Book* element also contains a *Title* element, but this element identifies the title of the book.

To prevent confusion, you can use namespaces to distinguish between different elements of the same name. A namespace associates elements or attributes with a unique identifier known as a Universal Resource Identifier (URI). A URI can be a URL or some other universally unique identifier. The namespace doesn't actually need to reference an actual Internet location; it just needs to be unique.

Declaring and Using Namespaces

You can declare namespaces in any element by using the *xmlns* attribute. You can declare a default namespace that will apply to the contents of the element in which you make the declaration. For example, the book order document could be rewritten as shown here:

```
<?xml version="1.0"?>
<BookOrder OrderNo="1234">
    <OrderDate>2001-01-01</OrderDate>
    <Customer xmlns="http://www.northwindtraders.com/customer">
        <Title>Mr.</Title>
        <FirstName>Graeme</FirstName>
        <LastName>Malcolm</LastName>
    </Customer>
    <Book xmlns="http://www.northwindtraders.com/book">
        <Title>Treasure Island</Title>
        <Author>Robert Louis Stevenson</Author>
    </Book>
</BookOrder>
```

This solves our duplicate name problem because all the elements in the *Customer* element belong to the *http://www.northwindtraders.com/customer* namespace while the elements in the *Book* element belong to the *http://www.northwindtraders.com/book* namespace.

However, what if we need to have a document containing multiple books or customers? Continually changing the default namespace throughout the document would soon become confusing. An alternative approach is to declare explicit abbreviations for multiple namespaces and to add as prefixes to element names the appropriate namespace abbreviation. With this approach, it is common to declare in the root element all the namespaces that will be used:

```
<?xml version="1.0"?>
<BookOrder xmlns="http://www.northwindtraders.com/order"
    xmlns:cust="http://www.northwindtraders.com/customer"
    xmlns:book="http://www.northwindtraders.com/book"
        OrderNo="1234">
    <OrderDate>2001-01-01</OrderDate>
    <cust:Customer>
        <cust:Title>Mr.</cust:Title>
        <cust:FirstName>Graeme</cust:FirstName>
        <cust:LastName>Malcolm</cust:LastName>
    </cust:Customer>
    <book:Book>
        <book:Title>Treasure Island</book:Title>
        <book:Author>Robert Louis Stevenson</book:Author>
    </book:Book>
</BookOrder>
```

Now the document references three namespaces: a default namespace of *http://www.northwindtraders.com/order*, the *http://www.northwindtraders.com/customer* namespace (abbreviated as *cust*), and the *http://www.northwindtraders.com/book* namespace (abbreviated as *book*). Elements and attributes with no abbreviations, such as *BookOrder*, *OrderNo*, and *OrderDate*, are assumed to belong to the default namespace. To indicate that an element or attribute belongs to a namespace other than the default, the abbreviation for the namespace is included in the element or attribute name.

Later in this appendix we'll see how to use namespaces to validate XML documents by referencing schemas, but for now let's look at how to process data in an XML document.

Navigating XML Documents with XPath

We've seen how easy it is to represent business data by using an XML document. The next step is to understand how an application processes that data. Of course, to process the data in an XML document, an application needs a way to navigate the document to retrieve the values from the document's elements and attributes. This is what XPath is designed for. In this section I'll cover some of the fundamentals of XPath. For a complete reference, view the specification at *http://www.w3c.org/TR/xpath*.

XPath provides a syntax for addressing the data in an XML document by treating the document as a tree of nodes. Each element, attribute, or value in the document is represented as a node in the tree, and XPath expressions are used to identify the node or nodes you want to process. To understand how this works, let's take a simple XML document as an example:

```
<?xml version="1.0"?>
<Order OrderNo="1234">
    <OrderDate>2001-01-01</OrderDate>
    <Customer>Graeme Malcolm</Customer>
    <Item>
        <Product ProductID="1" UnitPrice="18">Chai</Product>
        <Quantity>2</Quantity>
    </Item>
    <Item>
        <Product ProductID="2" UnitPrice="19">Chang</Product>
        <Quantity>1</Quantity>
    </Item>
</Order>
```

Figure A1-1 shows a node tree that could represent this document.

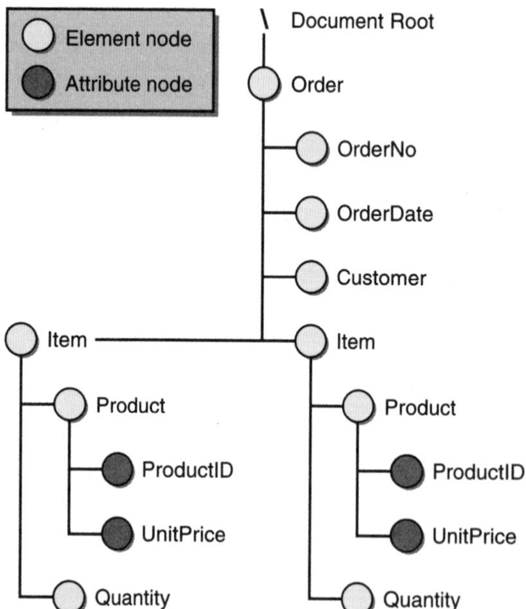

Figure A1-1 XML node tree

You can use XPath expressions to define location paths to nodes in the tree or to return a node or set of nodes that meet specified criteria. The expressions can be absolute paths or they can be relative to the currently selected node (known as the *context* node).

Specifying a Location Path

You can express XPath location paths by using either unabbreviated or abbreviated syntax. Both syntaxes define the root of the document by using a backslash (/) and allow forward and backward navigation through the nodes in the tree.

Absolute Location Paths

Let's examine some absolute location paths in the node tree produced by the order document described earlier. To select the *Order* element node by using unabbreviated syntax, we would use the following XPath expression:

```
/child::Order
```

Translated into abbreviated syntax, this expression becomes:

```
/Order
```

To drill further down into the document, we could retrieve the *Customer* node by using the following unabbreviated XPath expression:

```
/child::Order/child::Customer
```

Here's the abbreviated equivalent:

```
/Order/Customer
```

If you want to retrieve an attribute node, you must indicate this by using the *attribute* keyword in unabbreviated syntax or the @ character in abbreviated syntax. To retrieve the *OrderNo* attribute of the *Order* element, use the following unabbreviated syntax:

```
/child::Order/attribute::OrderNo
```

The abbreviated syntax for the *OrderNo* attribute is

```
/Order/@OrderNo
```

To retrieve descendant nodes—that is, nodes anywhere farther down the hierarchy—you can use the *descendant* keyword in unabbreviated syntax or a double slash (//) in abbreviated syntax. For example, to retrieve all the *Product* nodes in the order document, you could specify the following unabbreviated location path:

```
/child::Order/descendant::Product
```

The abbreviated equivalent is

```
/Order//Product
```

You can use wildcards to indicate nodes whose names aren't relevant. For example, the asterisk (*) wildcard indicates that any node name can be used. The following unabbreviated location path selects all the child elements of *Order*:

```
/child::Order/child::*
```

The equivalent abbreviated syntax is

```
/Order/*
```

Relative Location Paths

XPath location paths are often relative to a context node, in which case the path describes how to retrieve a node or set of nodes relative to the current one. For example, if the first *Item* element in the order document is the context node, the relative location path to retrieve the *Quantity* child element is

```
child::Quantity
```

In abbreviated syntax, the relative location path is

```
Quantity
```

Similarly, to retrieve the *ProductID* attribute of the *Product* child element, the location path is

```
child::Product/attribute::ProductID
```

This path translates to

```
Product/@ProductID
```

To navigate back up the tree, use the *parent* keyword. The abbreviated equivalent for this keyword is a double period (..). For example, if the context node is the *OrderDate* element, the *OrderNo* can be retrieved from the *Order* element using the following location path:

```
parent::Order/attribute::OrderNo
```

Note that this syntax will return a value only if the parent node is called *Order*. To retrieve the *OrderNo* attribute from the parent regardless of its name, you have to use the following unabbreviated syntax:

```
parent::*/attribute::OrderNo
```

The abbreviated version is simpler because you don't need to provide a specific identifier for the parent. The parent of the context node is simply referred to by using the double period, as shown here:

```
../@OrderNo
```

In addition, you can reference the context node itself by using either the *self* keyword or a single period. This can be useful in a number of circumstances, especially when you must determine the currently selected node.

Using Criteria in Location Paths

You can limit the nodes returned using an XPath expression by including search criteria in the location path. The criteria for the node or nodes to be returned are appended to the location path in square brackets.

For example, to retrieve all the *Product* elements with a *UnitPrice* attribute greater than 18, you can use the following XPath expression:

```
/child::Order/child::Item/child::Product[attribute::UnitPrice>18]
```

In abbreviated syntax, you can use the following expression:

```
/Order/Item/Product[@UnitPrice>18]
```

The criteria include a relative path to the node being retrieved, so you can use nodes from anywhere in the hierarchy in your criteria. The following example retrieves the *Item* nodes where the *Product* child element has a *ProductID* attribute of 1:

```
/child::Order/child::Item[child::Product/attribute::ProductID=1]
```

The abbreviated syntax for this expression is shown here:

```
/Order/Item[Product/@ProductID=1]
```

Now that you understand how to use XPath expressions to locate data in an XML document, you're ready to examine one of the most commonly used XML-related technologies, Extensible Stylesheet Language (XSL).

XSL Style Sheets

XML is a great way to describe data in order to exchange it between applications and organizations. However, as part of a business process the data in an XML document will likely need to be represented in a different format before it can be processed or presented. XSL is a language that you can use to transform an XML document into a different format, such as HTML, Wireless Markup Language (WML), or even an alternative XML representation. XSL was originally designed as a way to present XML data as HTML. However, it soon became clear that XML could be transformed to any output format. An enhanced version of XSL known as XSL Transformations (XSLT) has therefore evolved.

This section doesn't provide an exhaustive guide to XSL syntax, but it gives you enough information to start using XSL style sheets to process XML data. For a complete XSL reference, visit *http://www.w3.org/Style/XSL*.

XSL Style Sheet Documents

XSL documents define *style sheets* that you can apply to XML documents. A style sheet contains instructions that tell an XML parser how to generate an output document based on data in an XML document. The XSL style sheet is itself a well-formed XML document that contains XSL commands merged with literal output text.

For the parser to recognize the commands in an XSL document, you must declare a namespace in the root element, usually with the prefix *xsl*. One of two common namespaces is used in a style sheet: the original XSL namespace (*http://www.w3.org/TR/WD-xsl*) or the XSLT namespace (*http://www.w3.org/1999/XSL/Transform*). The Microsoft XML parser version 3.0 (MSXML3) supports both namespaces. However, you need to install MSXML3 in Replace mode by using a tool named Xmlinst.exe to enable support for the XSLT namespace in Internet Explorer 5.*x*. (Otherwise, Internet Explorer will use MSXML 2.5, which doesn't support the XSLT namespace.)

The root element in an XSL document is usually a *stylesheet* element. This element contains one or more *template* elements that are matched to specific XML data in the XML document being processed, such as the order document shown here:

```
<?xml version="1.0"?>
<Order OrderNo="1234">
    <OrderDate>2001-01-01</OrderDate>
    <Customer>Graeme Malcolm</Customer>
    <Item>
        <Product ProductID="1" UnitPrice="18">Chai</Product>
        <Quantity>2</Quantity>
    </Item>
    <Item>
        <Product ProductID="2" UnitPrice="19">Chang</Product>
        <Quantity>1</Quantity>
    </Item>
</Order>
```

Because an XSL style sheet is an XML document itself, it must obey all the rules for well-formed XML. The following example is a simple XSL style sheet that could be applied to the order document:

```
<?xml version="1.0"?>
<xsl:stylesheet xmlns:xsl="http://www.w3.org/1999/XSL/Transform"
```

```
    version="1.0">
    <xsl:template match="/">
        <HTML>
            <HEAD>
                <TITLE>Northwind Web Page</TITLE>
            </HEAD>
            <BODY>
                <P>Customer Order</P>
            </BODY>
        </HTML>
    </xsl:template>
</xsl:stylesheet>
```

This style sheet is based on the XSLT namespace and contains a single template that is applied to the root of an XML document and to all the elements within it. The actual template consists of a series of HTML tags that will appear in the output. This template doesn't actually do anything very useful; it simply outputs a hard-coded HTML document with none of the XML data from the input document merged into the results. To merge XML data into the template, you need to use some XSL commands.

The *value-of* Command

XSL defines a number of processing commands that are useful for extracting data from an XML document and merging it into an output document. The most basic of these commands (yet one of the most useful) is the *value-of* command. The *value-of* command selects a specific element or attribute value from the XML and merges it with the results. A *select* attribute is used with *value-of* to specify the XPath to the XML data you want to extract, so we could enhance the style sheet described earlier to include some data from the XML order document, as shown here:

```
<?xml version="1.0"?>
<xsl:stylesheet xmlns:xsl="http://www.w3.org/1999/XSL/Transform"
    version="1.0">
    <xsl:template match="/">
        <HTML>
            <HEAD>
                <TITLE>Northwind Web Page</TITLE>
            </HEAD>
            <BODY>
                <P>Customer Order</P>
                <P>Order No: <xsl:value-of select="Order/@OrderNo"/></P>
                <P>Date: <xsl:value-of select="Order/OrderDate"/></P>
                <P>Customer: <xsl:value-of select="Order/Customer"/></P>
            </BODY>
        </HTML>
    </xsl:template>
</xsl:stylesheet>
```

This version of the style sheet retrieves the *OrderNo* attribute and the *OrderDate* and *Customer* element values from the *Order* element by using an XPath location path. Notice that the XPath expressions are relative to the context node identified in the *template* element's *match* parameter (in this case the root element).

Applying the above style sheet to the XML order document we discussed earlier produces the following HTML. I'll explain how to apply a style sheet to an XML document later in this appendix.

```
<HTML>
    <HEAD>
        <TITLE>Northwind Web Page</TITLE>
    </HEAD>
    <BODY>
        <P>Customer Order</P>
        <P>Order No: 1234</P>
        <P>Date: 2001-01-01</P>
        <P>Customer: Graeme Malcolm</P>
    </BODY>
</HTML>
```

The *for-each* Command

In an XML document, multiple elements of the same name are commonly used to represent a list of entities. For example, our order document contains two *Item* elements to represent the two products being ordered. Most programming languages provide a mechanism for iterating, or *looping,* through a series of data entries. XSL is no exception. You can use the *for-each* command to loop through a collection of similarly named nodes, using a *select* attribute to identify the nodes you want to process.

For example, we could further enhance our style sheet to list each item in the order as an entry in a table:

```
<?xml version="1.0"?>
<xsl:stylesheet xmlns:xsl="http://www.w3.org/1999/XSL/Transform"
    version="1.0">
    <xsl:template match="/">
        <HTML>
            <HEAD>
                <TITLE>Northwind Web Page</TITLE>
            </HEAD>
            <BODY>
                <P>Customer Order</P>
                <P>Order No: <xsl:value-of select="Order/@OrderNo"/></P>
                <P>Date: <xsl:value-of select="Order/OrderDate"/></P>
                <P>Customer: <xsl:value-of select="Order/Customer"/></P>
                <TABLE Border="0">
```

```
                    <TR>
                        <TD>ProductID</TD>
                        <TD>Product Name</TD>
                        <TD>Price</TD>
                        <TD>Quantity Ordered</TD>
                    </TR>
                    <xsl:for-each select="Order/Item">
                        <TR>
                            <TD><xsl:value-of select="Product/@ProductID"/>
                            </TD>
                            <TD><xsl:value-of select="Product"/></TD>
                            <TD><xsl:value-of select="Product/@UnitPrice"/>
                            </TD>
                            <TD><xsl:value-of select="Quantity"/></TD>
                        </TR>
                    </xsl:for-each>
                </TABLE>
            </BODY>
        </HTML>
    </xsl:template>
</xsl:stylesheet>
```

In this version of the style sheet, the parser is told to loop through each *Item* element and extract the *ProductID* and *UnitPrice* attributes of the product element, as well as the values of the *Product* and *Quantity* elements, into a table. Notice that the relative XPath expression uses the node identified in the *for-each* command as the context node. (In this case it's the *Item* node.) Indicate the end of the loop by closing the *for-each* element. The preceding style sheet produces the following HTML when applied to the XML order document discussed earlier:

```
<HTML>
    <HEAD>
        <TITLE>Northwind Web Page</TITLE>
    </HEAD>
    <BODY>
        <P>Customer Order</P>
        <P>Order No: 1234</P>
        <P>Date: 2001-01-01</P>
        <P>Customer: Graeme Malcolm</P>
        <TABLE Border="0">
            <TR>
                <TD>ProductID</TD>
                <TD>Product Name</TD>
                <TD>Price</TD>
                <TD>Quantity Ordered</TD>
            </TR>
```

(continued)

```
            <TR>
                <TD>1</TD>
                <TD>Chai</TD>
                <TD>18</TD>
                <TD>2</TD>
            </TR>
            <TR>
                <TD>2</TD>
                <TD>Chang</TD>
                <TD>19</TD>
                <TD>1</TD>
            </TR>
        </TABLE>
    </BODY>
</HTML>
```

Generating Attributes with the *attribute* Command

Sometimes you might want to create an attribute in the output document that contains a value from the XML document being processed. For example, suppose that for each product name, you want to create a hyperlink that passes the *ProductID* to another Web page where you can display the details of that product. To create a hyperlink in an HTML document, you need to generate an *A* element containing an *href* attribute. You can use the *attribute* command to create an attribute, as shown in the following example:

```
<?xml version="1.0"?>
<xsl:stylesheet xmlns:xsl="http://www.w3.org/1999/XSL/Transform"
    version="1.0">
    <xsl:template match="/">
        <HTML>
            <HEAD>
                <TITLE>Northwind Web Page</TITLE>
            </HEAD>
            <BODY>
                <P>Customer Order</P>
                <P>Order No: <xsl:value-of select="Order/@OrderNo"/></P>
                <P>Date: <xsl:value-of select="Order/OrderDate"/></P>
                <P>Customer: <xsl:value-of select="Order/Customer"/></P>
                <TABLE Border="0">
                    <TR>
                        <TD>ProductID</TD>
                        <TD>Product Name</TD>
                        <TD>Price</TD>
                        <TD>Quantity Ordered</TD>
                    </TR>
                    <xsl:for-each select="Order/Item">
```

```
                    <TR>
                        <TD><xsl:value-of select="Product/@ProductID"/>
                        </TD>
                        <TD>
                            <A>
                                <xsl:attribute name="HREF">
                                Products.asp?ProductID=<xsl:value-of
                                    select="Product/@ProductID"/>
                                </xsl:attribute>
                                <xsl:value-of select="Product"/>
                            </A>
                        </TD>
                        <TD><xsl:value-of select="Product/@UnitPrice"/>
                        </TD>
                        <TD><xsl:value-of select="Quantity"/></TD>
                    </TR>
                </xsl:for-each>
            </TABLE>
        </BODY>
    </HTML>
  </xsl:template>
</xsl:stylesheet>
```

Applying this style sheet to the XML order document results in the following HTML:

```
<HTML>
    <HEAD>
        <TITLE>Northwind Web Page</TITLE>
    </HEAD>
    <BODY>
        <P>Customer Order</P>
        <P>Order No: 1234</P>
        <P>Date: 2001-01-01</P>
        <P>Customer: Graeme Malcolm</P>
        <TABLE Border="0">
            <TR>
                <TD>ProductID</TD>
                <TD>Product Name</TD>
                <TD>Price</TD>
                <TD>Quantity Ordered</TD>
            </TR>
            <TR>
                <TD>1</TD>
                <TD><A HREF="Products.asp?ProductID=1">Chai</A></TD>
                <TD>18</TD>
                <TD>2</TD>
            </TR>
```

(continued)

```
                <TR>
                    <TD>2</TD>
                    <TD><A HREF="Products.asp?ProductID=2">Chang</A></TD>
                    <TD>19</TD>
                    <TD>1</TD>
                </TR>
            </TABLE>
        </BODY>
</HTML>
```

Using Multiple Templates in a Style Sheet

So far all the style sheets we've seen include a single template that's applied to the root element of the document. XSL also allows us to use multiple templates in a single style sheet. You might want to do this for two reasons. First, you can easily separate the presentation logic for individual parts of the document, making it easier to debug or change your style sheets. Second, you can use XPath expressions to apply different formatting to XML data depending on the value of the data. When a style sheet contains multiple templates, you incorporate them into the presentation logic by using the *apply-templates* command. Usually you create a top-level template to process the document as a whole and use the *apply-templates* command to process elements within the scope of the top-level template. The additional templates can be called at any point, and the top-level template renders any data that isn't consumed by the additional templates. For example, the following style sheet includes multiple templates: a top-level template that applies to the root of the document, a template for *Product* elements with a *UnitPrice* attribute with a value greater than 18, a template for all other *Product* elements, and a template for *Quantity* elements:

```
<?xml version="1.0"?>
<xsl:stylesheet xmlns:xsl="http://www.w3.org/1999/XSL/Transform"
    version="1.0">
    <xsl:template match="/">
        <HTML>
            <HEAD>
                <TITLE>Northwind Web Page</TITLE>
            </HEAD>
            <BODY>
                <P>Customer Order</P>
                <P>Order No: <xsl:value-of select="Order/@OrderNo"/></P>
                <P>Date: <xsl:value-of select="Order/OrderDate"/></P>
                <P>Customer: <xsl:value-of select="Order/Customer"/></P>
                <TABLE Border="0">
                    <TR>
                        <TD>ProductID</TD>
                        <TD>Product Name</TD>
```

```
                    <TD>Price</TD>
                    <TD>Quantity Ordered</TD>
                </TR>
                <xsl:for-each select="Order/Item">
                    <TR>
                        <xsl:apply-templates/>
                    </TR>
                </xsl:for-each>
            </TABLE>
        </BODY>
    </HTML>
</xsl:template>

<xsl:template match="Product[@UnitPrice > 18]">
    <TD><xsl:value-of select="@ProductID"/></TD>
    <TD>
        <A>
            <xsl:attribute name="HREF">
            Products.asp?ProductID=<xsl:value-of select="@ProductID"/>
            </xsl:attribute>
            <xsl:value-of select="."/>
        </A>
    </TD>
    <TD>
        <FONT color="red">
            <xsl:value-of select="@UnitPrice"/>
        </FONT>
    </TD>
</xsl:template>

<xsl:template match="Product">
    <TD><xsl:value-of select="@ProductID"/></TD>
    <TD>
        <A>
            <xsl:attribute name="HREF">
            Products.asp?ProductID=<xsl:value-of select="@ProductID"/>
            </xsl:attribute>
            <xsl:value-of select="."/>
        </A>
    </TD>
    <TD><xsl:value-of select="@UnitPrice"/></TD>
</xsl:template>

<xsl:template match="Quantity">
    <TD><xsl:value-of select="."/></TD>
</xsl:template>

</xsl:stylesheet>
```

Applying this template to the XML order document described earlier results in the following HTML:

```
<HTML>
    <HEAD>
        <TITLE>Northwind Web Page</TITLE>
    </HEAD>
    <BODY>
        <P>Customer Order</P>
        <P>Order No: 1234</P>
        <P>Date: 2001-01-01</P>
        <P>Customer: Graeme Malcolm</P>
        <TABLE Border="0">
            <TR>
                <TD>ProductID</TD>
                <TD>Product Name</TD>
                <TD>Price</TD>
                <TD>Quantity Ordered</TD>
            </TR>
            <TR>
                <TD>1</TD>
                <TD><A HREF="Products.asp?ProductID=1">Chai</A></TD>
                <TD>18</TD>
                <TD>2</TD>
            </TR>
            <TR>
                <TD>2</TD>
                <TD><A HREF="Products.asp?ProductID=2">Chang</A></TD>
                <TD><FONT color="red">19</FONT></TD>
                <TD>1</TD>
            </TR>
        </TABLE>
    </BODY>
</HTML>
```

Applying Style Sheets

Now that you know how to create a style sheet, you need to understand how to apply a style sheet to an XML document. Applying a style sheet is a function of an XML parser. You can instruct the parser to apply a style sheet either by including a processing instruction in the XML document itself or by using some programmatic logic.

To include a style sheet–processing directive in an XML document, you simply need to add an *xml-stylesheet* processing instruction, as shown in the following example:

```
<?xml version="1.0"?>
<?xml-stylesheet type="text/xsl" href="Order.xsl"?>
<Order OrderNo="1234">
    <OrderDate>2001-01-01</OrderDate>
    <Customer>Graeme Malcolm</Customer>
    <Item>
        <Product ProductID="1" UnitPrice="18">Chai</Product>
        <Quantity>2</Quantity>
    </Item>
    <Item>
        <Product ProductID="2" UnitPrice="19">Chang</Product>
        <Quantity>1</Quantity>
    </Item>
</Order>
```

When an XML parser reads this document, the *xml-stylesheet* processing instruction tells the parser to apply the Order.xsl style sheet. The *type* attribute indicates the kind of style sheet to be applied, such as an XSL style sheet or a cascading style sheet (CSS). The *href* attribute specifies the absolute or relative path to the style sheet file. Opening a document such as this with an XML-aware browser such as Internet Explorer 5.5 causes the XML parser to load the style sheet and render the XML data accordingly.

The process of applying a style sheet varies programmatically from parser to parser. If you use the Microsoft XML parser, the document is loaded into a *Microsoft.XMLDom* object and the *transformNode* method is used to apply a style sheet loaded in another *XMLDom* object. For example, the following code could be used to apply a style sheet named Order.xsl to an XML document named Order.xml:

```
Dim objXML
Dim objXSL
Dim strResult

'Load the XML document.
Set objXML = CreateObject("Microsoft.XMLDom")
objXML.Async = False
objXML.Load "c:\Order.xml"

'Load the XSL style sheet.
Set objXSL = CreateObject("Microsoft.XMLDom")
objXSL.Async = False
objXSL.Load "c:\Order.xsl"

'Apply the style sheet.
strResult = objXML.transformNode(objXSL)
```

When this code has completed, *strResult* contains the output produced by the style sheet.

XML Data Schemas

One final XML-related technology that you should be aware of is the use of schemas to validate XML data. To understand what I mean by validate, consider the following scenario:

Company A is a retailer who wants to order goods from company B. To do this, companies A and B agree to exchange an XML order document. Company A sends an XML document containing order information to company B. When company B receives the order, the order must contain certain key pieces of information, such as products required, quantities required, and so on. Company B doesn't want to start processing the order if that information isn't there. In fact, if any of the required information is missing, the order can't be processed because it is invalid.

In this scenario, companies A and B need to agree beforehand on what information an order document must include. Then both companies must work according to a common definition that they can refer to in order to ensure that the documents being exchanged are valid based on this common definition.

A schema is an XML document that contains the definition for a particular type of XML document. You and your trading partners can create schemas to define the business documents you will exchange, thus guaranteeing that you can always refer to a common specification to ensure document validity. Schemas are a more flexible approach to solving the problem of document validation than an older technology called Document Type Definitions (DTDs). This section will discuss some of the important aspects of schemas. For a full explanation of schemas, consult the MSDN library at *http://msdn.microsoft.com/library*.

The syntax used to create schemas isn't yet fully approved by the World Wide Web Consortium (W3C). When the final specification is published, Microsoft is committed to supporting it in its products. Meanwhile, Microsoft does support a subset of a syntax named XML-Data, which was submitted as a proposal to the W3C in 1998. This subset is known as XML-Data Reduced (XDR).

Creating an XDR Schema

An XDR schema is an XML document containing declarations of the elements and attributes that can be used in an XML document based on that schema. The schema can also dictate the data types of the elements and attributes, the order in which these elements and attributes must appear, the minimum and maximum lengths of their values, and the minimum and maximum occurrences of these elements and attributes within a document. Furthermore, it can determine whether additional elements and attributes not defined in the schema can be included in a document based on that schema.

Schemas are based on the *xml-data* namespace. The *xml-data* namespace defines the syntax used to declare elements and attributes in a schema. The top-level element in a schema is the *schema* element, which can contain an optional *name* attribute. A minimal schema is shown here:

```
<?xml version="1.0"?>
<Schema name="orderschema"
    xmlns="urn:schemas-microsoft-com:xml-data">
</Schema>
```

Of course, this schema is fairly useless because it doesn't actually contain any declarations. To define a valid XML document, we must add element and attribute declarations to the schema. You declare elements and attributes by using the *ElementType* and *AttributeType* keywords. Elements are declared at the top level of the schema, while attributes can be declared globally, in which case the same attribute can be used in multiple elements or scoped locally within an element declaration. Once you've declared an element or an attribute, you can define an instance by using the *element* or *attribute* keyword.

Note Remember that XML is case sensitive. You *must* use the correct case for the *ElementType*, *AttributeType*, *element*, and *attribute* keywords.

The following example shows a schema that declares elements and attributes for an XML order document:

```
<?xml version="1.0"?>
<Schema name="orderschema"
    xmlns="urn:schemas-microsoft-com:xml-data">

    <ElementType name="OrderDate"/>
    <ElementType name="Customer"/>
    <ElementType name="Product">
        <AttributeType name="ProductID"/>
        <AttributeType name="UnitPrice"/>
        <attribute type="ProductID"/>
        <attribute type="UnitPrice"/>
    </ElementType>
```

(continued)

```
    <ElementType name="Quantity"/>
    <ElementType name="Item">
        <element type="Product"/>
        <element type="Quantity"/>
    </ElementType>

    <ElementType name="Order">
        <AttributeType name="OrderNo"/>
        <attribute type="OrderNo"/>
        <element type="OrderDate"/>
        <element type="Customer"/>
        <element type="Item"/>
    </ElementType>
</Schema>
```

Each element in the order document is declared in the schema. The first two element declarations, the *OrderDate* and *Customer* elements, are relatively simple, but the declaration for the *Product* element bears closer scrutiny. The *Product* element declaration includes two *AttributeType* declarations to specify the attributes that will be used in this element. The *attribute* keyword is then used to define an instance of a single attribute of each type declared in the element.

Next, the *Quantity* element is declared, followed by a declaration of the *Item* element, which contains an instance of the *Product* element and an instance of the *Quantity* element. Finally, the *Order* element is declared. This element contains an attribute declaration for the *OrderNo* attribute, and instances of the *OrderNo* attribute and the *OrderDate*, *Customer*, and *Item* child elements. An XML order document based on this schema could look like the following example:

```
<?xml version="1.0"?>
<Order OrderNo="1234">
    <OrderDate>2001-01-01</OrderDate>
    <Customer>Graeme Malcolm</Customer>
    <Item>
        <Product ProductID="1" UnitPrice="18">Chai</Product>
        <Quantity>2</Quantity>
    </Item>
    <Item>
        <Product ProductID="2" UnitPrice="19">Chang</Product>
        <Quantity>1</Quantity>
    </Item>
</Order>
```

Specifying a Content Model

By default, the content model for an XDR schema is *open*, meaning that elements and attributes not defined in the schema can still be included in documents based on the schema. For example, the following document could be based on the schema we defined earlier and would be considered valid, even though it includes a *DeliveryDate* element that isn't defined in the schema:

```
<?xml version="1.0"?>
<Order OrderNo="1234">
    <OrderDate>2001-01-01</OrderDate>
    <Customer>Graeme Malcolm</Customer>
    <DeliveryDate>2001-02-02</DeliveryDate>
    <Item>
        <Product ProductID="1" UnitPrice="18">Chai</Product>
        <Quantity>2</Quantity>
    </Item>
    <Item>
        <Product ProductID="2" UnitPrice="19">Chang</Product>
        <Quantity>1</Quantity>
    </Item>
</Order>
```

You can set the content model of each element in the schema by specifying a *model* attribute with a value of *open* or *closed*. For example, the schema could be enhanced to limit the possible elements and attributes by specifying a closed content model for each element, as shown here:

```
<?xml version="1.0"?>
<Schema name="orderschema"
    xmlns="urn:schemas-microsoft-com:xml-data">
    <ElementType name="OrderDate" model="closed"/>
    <ElementType name="Customer" model="closed"/>

    <ElementType name="Product" model="closed">
        <AttributeType name="ProductID"/>
        <AttributeType name="UnitPrice"/>
        <attribute type="ProductID"/>
        <attribute type="UnitPrice"/>
    </ElementType>

    <ElementType name="Quantity" model="closed"/>
    <ElementType name="Item" model="closed">
        <element type="Product"/>
        <element type="Quantity"/>
    </ElementType>

    <ElementType name="Order" model="closed">
        <AttributeType name="OrderNo"/>
        <attribute type="OrderNo"/>
        <element type="OrderDate"/>
        <element type="Customer"/>
        <element type="Item"/>
    </ElementType>
</Schema>
```

This subtle alteration ensures that a document based on this schema must contain *only* the elements and attributes defined in the schema. No additional data is allowed.

Limiting the Content of an Element

Elements can contain text values and subelements. You can use the *content* attribute in a schema to limit the kind of data that can be used in an element. You can use the following values for the *content* attribute:

- ***textOnly*** Only text is allowed.
- ***eltOnly*** Only subelements are allowed.
- ***mixed*** Both text and subelements are allowed.
- ***empty*** The element must not contain any text or subelements.

The following enhanced order schema shows how you can use the *content* attribute to limit the types of XML data representation allowed in an XML document:

```
<?xml version="1.0"?>
<Schema name="orderschema"
    xmlns="urn:schemas-microsoft-com:xml-data">

    <ElementType name="OrderDate" model="closed" content="textOnly"/>
    <ElementType name="Customer" model="closed" content="textOnly"/>

    <ElementType name="Product" model="closed" content="mixed">
        <AttributeType name="ProductID"/>
        <AttributeType name="UnitPrice"/>
        <attribute type="ProductID"/>
        <attribute type="UnitPrice"/>
    </ElementType>

    <ElementType name="Quantity" model="closed" content="textOnly"/>
    <ElementType name="Item" model="closed" content="eltOnly">
        <element type="Product"/>
        <element type="Quantity"/>
    </ElementType>

    <ElementType name="Order" model="closed" content="mixed">
        <AttributeType name="OrderNo"/>
        <attribute type="OrderNo"/>
        <element type="OrderDate"/>
        <element type="Customer"/>
        <element type="Item"/>
    </ElementType>
</Schema>
```

In this version of the schema, the *OrderDate*, *Customer*, and *Quantity* elements can contain only text, while the *Item* element can contain only subelements.

Determining the Required Occurrences of Data

Another important constraint you can enforce by using schemas is the definition of what data is required in a document and what the minimum and maximum occurrences of each piece of data are. You can omit elements and attributes declared in a schema from documents based on the schema or they can appear multiple times. To define the rules for data occurrence use the *required*, *default*, *minOccurs*, and *maxOccurs* attributes.

Requiring Attributes

An attribute can appear only once in its parent element, so the question of minimum or maximum occurrences is academic—either the attribute appears or it doesn't. You can force the inclusion of an attribute by specifying a *required* attribute with a value of *yes*. The parser will consider invalid any documents that omit the attribute.

You can also specify a default value for an attribute. This value is used when the attribute is omitted in a document based on the schema. To declare a default value you must use the *default* attribute in the instance of the attribute for which you want to define a default value. Note that the default declaration goes in the instance tag for the attribute (*attribute*), rather than the declaration (*AttributeType*).

Limiting Occurrences of Elements

To control the number of times an element can be used in a document based on the schema, use the *minOccurs* and *maxOccurs* attributes. These attributes take an integer value to define how many times the element can appear or a wildcard asterisk (*) value to specify that it can appear an infinite number of times. To ensure that an element appears in the document, set the *minOccurs* attribute to 1. You can use the *maxOccurs* attribute to specify the maximum number of instances allowed for a particular element.

The following example shows how you can use a schema to constrain the occurrences of attributes and elements:

```
<?xml version="1.0"?>
<Schema name="orderschema"
    xmlns="urn:schemas-microsoft-com:xml-data">

    <ElementType name="OrderDate" model="closed" content="textOnly"/>
    <ElementType name="Customer" model="closed" content="textOnly"/>
```

(continued)

```
    <ElementType name="Product" model="closed" content="mixed">
        <AttributeType name="ProductID" required="yes"/>
        <AttributeType name="UnitPrice"/>
        <attribute type="ProductID"/>
        <attribute type="UnitPrice" default="10.00"/>
    </ElementType>

    <ElementType name="Quantity" model="closed" content="textOnly"/>
    <ElementType name="Item" model="closed" content="eltOnly">
        <element type="Product" minOccurs="1" maxOccurs="1"/>
        <element type="Quantity" minOccurs="1" maxOccurs="1"/>
    </ElementType>

    <ElementType name="Order" model="closed" content="mixed">
        <AttributeType name="OrderNo" required="yes"/>
        <attribute type="OrderNo"/>
        <element type="OrderDate" minOccurs="1" maxOccurs="1"/>
        <element type="Customer" minOccurs="1" maxOccurs="1"/>
        <element type="Item" minOccurs="1" maxOccurs="*"/>
    </ElementType>
</Schema>
```

In this schema, the *OrderNo* attribute of the *Order* element and the *ProductID* attribute of the *Product* element are both required. The *UnitPrice* attribute of the *Product* element has a default value of *10.00*. The *Product* and *Quantity* elements in an *Item* element must appear exactly once, as must the *OrderDate* and *Customer* elements in the *Order* element. The *Item* element, however, must appear a minimum of once, but can appear as many times as necessary.

Specifying Data Types

You can use a schema to define the data types of the elements and attributes in a valid XML document. This ensures that the data exchanged in XML documents can be processed correctly, and helps minimize the chance of an error caused by invalid data. To specify data types, your schema must refer to the *datatypes* namespace. Supported data types for elements include the primitive XML data types specified by the W3C (*string*, *id*, *idref*, *idrefs*, *entity*, *entities*, *nmtoken*, *nmtokens*, and *notation*) as well as more common data types such as *boolean*, *char*, *dateTime*, *int*, *float*, and others. You can declare attributes as XML primitive types, including *enumeration*, and the common data types.

> **Note** Earlier versions of the Microsoft XML parser supported only a subset of data types for attributes. For full support make sure you are using the latest version of the parser.

The following schema shows how to declare data types for elements and attributes:

```
<?xml version="1.0"?>
<Schema name="orderschema"
    xmlns="urn:schemas-microsoft-com:xml-data"
    xmlns:dt="urn:schemas-microsoft-com:datatypes">

    <ElementType name="OrderDate" model="closed" content="textOnly"
        dt:type="date"/>
    <ElementType name="Customer" model="closed" content="textOnly"
        dt:type="string"/>

    <ElementType name="Product" model="closed" content="mixed">
        <AttributeType name="ProductID" required="yes" dt:type="int"/>
        <AttributeType name="UnitPrice" dt:type="fixed.14.4"/>
        <attribute type="ProductID"/>
        <attribute type="UnitPrice" default="10.00"/>
    </ElementType>

    <ElementType name="Quantity" model="closed" content="textOnly"
        dt:type="int"/>
    <ElementType name="Item" model="closed" content="eltOnly">
        <element type="Product" minOccurs="1" maxOccurs="1"/>
        <element type="Quantity" minOccurs="1" maxOccurs="1"/>
    </ElementType>

    <ElementType name="Order" model="closed" content="mixed">
        <AttributeType name="OrderNo" required="yes" dt:type="int"/>
        <attribute type="OrderNo"/>
        <element type="OrderDate" minOccurs="1" maxOccurs="1"/>
        <element type="Customer" minOccurs="1" maxOccurs="1"/>
        <element type="Item" minOccurs="1" maxOccurs="*"/>
    </ElementType>
</Schema>
```

This version of the schema requires that the *OrderNo*, *ProductID*, and *Quantity* values are integer numbers, the *OrderDate* value is a date, the *Customer* value is a string, and the *UnitPrice* value is a fixed decimal number (with up to 14 digits in front of the decimal point and up to 4 digits behind the decimal).

Validating an XML Document

To ensure that a document is validated using an appropriate schema, you can reference the schema in the document namespace by using the *x-schema* keyword. For example, the following document references a schema named Orderschema.xml:

```
<?xml version="1.0"?>
<Order OrderNo="1234" xmlns="x-schema:Orderschema.xml">
    <OrderDate>2001-01-01</OrderDate>
    <Customer>Graeme Malcolm</Customer>
    <Item>
        <Product ProductID="1" UnitPrice="18">Chai</Product>
        <Quantity>2</Quantity>
    </Item>
    <Item>
        <Product ProductID="2" UnitPrice="19">Chang</Product>
        <Quantity>1</Quantity>
    </Item>
</Order>
```

The file name given in the *x-schema* namespace is a relative or absolute path to the schema file. In this case the schema is saved as Orderschema.xml in the same folder as the document. When the parser loads a document referencing a schema, that document can be validated against the schema to ensure that it meets all the requirements for documents of that type. If you use the Microsoft XML object library to load the document into an *XMLDom* object, the default behavior is for the document to be validated as it is parsed. You can check the value of the *parseError* property to determine if any errors occurred while loading the document, which will result in a nonzero value. The following Microsoft Visual Basic code shows how to check for a parse error:

```
Dim objXML As MSXML2.DOMDocument30
Set objXML = CreateObject("Microsoft.XMLDom")
objXML.async = False
objXML.Load "C:\Order.xml"
If Not objXML.parseError = 0 Then
    MsgBox "Error parsing XML"
End If
```

As an alternative approach, you can alter this behavior by setting the *validateOnParse* property to False. Then you can use the *Validate* method to validate the document against the schema:

```
Dim objXML As MSXML2.DOMDocument30
Set objXML = CreateObject("Microsoft.XMLDom")
objXML.async = False
objXML.validateOnParse = False
objXML.Load "C:\Order.xml"
If Not objXML.Validate = 0 Then
    MsgBox "The document is invalid."
End If
```

One potential area for confusion is the fact that Internet Explorer doesn't automatically validate XML documents when you load them in the browser. It merely checks to ensure that the document is well formed. You can install the XML Validation Tool from the MSDN site at *http://msdn.microsoft.com/downloads* to enable document validation from within Internet Explorer. After you install this tool, right-click in an XML document in Internet Explorer and choose to validate the XML against a schema.

Summary

This appendix covers some basic XML technologies and issues. I hope that it has given you enough XML knowledge to feel comfortable using XML for representing data. You should use the rest of the material in this book to build on what you have learned and to see how you can use the XML support in SQL Server 2000 to build powerful integration solutions.

Index

Note: Page numbers in italics refer to figures or tables.

Numbers and Symbols

A

Index

D

J

K

L

M

N

Q

R

S

T

V

W

X

Graeme Malcolm

Graeme Malcolm is Principal Technologist for Content Master Ltd., a technical authoring company based in the United Kingdom. He has written several training courses for Microsoft and regularly speaks at conferences and other events. He has worked with SQL Server since version 4.2 and holds Microsoft MCSE, MCSD, MCDBA, and MCT certifications, having spent six years as a professional trainer.

Snips or Shears

The first recorded use of snips or shears dates back to Roman toolmakers around AD 120. The design for those early snips has lasted centuries—their basic straight jaw and pivot equipped with either straight handles or scissor-like grips. Tin snips or metal shears are most often used for cutting sheet metal and wire screen. Of the different types of shears and snips are snips designed make internal or concave cuts, shears with curved blades for cutting sharp angles without distorting the metal, and specialty aviation snips. Many modern snips are made of aluminum alloy with replaceable blades of high-carbon steel; such cutters are more corrosion-resistant than traditional forged snips and have a high-leverage ratio, which makes cutting metal easier.

Tools are central to the progress of the human race. People are adept at building and using tools to accomplish important (and unimportant) tasks. Software is among the most powerful of tools moving us forward, and Microsoft is proud to create tools used by millions worldwide and to contribute to continuing innovation.

The manuscript for this book was prepared and galleyed using Microsoft Word 2000. Pages were composed by Microsoft Press using Adobe PageMaker 6.52 for Windows, with text in Garamond and display type in Helvetica Condensed. Composed pages were delivered to the printer as electronic prepress files.

Cover Designer:	Methodologie, Inc.
Interior Graphic Designer:	James D. Kramer
Principal Compositor:	Dan Latimer
Interior Artist:	David Holter
Principal Copy Editor:	Holly M. Viola
Indexer:	Bill Meyers

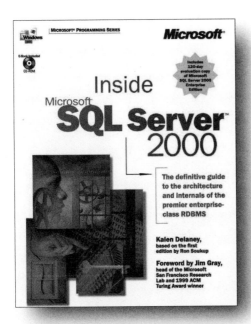

Get a **Free**
e-mail newsletter, updates, special offers, links to related books, and more when you

register on line!

Register your Microsoft Press® title on our Web site and you'll get a FREE subscription to our e-mail newsletter, *Microsoft Press Book Connections.* You'll find out about newly released and upcoming books and learning tools, online events, software downloads, special offers and coupons for Microsoft Press customers, and information about major Microsoft® product releases. You can also read useful additional information about all the titles we publish, such as detailed book descriptions, tables of contents and indexes, sample chapters, links to related books and book series, author biographies, and reviews by other customers.

Registration is easy. Just visit this Web page and fill in your information:

http://mspress.microsoft.com/register

Microsoft

Proof of Purchase

Use this page as proof of purchase if participating in a promotion or rebate offer on this title. Proof of purchase must be used in conjunction with other proof(s) of payment such as your dated sales receipt—see offer details.

Programming Microsoft® SQL Server™ 2000 with XML

0-7356-1369-9

____

CUSTOMER NAME

Microsoft Press, PO Box 97017, Redmond, WA 98073-9830

MICROSOFT LICENSE AGREEMENT

Book Companion CD

IMPORTANT—READ CAREFULLY: This Microsoft End-User License Agreement ("EULA") is a legal agreement between you (either an individual or an entity) and Microsoft Corporation for the Microsoft product identified above, which includes computer software and may include associated media, printed materials, and "online" or electronic documentation ("SOFTWARE PRODUCT"). Any component included within the SOFTWARE PRODUCT that is accompanied by a separate End-User License Agreement shall be governed by such agreement and not the terms set forth below. By installing, copying, or otherwise using the SOFTWARE PRODUCT, you agree to be bound by the terms of this EULA. If you do not agree to the terms of this EULA, you are not authorized to install, copy, or otherwise use the SOFTWARE PRODUCT; you may, however, return the SOFTWARE PRODUCT, along with all printed materials and other items that form a part of the Microsoft product that includes the SOFTWARE PRODUCT, to the place you obtained them for a full refund.

SOFTWARE PRODUCT LICENSE

The SOFTWARE PRODUCT is protected by United States copyright laws and international copyright treaties, as well as other intellectual property laws and treaties. The SOFTWARE PRODUCT is licensed, not sold.

1. **GRANT OF LICENSE.** This EULA grants you the following rights:
   - a. **Software Product.** You may install and use one copy of the SOFTWARE PRODUCT on a single computer. The primary user of the computer on which the SOFTWARE PRODUCT is installed may make a second copy for his or her exclusive use on a portable computer.
   - b. **Storage/Network Use.** You may also store or install a copy of the SOFTWARE PRODUCT on a storage device, such as a network server, used only to install or run the SOFTWARE PRODUCT on your other computers over an internal network; however, you must acquire and dedicate a license for each separate computer on which the SOFTWARE PRODUCT is installed or run from the storage device. A license for the SOFTWARE PRODUCT may not be shared or used concurrently on different computers.
   - c. **License Pak.** If you have acquired this EULA in a Microsoft License Pak, you may make the number of additional copies of the computer software portion of the SOFTWARE PRODUCT authorized on the printed copy of this EULA, and you may use each copy in the manner specified above. You are also entitled to make a corresponding number of secondary copies for portable computer use as specified above.
   - d. **Sample Code.** Solely with respect to portions, if any, of the SOFTWARE PRODUCT that are identified within the SOFTWARE PRODUCT as sample code (the "SAMPLE CODE"):
     - i. **Use and Modification.** Microsoft grants you the right to use and modify the source code version of the SAMPLE CODE, *provided* you comply with subsection (d)(iii) below. You may not distribute the SAMPLE CODE, or any modified version of the SAMPLE CODE, in source code form.
     - ii. **Redistributable Files.** Provided you comply with subsection (d)(iii) below, Microsoft grants you a nonexclusive, royalty-free right to reproduce and distribute the object code version of the SAMPLE CODE and of any modified SAMPLE CODE, other than SAMPLE CODE, or any modified version thereof, designated as not redistributable in the Readme file that forms a part of the SOFTWARE PRODUCT (the "Non-Redistributable Sample Code"). All SAMPLE CODE other than the Non-Redistributable Sample Code is collectively referred to as the "REDISTRIBUTABLES."
     - iii. **Redistribution Requirements.** If you redistribute the REDISTRIBUTABLES, you agree to: (i) distribute the REDISTRIBUTABLES in object code form only in conjunction with and as a part of your software application product; (ii) not use Microsoft's name, logo, or trademarks to market your software application product; (iii) include a valid copyright notice on your software application product; (iv) indemnify, hold harmless, and defend Microsoft from and against any claims or lawsuits, including attorney's fees, that arise or result from the use or distribution of your software application product; and (v) not permit further distribution of the REDISTRIBUTABLES by your end user. Contact Microsoft for the applicable royalties due and other licensing terms for all other uses and/or distribution of the REDISTRIBUTABLES.

2. **DESCRIPTION OF OTHER RIGHTS AND LIMITATIONS.**
   - **Limitations on Reverse Engineering, Decompilation, and Disassembly.** You may not reverse engineer, decompile, or disassemble the SOFTWARE PRODUCT, except and only to the extent that such activity is expressly permitted by applicable law notwithstanding this limitation.
   - **Separation of Components.** The SOFTWARE PRODUCT is licensed as a single product. Its component parts may not be separated for use on more than one computer.
   - **Rental.** You may not rent, lease, or lend the SOFTWARE PRODUCT.
   - **Support Services.** Microsoft may, but is not obligated to, provide you with support services related to the SOFTWARE PRODUCT ("Support Services"). Use of Support Services is governed by the Microsoft policies and programs described in the

user manual, in "online" documentation, and/or in other Microsoft-provided materials. Any supplemental software code provided to you as part of the Support Services shall be considered part of the SOFTWARE PRODUCT and subject to the terms and conditions of this EULA. With respect to technical information you provide to Microsoft as part of the Support Services, Microsoft may use such information for its business purposes, including for product support and development. Microsoft will not utilize such technical information in a form that personally identifies you.

- **Software Transfer.** You may permanently transfer all of your rights under this EULA, provided you retain no copies, you transfer all of the SOFTWARE PRODUCT (including all component parts, the media and printed materials, any upgrades, this EULA, and, if applicable, the Certificate of Authenticity), **and** the recipient agrees to the terms of this EULA.
- **Termination.** Without prejudice to any other rights, Microsoft may terminate this EULA if you fail to comply with the terms and conditions of this EULA. In such event, you must destroy all copies of the SOFTWARE PRODUCT and all of its component parts.

3. **COPYRIGHT.** All title and copyrights in and to the SOFTWARE PRODUCT (including but not limited to any images, photographs, animations, video, audio, music, text, SAMPLE CODE, REDISTRIBUTABLES, and "applets" incorporated into the SOFTWARE PRODUCT) and any copies of the SOFTWARE PRODUCT are owned by Microsoft or its suppliers. The SOFTWARE PRODUCT is protected by copyright laws and international treaty provisions. Therefore, you must treat the SOFTWARE PRODUCT like any other copyrighted material **except** that you may install the SOFTWARE PRODUCT on a single computer provided you keep the original solely for backup or archival purposes. You may not copy the printed materials accompanying the SOFTWARE PRODUCT.

4. **U.S. GOVERNMENT RESTRICTED RIGHTS.** The SOFTWARE PRODUCT and documentation are provided with RESTRICTED RIGHTS. Use, duplication, or disclosure by the Government is subject to restrictions as set forth in subparagraph (c)(1)(ii) of the Rights in Technical Data and Computer Software clause at DFARS 252.227-7013 or subparagraphs (c)(1) and (2) of the Commercial Computer Software—Restricted Rights at 48 CFR 52.227-19, as applicable. Manufacturer is Microsoft Corporation/One Microsoft Way/Redmond, WA 98052-6399.

5. **EXPORT RESTRICTIONS.** You agree that you will not export or re-export the SOFTWARE PRODUCT, any part thereof, or any process or service that is the direct product of the SOFTWARE PRODUCT (the foregoing collectively referred to as the "Restricted Components"), to any country, person, entity, or end user subject to U.S. export restrictions. You specifically agree not to export or re-export any of the Restricted Components (i) to any country to which the U.S. has embargoed or restricted the export of goods or services, which currently include, but are not necessarily limited to, Cuba, Iran, Iraq, Libya, North Korea, Sudan, and Syria, or to any national of any such country, wherever located, who intends to transmit or transport the Restricted Components back to such country; (ii) to any end user who you know or have reason to know will utilize the Restricted Components in the design, development, or production of nuclear, chemical, or biological weapons; or (iii) to any end user who has been prohibited from participating in U.S. export transactions by any federal agency of the U.S. government. You warrant and represent that neither the BXA nor any other U.S. federal agency has suspended, revoked, or denied your export privileges.

DISCLAIMER OF WARRANTY

NO WARRANTIES OR CONDITIONS. MICROSOFT EXPRESSLY DISCLAIMS ANY WARRANTY OR CONDITION FOR THE SOFTWARE PRODUCT. THE SOFTWARE PRODUCT AND ANY RELATED DOCUMENTATION ARE PROVIDED "AS IS" WITHOUT WARRANTY OR CONDITION OF ANY KIND, EITHER EXPRESS OR IMPLIED, INCLUDING, WITHOUT LIMITATION, THE IMPLIED WARRANTIES OF MERCHANTABILITY, FITNESS FOR A PARTICULAR PURPOSE, OR NONINFRINGEMENT. THE ENTIRE RISK ARISING OUT OF USE OR PERFORMANCE OF THE SOFTWARE PRODUCT REMAINS WITH YOU.

LIMITATION OF LIABILITY. TO THE MAXIMUM EXTENT PERMITTED BY APPLICABLE LAW, IN NO EVENT SHALL MICROSOFT OR ITS SUPPLIERS BE LIABLE FOR ANY SPECIAL, INCIDENTAL, INDIRECT, OR CONSEQUENTIAL DAMAGES WHATSOEVER (INCLUDING, WITHOUT LIMITATION, DAMAGES FOR LOSS OF BUSINESS PROFITS, BUSINESS INTERRUPTION, LOSS OF BUSINESS INFORMATION, OR ANY OTHER PECUNIARY LOSS) ARISING OUT OF THE USE OF OR INABILITY TO USE THE SOFTWARE PRODUCT OR THE PROVISION OF OR FAILURE TO PROVIDE SUPPORT SERVICES, EVEN IF MICROSOFT HAS BEEN ADVISED OF THE POSSIBILITY OF SUCH DAMAGES. IN ANY CASE, MICROSOFT'S ENTIRE LIABILITY UNDER ANY PROVISION OF THIS EULA SHALL BE LIMITED TO THE GREATER OF THE AMOUNT ACTUALLY PAID BY YOU FOR THE SOFTWARE PRODUCT OR US$5.00; PROVIDED, HOWEVER, IF YOU HAVE ENTERED INTO A MICROSOFT SUPPORT SERVICES AGREEMENT, MICROSOFT'S ENTIRE LIABILITY REGARDING SUPPORT SERVICES SHALL BE GOVERNED BY THE TERMS OF THAT AGREEMENT. BECAUSE SOME STATES AND JURISDICTIONS DO NOT ALLOW THE EXCLUSION OR LIMITATION OF LIABILITY, THE ABOVE LIMITATION MAY NOT APPLY TO YOU.

MISCELLANEOUS

This EULA is governed by the laws of the State of Washington USA, except and only to the extent that applicable law mandates governing law of a different jurisdiction.

Should you have any questions concerning this EULA, or if you desire to contact Microsoft for any reason, please contact the Microsoft subsidiary serving your country, or write: Microsoft Sales Information Center/One Microsoft Way/Redmond, WA 98052-6399.

PN 097-0002296